IAN INSKIP served in HMS *Glamorgan* a
the Falklands War in 1982 and in that po
insight into the conduct of the naval ope
most. He left the ship at the end of the war to become Staff
Navigating Officer to the Flag Officer Sea Training before being
promoted Commander. His postings as Commander included
appointments as Fleet Navigating Officer at Northwood. He
completed his active service in Naval Security.

Ordeal by Exocet

HMS *Glamorgan* and the Falklands War 1982

Commander Ian Inskip RN

FRONTLINE BOOKS, LONDON

A Greenhill Book

Greenhill Books

First published in Great Britain in 2002 by Chatham Publishing, an
imprint of Greenhill Books, Lionel Leventhal Limited
www.greenhillbooks.com

This edition published in 2012 by Frontline Books

an imprint of
Pen & Sword Books Ltd.
47 Church Street, Barnsley, S. Yorkshire, S70 2AS.

Visit us at www.frontline-books.com, email info@frontline-books.com
or write to us at the above address.

ISBN 978-1-84832-131-1

CIP data records for this title are available from the British Library.

Printed and Bound by CPI Group (UK) Ltd, Croydon, CR0 4YY

Typeset in 11pt Ehrhardt by Mac Style, Beverley, East Yorkshire

Contents

Foreword

By Captain M E Barrow, DSO, Royal Navy

Ian Inskip and I joined *Glamorgan* at about the same time in 1980. In the intervening years we became, and have remained, firm friends; it is a great pleasure to be invited to contribute a foreword to his book.

I soon learned that Ian's somewhat piratical appearance, his wry smile and buccaneering 'press on' attitude concealed a most likeable, professional, painstaking and efficient personality whom I came to respect and trust. His considerable navigational expertise and experience, together with his sense of fun and physical stamina, proved invaluable to us all, especially during the stresses of war.

Ordeal by Exocet is Ian's – and others' – tale of *Glamorgan* during the time he was her Navigating Officer; a detailed account of the comings and goings of our 500 company and, unusually also, snapshots of what our families were doing 'back home'.

I warmly commend this story about the people in just one of the many ships and units deployed in 1982 to regain the sovereignty of the Falkland Islands.

Michael Barrow
Captain, Royal Navy
President, *Glamorgan* 1982 Association.
June 2001

Author's Note

The Task Force used GMT for both operational and domestic reasons and those times are used in the book. This gave sunrise at about 1100 GMT (11 am) and sunset at 1900 GMT (7 pm). It allowed breakfast and domestic routines to be completed before the air threat went up at dawn, and allowed the evening meal to take place once the air threat had lessened and before we went inshore for the night's dirty work. Operationally, the RAF worked in GMT as their aircraft crossed several time zones and it avoided confusion if everyone was in the same time zone.

It is worth making the point that we were operating in 16 hours of darkness and only 8 hours of daylight and that weather conditions in winter in the South Atlantic are considerably worse than those in the North Atlantic at similar latitudes. Colder temperatures and higher wind speeds are due to the absence of the warming effects of the Gulf Stream and the relative lack of land masses.

Leading Weapons Electrical Mechanic on HMS *Glamorgan*, James Spence, wrote in his copy of *Up the Line to Death - The War Poets 1914-1918* the following poignant lines shortly after the ship was hit by Exocet missile, 12 June 1982.

Blinding light, searing heat,
We step forward, our Maker greets
Us with a smile says, 'Welcome boys,
You'll play no more with lethal toys!'

Friend and foe, enemy, ally,
The politicians watch you die
Then speak words with frozen tongue
'What's gone is gone, what's done is done.'

Gone now husband, sons and brothers,
Leaving widows, sisters, mothers.
Where lies the blame for all their sorrow?
Read it in the news tomorrow!

Soldier, sailor, airman dying
Ever after mothers trying
To understand decisions made
That sent their sons to early graves.

Introduction

At 0636 on 12 June 1982, the faintest of 'blips' appeared on *Glamorgan*'s bridge radar display. A little over 30 seconds later, an Exocet missile clipped the side of the upper deck, exploded and blasted holes down through two decks. The missile body penetrated the hangar door and hit the fully fuelled and armed Wessex helicopter inside. A second later the helicopter blew up and a massive explosion, with accompanying fireball, erupted from the hangar. No ship had ever survived a hit by Exocet and those watching from nearby consorts believed that *Glamorgan* had blown up and gone the way of *Hood*. Our bows then emerged from the smoke, 'going like a bat out of hell', and the battle to save the ship began.

In 1982, the Cold War with Russia was at its height and the Royal Navy had for decades prepared to counter the Soviet threat. To many it came as something of a surprise to find ourselves heading south to fight Argentina, a country with whom we traditionally had maintained good relations. Despite the fact that the Royal Navy had fought and won famous naval battles off the Falklands in both the First and Second World Wars, few people knew much about the Falklands and even fewer understood the controversial claims made by both Britain and Argentina to the islands. These claims were to become a ticking bomb when General Galtieri sought to divert attention away from his unpopular government in an attempt to realise an Argentine dream – sovereignty of the 'Malvinas'. The excuse for war was the incident surrounding Davidoff and his scrap merchants who had been given conditional permission to dismantle a whaling station in South Georgia. When those conditions were broken, *Endurance* was sent to evict the scrap merchants and Argentina responded.

In April 1982, Argentina invaded the Falklands. With less than fifty Royal Marines defending the Islands, resistance was token. The

First Sea Lord, Admiral Sir Henry Leach, persuaded Margaret Thatcher that a naval task force could be deployed and could re-capture the islands. Historically, such long-range deployments have generally failed. It would take weeks for the force to sail the 8,000) miles to the South Atlantic, by which time the Argentinians would be well dug in and supported by a large air force. Doctrine stated that for a successful amphibious landing you needed air superiority and an advantage of three to one on the ground. At best, air superiority would be disputed and the defenders would out-number the attackers. Once again, the Royal Navy would be called upon to face overwhelming odds in the ensuing air battle and high losses could be anticipated. Despite all these odds, for the third time in seventy years, the Royal Navy won a famous victory off the Falklands.

Glamorgan, a 'County' class destroyer, was not a new ship. She had been designed to protect fixed-wing aircraft carriers against the Soviet threat before the defence review of 1966 did away with fleet carriers. (*Ark Royal*, the last fleet carrier, was paid off in December 1978.) Her main armament was the Seaslug missile system which was ideal for downing high flying aircraft in the open ocean but was not designed for use against low flying aircraft and sea skimming missiles. Nor was *Glamorgan* suited for inshore operations. However, with good command facilities, a twin turret and four Exocet launchers she was ideal as leader of the surface attack unit tasked with taking the fight to the enemy. On the close screen by day, *Glamorgan*'s high speed dashes inshore by night made her a veritable thorn in the side of the enemy and a true friend to our own troops fighting ashore. Yet, in the greater scheme of things, like pawns on a chessboard, escorts were expendable for the common good even though they were capable of inflicting severe damage upon the enemy. And so it was, faced once more with conflicting orders, that *Glamorgan* again put the common good before her own safety. Some say that it was luck which saved *Glamorgan* from complete destruction. Yes, it was a very close run thing but it was courage, dedication and skill which actually saved the ship.

When the crisis arose, Exercise Springtrain was taking place off Gibraltar and *Glamorgan* was one of the first group of ships to be deployed south on 2 April. With mixed feelings of elation and fear, I checked *Jane's All the World's Aircraft* to assess the opposition. They had 400 military aircraft, 200 of which were front line aircraft. I thought, 'If all six of us have a good day and shoot down ten apiece, that only leaves another 140 to attack us!' My fears were justified because of that initial group of six ships, every one was to either be seriously damaged or sunk by air attack. Some on board did not consider the Argentine armed forces to be particularly capable and I had no doubt that the Royal Navy was the best in the world. However, I realised that, fighting 8,000 miles from home in the most inhospitable waters in the world against an enemy who had modern ships and aircraft, this war was to be deadly serious and that we would need to prepare and keep our wits about us if we were to survive.

As a Sub-Lieutenant, I had read that records in war were even more important than records in peacetime. I also knew that I would be required to draft our Reports of Proceedings and for these reasons I started a daily journal, recording everything I possibly could. Two years after the Falklands War, I allowed Lieutenant Commander Berry Reeves, who was relieving me at Portland, to read the journal. It was he who first said, "You have got to put this in a book.' With over 200 sides of foolscap in my journal I had the basis for one, one which would be a view from the bridge, portraying daily life aboard an 'expendable' escort under wartime conditions. At *Glamorgan*'s Falklands 15th Anniversary reunion, I asked my fellow shipmates for any input they might have. I received a number of letters and four complete diaries which I was able to match with my own journal. I now had a wider perspective of first-hand accounts upon which this book could be based.

The book takes the reader, day by day, through the build-up of the crisis as Flagship, down into the South Atlantic and to war as one of the escorts tasked to take the fight to the enemy. It concludes with the aftermath and our return to Portsmouth. I have tried to explain what we did, why we did it, and how we went about it, including the impact of the war upon our families. No-one on board had the full picture and we did our best based upon the information we had at the time. I have not tried to hide the mistakes which, with the benefit of hindsight, were made. Everyone was working incredibly long hours under, sometimes, extreme stress. Upon reflection, we may wish that we had acted differently. We cannot change the past, but everyone should heed the lessons of history.

I hope that this book, which is dedicated to those who lost their lives in the South Atlantic, will both help ease the suffering of those who have been searching for answers as to 'why?' and allow others to understand what the war at sea was really like. For us, the war did not end on 14 June 1982 – the images of war remain to this day, vivid in our minds. The day will come when the ship is broken up for scrap. However, the bonds of comradeship and support cannot be broken. They remain very evident in the *Glamorgan* website which I would encourage the reader to visit.

IAN INSKIP
Goonhavern
November 2001

Update to the 2012 Edition

Ten years have passed since writing *Ordeal by Exocet* in 2001, but the story of *Glamorgan* and her crew continues. The ship was sold to the Chilean Navy in 1986 and became the *Almirante Latorre*. She was withdrawn from service in 1998 and sold for scrap in 2005, but whilst being towed to a breaker's yard she sank off Arica. However, the memory of *Glamorgan* lives on. There is a *Glamorgan* memorial window in Portsmouth Cathedral and her final battle ensign is on display in the Falklands Memorial Chapel at Pangbourne.

New information about the firing of the Exocet has also come to light. In 2006, I visited Argentina and met Captain Norberto Dimeglio, the leader of the Torno Squadron, which bombed *Glamorgan* on 1 May 1982. I also met José Scaglia, who both drove the Exocet launcher trailer and pushed the missile fire button on 12 June 1982. He informed me that the Exocet missile had not been fired from Eliza Cove but from a position just off the Stanley Airport road. It later emerged that the firing location, which is now in the middle of an industrial estate, was near Hookers Point. José Scaglia also informed me that on the very frosty morning of 11 June 1982, when he was driving the launcher back into Stanley, the entire rig started slipping on ice down the steep hill and nearly ended up in the harbour!

The Falkland Islands remain a place of pilgrimage for many. My wife, Marianne, and I visited in 2003, and whilst there we noted that there were memorials in the Islands for all units which had suffered significant losses, except for *Glamorgan*. On my return I put forward a case, to the Glamorgan Falklands Association, for a memorial to be erected in the Falkland Islands. Other crew members, who subsequently visited the Islands, came to the same conclusion and also contacted the Association. In 2009, the Association started raising the necessary funds, and a total of over £15,000 was raised mainly by former crew members. A memorial made from polished Welsh granite was dedicated on 15 February 2011 at Hookers Point and overlooks the spot 19 miles away where *Glamorgan* was hit.

As a tribute to the surviving crew, who saved their ship, an oil painting has been commissioned from the military artist Mark Littlejohn to record *Glamorgan*'s fight for survival.

The HMS *Glamorgan* Falklands Association website http://www. hmsglamorgan.co.uk contains a huge amount of information, including photographs of the ship and her memorials. The Association also holds reunions for the crew and their families every five years.

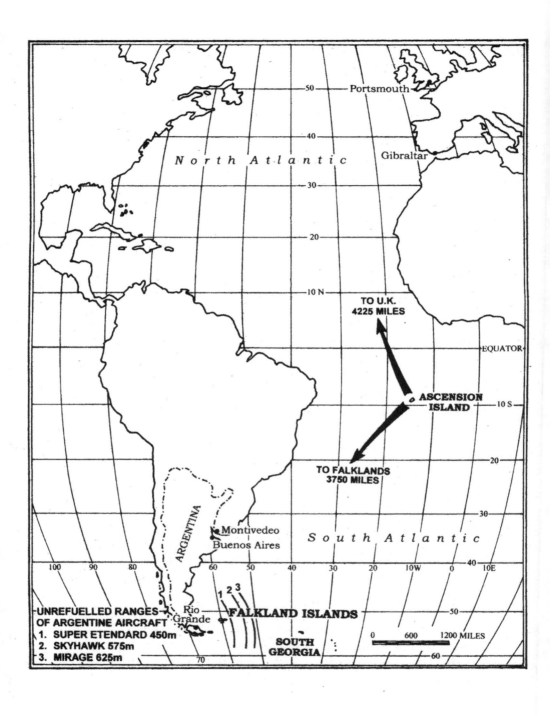

Chapter 1

The Road to *Glamorgan*

I fyny bo'r nod – To aim high

On 17 March 1982, *Glamorgan* sailed from Portsmouth for Exercise Springtrain off Gibraltar. Every member of the crew had a different story to tell as to how they found themselves in *Glamorgan* that day. For me, a navigation specialisation led me to the ship. I had honed my navigational skills initially under Captain George Vallings 'in accordance with Queen's Regulations for the Royal Navy'. His successor, Captain 'Jas' Briggs, was probably the most notable maverick in the Royal Navy and he taught me everything about navigation, including a lot which was not in the book. His idea of navigation was to go as close and as fast as physically possible to everything, which required precision and meticulous planning.

On qualifying as an advanced specialist navigator I was appointed to *Glamorgan* in August 1980 and Captain Mike Barrow, a very experienced captain, joined shortly afterwards. He delegated authority whilst always retaining responsibility, and gave us tremendous job satisfaction and the drive to do that little bit better. He made a point of getting to know every member of the crew and one felt that the Captain took a personal interest: in short, he was a born leader and the most caring Captain under whom I have served. The entire crew was behind Mike Barrow and if anyone was to ask me what was meant by leadership, I could do no better than advise them to observe Mike at work. Thus *Glamorgan* soon enhanced her existing reputation both as a happy ship and an efficient one.

In October 1981, *Glamorgan* had sailed for the Persian Gulf. On completion of an exercise with the Omani Navy, we had planned to anchor off a small bay called Bandar Jissah. The bay had been surveyed in 1849 but the Sailing Directions had recently been amended, indicating that the Royal Navy had been inside the Bay during the previous year. We also knew that the Sultan of Oman's yacht regularly visited the Bay. There were advantages of going inside the bay which outweighed the cons of limited space and the survey date and so, with the Admiral's approval, we carefully entered the bay and safely came to anchor. I sent the Gemini boat away to take soundings around the ship, the only time I had ever gone to this degree of trouble, and the bottom appeared completely flat. Unfortunately, there was a large uncharted rock right under the ship and when we came to leave our propellers grounded. Whilst considering our position, Chief Yeoman Richardson said to the Captain, 'Do you realise, sir, not only are you the Senior Captain Afloat, you are also the Senior Captain Aground!' Mike Barrow was not amused. *Ambuscade*, demonstrating superb seamanship, made a sternboard into the bay and towed us to Muscat where clearance divers, assisted by our ship's divers, did their best to balance the port screw. This was the first time such a solution had been attempted and it was not a complete success, reducing our best speed on the voyage back to Portsmouth to 13 knots.

We docked down after Christmas and whilst the engineers changed the propellers Mike Barrow and I were explaining our grounding to the Board of Inquiry. With new propellers, we resumed operations. As we passed Outer Spit buoy we received a signal from the Commander-in-Chief, Fleet, saying that the Captain and I were to be court martialled immediately on return to Portsmouth. Due to our programme, we would have no time to speak to our defence team before the trial and we protested that this was unfair, so the Court Martial was postponed until after our programmed return in April. We sailed for exercises off Scotland. February off Scotland is renowned for rough weather and inhospitable seas. Shiphandling becomes difficult and when ships attempt to re-fuel, for instance, crew were liable to be injured. Admiral Woodward remarked, however, that 'This is our battlefield, we have to learn to live with it,' and within a few months, our battlefield was to be 8,000 miles away in the South Atlantic where the weather was, if anything, worse.

Not everyone had been on board since the end of refit. Sub-Lieutenant John Holden, our Damage Control Engineering Officer, joined before sailing from Portsmouth. He had just finished a course at the Royal Naval Engineering College on which, during the damage control phase, he had been lectured by the college's resident Pakistani Shipwright Officer who gave the course the benefits of his personal experience in the Indo–Pakistan war when his ship had been hit by three missiles and sunk in a matter of minutes.

On joining, John quickly discovered his place in the engineering hierarchy. He concluded that Lieutenant Commander Keith Smith, the Senior Engineer, was a highly competent engineer who ran a tight but happy department for Commander Jim Butterfield, the Commander 'E' (head of the engineering department). After the war, Keith Smith was to move to the Damage Control School *Phoenix* and to lecture on how to survive a missile attack.

. We arrived in Gibraltar on 24 March to an impressive gathering of ships and someone remarked that this would be the last time we would see so many British warships gathered together. In little over a month, however, there would be a mightier gathering in the South Atlantic. Whilst we were enjoying ourselves in Gibraltar, events were unfolding in the South Atlantic. Five years earlier an Argentine businessman, Constantino Davidoff, had approached the firm of Christian Salvesen regarding the scrap metal at the old whaling stations in South Georgia and an agreement had been signed in September 1979 whereby Davidoff was authorized to dismantle and take away buildings and equipment at Leith, Husvik and Stromness by March 1982. Grytviken was not included in the agreement. Due to delays, Davidoff was allowed to extend his work until the end of the season provided that he complied with British regulations in South Georgia, took all necessary provisions with him and did not make any use of the facilities at Grytviken.

Davidoff's party sailed to South Georgia on 11 March in the Argentine Navy Transport *Bahia Buen Suceso*, the Captain and crew of which were all members of the Argentine Merchant Navy. Davidoff had reported the sailing of his expedition to the British Embassy in Buenos Aires but had lacked time to obtain a landing permit, so, in lieu of one he had agreed with the British Embassy that a representative from his party would report to the British Antarctic Survey (BAS) base at Grytviken. On 16 March Davidoff's expedition arrived in Stromness Bay, without reporting at Grytviken and on 19 March a British scientist noted the Argentinians in Stromness Bay. The Argentine Flag was flying and shots were being fired contrary to British regulations. The British magistrate in Grytviken reported this to Sir Rex Hunt, governor of the Falklands, in Stanley, and he replied on 20 March that the Argentine party were to lower the flag and come to Grytviken for a landing permit. The flag was lowered but no–one visited Grytviken. The next day, with all stores ashore for the winter, the *Bahia Buen Suceso* sailed. Believing (incorrectly) that Argentine naval personnel were ashore, the British government protested to the Argentine government and insisted the *Bahia Buen Suceso* returned to Leith to collect the entire party. The Royal Navy's Antarctic survey vessel, *Endurance*, with marines embarked, sailed from Stanley to be poised to enforce the removal of Davidoff's expedition if necessary but the next day, the Argentine government informed the British government of its assumption that the entire expedition had sailed in the *Bahia Buen Suceso*. *Endurance* returned to the Falklands and the situation eased.

On 22 March, the British government learned from the British Antarctic Survey that the Argentinians were still there and that no-one had reported to Grytviken. Lord Carrington informed the Argentinians that if Davidoff's expedition was not immediately removed, they would be forcibly removed and *Endurance* once again sailed for South Georgia, arriving at Grytviken on 24 March, landing her twenty-two Royal Marines. The same day, the Argentine Navy sailed a corvette to station between the Falklands and South Georgia, ready to intercept *Endurance* and the following day, the Argentine Navy's ship *Bahia Paraiso* arrived at Leith and landed fourteen armed naval personnel and marines. It was Lord Carrington's ultimatum which prompted the Argentine junta to try to exploit the situation and seize the Falklands and their dependencies. *Endurance* monitored events in Leith, hoping for an Argentine withdrawal. The *Bahia Paraiso* departed Leith on 26 March and patrolled off South Georgia while the Junta took the final decision that day to invade the Falklands; by the evening of 28 March, the invasion troops had sailed.

Meanwhile, *Fort Austin* and *Brilliant* deployed from Gibraltar to support *Endurance*. Diplomatic and media activity increased and on 29 March the British government decided to deploy a nuclear submarine in support of *Endurance*. However, the press had noted the unexpected departure of *Superb* from Gibraltar and assumed she was heading south and the government did nothing to correct this supposition. In fact, *Superb* had been tasked to monitor a Soviet naval deployment emerging around North Cape but except for very few people with a need to know, the rest of us on board also made the assumption that *Superb* was dashing south. It was some considerable time before we appreciated the truth.

Back in Gibraltar, we were well aware of the growing crisis. On 26 March I wrote home to Marianne, 'We are expecting a big change to the exercise programme because the nuclear submarine has been withdrawn "to do something else". When the signal [the signal listing all the changes to programme due to the withdrawal of *Superb*] comes in I shall have to insert a huge change into the serialized programme.'

* * *

The Falklands sovereignty issue stretched back a long way. Argentina based its claim on the papal grants of 1493 and 1494 which gave Spain dominion over all South America except for the parts occupied by Portugal. It was not until a century later that the Falkland Islands were discovered by Captain John Davies in 1592 while Captain John Strong made the first recorded landing in 1690. The channel dividing the two islands was named Falkland Sound after Viscount Falkland, First Lord of the Admiralty at the time.

In 1764 the French established a settlement on East Falkland at Port Louis. Unaware of this activity, in 1765 the British government dispatched Captain John Byron to take formal possession of the islands at Port Egmont on West Falkland 'for the Crown of Great Britain, his heirs and successors'. Fourteen years later, the Spanish governor in Buenos Aires bought out the French and then sent a force to oust the British from Port Egmont. There then followed a flurry of diplomatic activity during which Spain claimed that the governor had acted upon his own initiative and handed Port Egmont back to the British. This suggested that the papal decrees no longer had any credence or significance. By 1811, both the Spanish and the British had withdrawn on the grounds of economy, leaving the islands to passing whalers and sealers. When Spain withdrew her settlement, she left for all time and never assumed any ongoing rights to the islands. The Argentinians claim to have asserted those rights when the Spaniards departed despite the fact that there was never any direct hand-over or any legal transfer of title.

In 1824, a German, Louis Vernet, attempted to re-establish a settlement at Port Louis with the approval of the government in Buenos Aires. Four years later, the government of the United Provinces of La Plata granted him full sovereignty over East Falkland and one year later gave him the title of governor. Britain immediately protested and Lord Palmerston stated that Britain was not prepared to permit 'any state to exercise a right as derived from Spain which Britain had denied to Spain itself'. The issue was further complicated in 1831 when the United States intervened. They sent the *Lexington* to Port Louis, declared Louis Vernet a pirate and destroyed the settlement. The islands remained unpopulated for the next two years until Britain occupied and asserted her full rights in the Falklands with a naval garrison at Port Louis. The British administration in the islands remained unbroken until the Argentine invasion in 1982.

Argentina's other argument was based upon the geographical location but their argument would only be valid if the islands were uninhabited and even 'proximity' would embarrass many countries since the islands are 300 miles from Argentina while South Georgia is a further 800 miles away. The Argentinians also claimed that the islands were a symbol of British colonialism. If colonialism infers that control of the land has been taken from its native people, this was never the case since there was never an indigenous population.

As far as the Islanders were concerned, they believed that they had an absolute historical, legal and moral title to the islands, and they resented the Argentine assertion that the islands were 'disputed territory'. Happy in the knowledge that if there was a fight, I was on the side of democracy, I had no misgivings about being sent south.

Chapter 2

South to Ascension

Monday, 29 March

The Springtrain forces sailed from Gibraltar for the high seas firing areas and the tactical phase of the exercise. Commander-in-Chief, Fleet, Admiral Sir John Fieldhouse, was embarked in *Glamorgan* observing the exercise while Rear Admiral Woodward, embarked in *Antrim*, was running the tactical phase.

Tuesday, 30 March

As the crisis developed, *Glamorgan* closed Gibraltar to disembark the Commander-in-Chief by helicopter but not before Admiral Woodward had flown from *Antrim* for an urgent meeting. Together, with Captain Mike Barrow and Commander Jeremy Sanders (Staff Officer Operations to Admiral Woodward), they decided which ships should go south. The rest of us were aware that something was afoot and intelligence reports were indicating that a number of Soviet vessels were emerging from the north. We were not sure whether the two events, north and south, were linked.

Having disembarked Admiral Fieldhouse, we rejoined the exercise to rendezvous with *Euryalus*, *Coventry*, *Glasgow*, *Antrim* and *Sheffield*. Little did we realise that, except for *Euryalus* which returned to the UK, all of the rest of our group would either be sunk or severely damaged within the next ten weeks. Since *Glamorgan* was a fully operational air defence ship, we stood a good chance of being selected to deploy south and this, for me as navigator, presented a specific problem; we only carried the standard UK based chart outfit which did not even reach Ascension, let alone the South Atlantic. Mindful that the Captain and I were to be court martialled for using an 1849 chart, the Commander-in-Chief would take even less kindly to me navigating from a school atlas. The tanker RFA *Tidespring* was still in Gibraltar where there was a chart depot and I suggested to Captain Barrow that we signal Flag Officer Gibraltar for the appropriate folios and associated publications to be embarked in *Tidespring* for us. Mike readily agreed and a priority special handling signal was sent to

Gibraltar requesting hydrographic material and copied to Admiral Woodward who immediately accused us of breaching security. This seemed most unjust since I had based my chart demand on information received via the BBC World Service; I was not party to the flurry of highly classified signal traffic or meetings concerning events in the South Atlantic. However, we received a signal from *Antrim*, referring to our chart demand, 'cancel demand forthwith', but by the time our cancellation signal was received by Gibraltar, *Tidespring* had sailed with our charts embarked.

Wednesday, 31 March
Our helicopter collected the charts and by nightfall, as events escalated, we were the only ship in the group with South Atlantic charts. The other notable event was our Seaslug missile firings. The Seaslug missiles, weighing two tons apiece, leapt skywards. Once the four wrap-round boosters dropped off two miles down range, the sustainer motors took the missiles towards the Chukka targets, riding the radar beam, and both firings were successful.

Thursday, 1 April
Early on, the Navigating Officer of *Antrim* requested on secure voice, 'Where are my charts?' I informed him that the charts ordered by *Glamorgan*, for *Glamorgan*, were on board and I knew nothing about any charts ordered for *Antrim*. A few minutes later came the directive to transfer our charts as soon as possible and despite eight hours of sundry delays, they were eventually stolen for *Antrim*. Before surrendering them I photocopied the relevant ones for South Georgia and Ascension and then placed inside the bag of charts a rude note for *Antrim* referring to Matthew 25, the parable of the wise and foolish virgins. Operational readiness reports were requested from all ships and since all our kit worked and the ship was recently refitted with good command facilities I assessed that we would be selected to deploy south.

Friday, 2 April
At 0400 *Glamorgan* was ordered south. My immediate feeling was one of elation, quickly followed by fear. Fighting far from home on someone else's doorstep was fraught with problems, as the Russians found out to their cost at Tsushima in 1905, and in a few days I would be outside my chart coverage. There was one benefit of disappearing

south, however; the war would take precedence over the courts martial. I informed the Captain that we would be without proper charts to reach Ascension, exposing us to further charges of negligence, but assured him that, having previously visited Ascension, and having photocopied the charts, I could bring the ship safely to anchor. I need not have worried. The Admiral had already detached *Plymouth* to return to Gibraltar to collect the entire stock of South Atlantic folios held in the chart depot there.

Our diversion south also impacted upon domestic plans. For example, Leading Seaman Eon Matthews and some messmates had planned a boating holiday on the Thames for mid April. Eon managed to contact his wife, who fortunately was able to organise families and friends to take up the now vacant places.

At 1115 we met up with the *Antrim* group. All ships were carrying out vertical replenishments by helicopter (Vertreps), with stores and personnel travelling in all directions. Vertreps continued until sunset to get all the war essentials onto the 'south goers' and all the peacetime impedimenta off-loaded onto the 'north goers'. We collected Seacat missiles and torpedoes from *Euryalus*, and food from anyone who had some to spare.

Over lunch there were reports that Argentine soldiers had landed on the Falklands. War loomed ominously closer. If *Superb* had been routed south at 24 knots she could have been within forty-eight hours of the Falklands by now and assuming that the Argentinians would be working along similar presumptions it is safe to say that the media were inadvertently helping the deception. After lunch, we began rigging the light jackstay to receive shells from *Ariadne*. Suddenly our machinery control room (MCR) rang up 'Emergency Slow' after lub oil had been lost to the port main circulator. Fifteen minutes later first aid action had been completed and we resumed station but we were left with the nasty thought that it might have been sabotage. The sump drain cock to the main circulator was found open, having been checked shut earlier in the afternoon. It happening so soon after news of the invasion of the Falklands left little doubt in my mind. To survive in war we needed maximum teamwork. *Ariadne* was soon ready for the jackstay transfer during which we received two hundred shells and fifty cartridges. We then closed *Engadine* for a jackstay transfer whilst helicopters delivered further stores. I took the opportunity to write to Marianne, 'At 0400 this morning we heard that we were going south. Where we are, where we are going and what we are going to do, I cannot tell you. You know where the trouble is brewing and *Glamorgan* is a powerful ship and likely to be in the front line. I hope to be home soon but we really have no idea at all how long this will go on for or what will be the outcome. If it does turn into a shooting war, we are well equipped to deal with the situation, but at the same time we must never underestimate the other side. They have some very similar ships to us. If anything should happen to me, please remember I was thinking of the family all the time. Remember *Glamorgan* with pride.'

Having posted the letter I visited the ops room to look at *Jane's All the World's Aircraft*. Argentina had about four hundred aircraft of which two hundred were front line. Just six ships had been diverted south. If we all shot down ten apiece that would leave another 140 to attack us. Morale on board was high, perhaps even overconfident, and I felt it important to maintain a cheerful exterior and keep my inner fears to myself.

After replenishing from *Blue Rover*, we were fully fuelled, stored and ammunitioned. Our Flight Commander, Lieutenant Commander Gerry Hunt, had flown eight hours that day and our Second Pilot, Sub-Lieutenant Mike De Winton, for half as long – far exceeding peacetime procedural rules.

The passage intentions were to follow a covert passage through the Canary Islands to a waiting position off Ascension where we would await reinforcement. As I read the intentions signal the BBC reported that the Falklands had fallen and a cabinet meeting was scheduled for the following morning with an emergency meeting of the House of Commons. I believed that we would see an ultimatum issued before the outbreak of official war but I could not envisage the Argentinians backing down.

Admiral Woodward's directive was received on how to prepare ourselves for war. The nuclear submarine (SSN) would be tasked against their aircraft carrier, *Veinticinco De Mayo*. Our biggest problem would be in dealing with their Exocet-armed surface ships and aircraft and it did not escape my mind that we had a massive Seaslug missile magazine at vulnerable Exocet height above the waterline. To survive and win, we would have to get our drills right.

Overnight we learned that Admiral Woodward and his staff would be transferring to *Glamorgan*. The 'north goers' departed at midnight and the 'south goers' adopted a dispersed formation under radar silence. Only three sweeps of navigational radar were permitted every thirty minutes: upper decks were darkened and the ship displayed no navigation lights.

Saturday, 3 April
This was a day of consolidation and moving stores. Mrs Thatcher announced that the government intended to re-take the Falkland Islands, that a task force led by *Invincible* would sail on Monday and that 'other warships were already at sea'. That was us.

During the forenoon our guns were test fired, systems oiled, greased, and functionally checked. Damage control equipment was checked and all hatches and doors inspected. Merchant ship lighting was rigged for deception purposes and food control started. Enforced diets began and in the following six weeks I would lose a stone and a half.

Plymouth re-joined and stationed three miles away while *Antrim* was over the horizon ahead of us, part of the group's dispersed cart-wheel formation. We continued towards the Canaries, only altering course to avoid merchant ships. At sunset, we increased speed to close *Antrim* for the next day's transfers.

Sunday, 4 April
At 0100 *Glamorgan* passed between Tenerife and Gran Canaria, and detected Soviet radar transmissions which indicated that we might have picked up a Soviet tail. Fortunately, it was a false alarm, the radar coming from a Soviet merchant ship. The morning BBC World Service news announced that Argentina would go into battle with all the means at her disposal in the defence of the Malvinas. We would use all the means at our disposal to re-take the Falklands. The previous day the Royal Marine garrison and Sir Rex Hunt had surrendered and been taken to Montevideo for onward passage back to the UK.

Vertreps soon resumed, bringing in one load a set of South Atlantic folios, followed shortly afterwards by Admiral Woodward's staff. With half of the staff and their equipment embarked, we paused from helicopter operations to replenish from *Tidespring*. On completion, Admiral Woodward embarked and *Glamorgan* became the Flagship of the South Atlantic Task Force. In addition to *Glamorgan*'s signal traffic we now also received the signal traffic for the Flag which gave us an excellent overview of events.

The naval task organisation had a recognisable hierarchy but was designed to be flexible and able to adapt. The Commander of the Task Force was Admiral Fieldhouse at the Fleet Headquarters at Northwood and the task force itself was broken down into a number of Task Groups. The South Atlantic Battle Group was under Rear Admiral Woodward and the Amphibious Group under Commodore Amphibious Warfare. Each group could be further subdivided into task units. The surface action group (SAG) was formed into one such task unit. These task units could be further sub-divided into task elements. The organisation could be changed at any time to suit the operational situation and ships frequently went from one group or unit to another. It was important to keep the task organisation up to date since signals were addressed to groups, units or elements in preference to individual ships.

Over lunch we learned that South Georgia had been captured and in the process the Royal Marine garrison under Lieutenant Mills had downed a Puma helicopter, hit an Alouette helicopter and put a Carl Gustav round and three anti-tank rockets through the side of the Argentine frigate *Guerrico* which was also peppered with over 1,000 rounds of small arms ammunition. With the loss of South Georgia, there was no point in keeping *Endurance* exposed in theatre and she was withdrawn towards Ascension.

The day had been designated a rest day but not for *Glamorgan*, where the Admiral's day cabin was converted into a war room. Whilst his staff concentrated on planning 'Operation Corporate', ship's staff would organise and run the group's day-to-day programme. Some extraordinary plans had been considered including the sending of *Plymouth* into Stanley under a white flag to parley, and even the bombardment of Argentine mainland ports. In the end the choice was a night amphibious landing after a period of softening up. The priority list for the SSNs was *Veinticinco De Mayo*, tankers and Exocet firers while *Glamorgan* was tasked as the leader of the Exocet surface action group (SAG). When the carriers eventually arrived, the Flag would transfer to *Hermes*.

Throughout the group a more warlike appearance was becoming evident as ships toned down, and all the brightwork and fancy paintwork was overpainted grey, including pennant numbers. Darken ship procedures improved and the group's efficiency increased.

Monday, 5 April

Hermes and *Invincible* sailed from Portsmouth and the SSN *Conqueror* sailed from Faslane. The government's decision a decade earlier to scrap full-sized aircraft carriers would be felt badly, particularly the lack of airborne early warning. The decision was made on the grounds that the RAF could always fulfil this function but somehow the possibility of fighting outside the range of RAF support escaped the decision makers' notice. People would die as a result.

The Argentinians reacted with alarm and amazement at the British response to their invasion but despite their personal fears there was a grim determination to do whatever was necessary. The sooner we received the necessary rules of engagement (ROE) the better. I surmised that *Superb* must now be on station but later that evening I discovered she had deployed north to conduct Cold War operations. That left *Spartan*, in transit close to our current position and *Conqueror* just leaving Scotland.

We received much encouragement from home including one telegram from West Glamorgan: 'The thoughts and prayers of the people of West Glamorgan are with you.' It was just one line but the very fact that West Glamorgan had taken the trouble to wish us well meant a lot. Less encouraging was news that our mail, instead of being flown to Ascension had been embarked in *Invincible*. It would be weeks before it arrived.

Tuesday, 6 April

Every department was making its own preparations. Equipment never previously used, suddenly appeared. New stateboards were displayed everywhere, toning down continued and additional signal logs were rapidly being filled. I was tasked to prepare anchor berths for Ascension and the Falklands, safely fitting as many ships as possible into a confined space. Having prepared thirty anchorages around Ascension I had them approved by the Admiral. Afterwards, I was shown an exclusive signal from Commander-in-Chief, Fleet, who was concerned over the delay to our courts martial and offered 'administrative action'. Instead of being given the opportunity to answer the charges we were being offered the chance of being administratively censured, based upon a flawed Board of Inquiry report which had moved lines on the chart, ignored minimum heights of tide, and was contradictory. I objected strongly to Captain Barrow, saying I was fully prepared to answer to a court martial and so, forever the diplomat, he thanked CINCFLEET for his consideration but politely declined the kind offer.

Wednesday, 7 April

The group continued south, topping up with fuel and practising surface action group procedures.

Thursday, 8 April

A 200-mile exclusion zone around the Falklands was declared to become effective at 0400 on Monday 12 April, giving Argentinian warships three days to clear the area. I calculated that *Spartan* would then be 200 miles from the Falklands, hence the significance of the deadline. *Plymouth* and *Antrim* detached to join *Tidespring*. Mention was also made of the Special Boat Squadron (SBS) so it seemed likely that these units were being tasked against South Georgia and I also surmised that an SSN would be in attendance.

We would probably sail from Ascension sometime between 17 April and 20 April and although it was possible for an Argentine submarine to reach Ascension, intelligence indicated that one was in the Falklands, one off Argentina and two in their home port. Ascension, however, could offer rich pickings for a submarine and a submarine on our supply line would create major problems.

That night, as we practised SAG action with *Brilliant*, fully darkened and silent, and supposedly maintaining visual contact, we ended up sixteen miles from the guide. It was just as well that it was an exercise. The night was further disturbed by problems of transferring an essential computer spare to *Antrim*.

Gradually the Admiral's plan for South Georgia unfolded. *Antrim* and *Plymouth* were to provide support for *Endurance* and *Tidespring* and there was to be a landing in force to take over the island. Having achieved this, we would have a forward operating base 800 miles from the Falklands, out of range of Argentinian fighter-bombers. In response to our 200-mile exclusion zone the Argentinians declared one of their own and while ours was based upon a point in Falkland Sound, theirs was based upon the coastline and was consequently a larger area.

We were fortunate in *Glamorgan* to be fitted with satellite navigation (SATNAV), the forerunner to the Global Positioning System (GPS). When asked by the Admiral whether there were any particular navigational items which the Task Force needed I urged him to press for SATNAV for all ships and for many years after the Falklands War navigators benefitted from this emergency procurement.

Friday, 9 April

Preparations continued, and anything not wanted on board was ditched, including the Wardroom piano. Many compartments had been finished with unbonded formica which was liable, if hit, to shatter into razor-sharp shards. For safety reasons it was removed from all compartments except in the galley and sick-bay. The rationale for these exceptions was that, in addition to cleanliness and hygiene, the galley would not be occupied in action and little use would be made of the sick bay until after a hit.

We were due to arrive at Ascension on Sunday 11 April, working up until 15 April before heading north to rendezvous with *Hermes* to transfer the Admiral and his staff. At 1745 we crossed the Line, deeming it inappropriate to pay due reverence to Neptune, though we did allow ourselves a moment of light relief. We followed a figure of eight and 'tied a knot' in the Line so that in effect, we crossed the equator five times. The helicopters, the Lynx in particular, were suffering from the heat but heat was not to be our problem for much longer.

Intelligence reports showed that Russia was taking an active interest and though Argentina had turned down an offer of help from Libya she might well accept help from the Soviets, and if that happened the Third World War might not be far away. Intelligence also reported an Argentine frigate on patrol in the exclusion zone and an auxiliary ferrying troops.

Saturday, 10 April

I was on the go until nearly midnight. We closed down to wartime cruising state for a twenty-four hour period during which the group replenished from *Appleleaf*. *Glamorgan* lay uncomfortably alongside *Appleleaf* due to the latter's bulbous bow and I had to remain pretty alert, detecting trends before they developed into excursions, but conditions were good on this occasion and I gained valuable experience.

It seemed that the Supply Department were in league with the NBCD Department (Nuclear, Biological and Chemical Defence) – exercising action stations at 1545, just in time to miss tea. Closing

for action stations was fine for the upper deck crews in the
, ... , but for those below decks it was hot and sticky.

Sunday, 11 April

Easter Sunday, and at 0700 we closed *Appleleaf* for the first serial of
'Pass the Padre', to other ships by helicopter. Martin Culverwell, a
young padre, was embarked in *Glamorgan*, his first ship. He was a
pleasant character and the only honest soul on board. On 1 April the
previous year a note had been placed on Daily Orders regarding
payment of 'bunk light electricity bills' and he was the only individual
to turn up at the ship's office with his cheque book.

At 1100, with Ascension in sight, all the captains and ops officers
embarked for discussions and de-briefing on tactics. Back in London,
further talks were about to take place between American Secretary of
State General Haig and the government. There were indications of
the Argentinians wishing to compromise and hopeful though this
was, I did not believe that Margaret Thatcher would back down. The
other consideration was that only eighteen hours remained before
Spartan entered the exclusion zone and the shooting might start.
According to the press, we were 'in the vicinity with some nuclear
submarines' but the truth was that *Spartan* was about 200 miles from
the Falklands and the rest of us were still around Ascension.
Operation Paraquat, the recovery of South Georgia by *Antrim*,
Plymouth, *Tidespring* and *Endurance* was just getting under way.
Intelligence reported that all four Argentine submarines were now in
harbour so that for the next two weeks the Ascension anchorage
would be safe from submarine attack.

I arranged a spot of 'dentology', the science of identifying ships by
their dents and other unique peculiarities which stemmed from the
Cold War when the Russians regularly changed pennant numbers but
could do little about their mishaps. Now, we circled each other at
close range taking note of all the minor differences we could. If you
knew what to look for, recognition was a lot easier. Differentiating
between the Type 42 destroyers turned out to be simple. *Sheffield* was
the only one with 'Mickey Mouse ears' in her funnel. *Coventry* and
Glasgow were seemingly similar until you looked at the main roof
aerial. In *Coventry* these aerials were strung from foremast to funnel
to mainmast: in *Glasgow* they were strung mast to mast. This
significant difference made painting large vertical black recognition
bands down the funnel to waterline of the Type 42s to distinguish

them from the Argentinian ships unnecessary; but as people were busy toning down the ships and aircraft, others were painting these large black 'aiming marks' on the Type 42s. The Argentinian *Hercules* and *Santissima Trinidad* both had 'Mickey Mouse ears'. Their other recognition features were their Exocet launchers by the after 909 radar. Both *Glasgow* and *Coventry* were bombed and I cannot help wondering just how much help the enemy were given in picking out their targets by the highly visible and distinctive markings.

Although we were generally in good shape, the maintainers were busy resolving equipment problems. One of our compass stabilizer systems was defective, and in the steam turbine room a valve had blown out and we had to resort to fuel-guzzling gas turbines. In addition, niggling little difficulties remained unresolved. Once again I asked for a long lead headset for Command Open Line (COL) at the chart table on the bridge but it was never forthcoming as it was not deemed to be a priority. Sometimes, though, the 'nice to have' turn out to be essential and certainly the lack of a long lead headset was to have significant consequences.

The receipt of mail always boosted morale. Letters to and from the ship arrived in batches as opportunities to send and receive mail were limited but this did not stop many people from writing on a daily basis. The message we received was that the country was right behind us and the families seemed to have a pretty good idea as to where we were. Marianne wrote on Sunday, 4 April, 'We heard on Friday that you have been diverted south and now we know that you will be continuing south. Please do not worry about us, we are fine and can cope and we are keeping in close contact with other wives.' Marianne also commented upon the media hype about the war, the sight of Harriers and helicopters flying over Gosport en route to embark in the carriers, and watching from the Gosport ferry terminal as the Task Force sailed. On 8 April, Marianne wrote informing me of a meeting at Elizabeth Gotto's (the Commander's wife) on the following Wednesday for a picnic lunch and an opportunity to discuss matters.

The opportunity for us to send mail posed a dilemma. What do you write and send, and what do you keep to yourself? None of our group had had the opportunity to say goodbye to our families and loved ones and perhaps in some respects it was better that way. Knowing that the families were rallying round together was a big help.

Monday, 12 April

Whilst TV programmes upset the families with wild speculation, the Royal Navy quietly went about its business. At 0100 *Antrim* was detached for Operation Paraquat. At 0400 the maritime exclusion area (MEXA) around the Falklands came into effect. The public were hopeful of a peaceful solution but aboard *Glamorgan*, the Carrier Battle Group (CVBG) Flagship, we were focussed on recapturing the Falklands.

Late that morning, *Glamorgan* anchored off Ascension. Underslung helicopter loads were arriving from Wideawake airfield and one such load included a large bundle of charts which were quickly sorted and re-packaged for individual ships. In mid afternoon we sailed to practise naval gunfire support (NGS). NGS was exercised during work-up but range safety constraints made these serials both difficult and frustrating. Runs were usually conducted on a steady course at slow speed so that rounds could be fired before firing limits were exceeded. But my previous Captain, Jas Briggs, had forced me to undertake runs at 20 knots with three zigs and Mike Barrow encouraged me to achieve similar results, as slow straight runs under enemy fire from shore batteries invited disaster.

The problem with NGS was the time it took to set the fire control box (the box). A grid had to be drawn upon the navigational chart. A call for fire would come in giving the target grid location and target height. This would be plotted on the chart and from a point ahead of the ship I would calculate an initial range and bearing for the gunnery system transmitting station (TS). I would pass the parameters down to the Master Gunner, Brian Lister, in the ops room. He would repeat back the co-ordinates in confirmation. There would then be a pause of about half a minute whilst the settings were applied to the box in the TS. 'Box set' would then be reported. If very close to my chosen position I could report 'no initial firing correction, start the box'. More often, taking account of the gun-target line, I would have to order a correction. This correction was reported and the revised settings applied. I could then order 'start the box' by which time the ship had once again moved. The secret was to guess how long the TS would take to apply settings. When 'box started' was reported I then had to check how far we were from my chosen point, applying a further correction if necessary. As the drill improved, we became slicker and more accurate.

Tuesday, 13 April
Hopes for peace faded and bad news was mind sapping, both for ships' crews and their families. The Russians were also causing us concern. We had a 'Krivak' frigate on the plot southeast of Ascension and *Invincible* was being trailed by a Soviet spy ship. All we could hope was that they were not passing information onto the Argentinians.

The morning was programmed as a group replenishment for fuel, stores, ammunition and, most importantly, beer. No one had any intention of getting drunk but an occasional beer was a wonderful cure for stress!

Wednesday, 14 April
Overnight we again exercised SAG procedures and electronic warfare exercises. Our final activity was to launch our Wessex helicopter, nicknamed 'Willie', to collect stores from Ascension. Willie eventually re-embarked shortly before 0800. Since I had to be up for most of the night I took the opportunity of reading the intelligence assessment of the Argentine order of battle which was not very heartening. Provided that we could deploy our 3in chaff delta (decoy) rockets in time, we had a good chance of seducing Exocet. The problem was that these rockets were fired in salvos of sixteen and we only had enough rockets for four complete salvos. Chaff delta had been an addition after the 'County' class ships had been designed and stowages for reloads were the limiting factor. Four false alarms and all reloads were gone – but how do you tell a false alarm from the real thing? One evasive option was to take the Exocet at a very fine inclination so that with luck, the missile would bounce off the ship's side. This would enable the ship to escape much of the blast cone, the kinetic energy and residual fuel of the missile. I produced some time/range/turn data for use if necessary. One signal explored the possibility of tapping into the Argentinian data link between their ships. If we could manage it, enemy ship positions would appear on our screens! I wondered – could they participate in our link? In this electronic age, communications security was going to be vital.

In the morning we had planned to conduct a Sea Wolf (a new anti-aircraft missile system) anti-Exocet trial, using our 4.5in gun to simulate an Exocet. The trial was suspended when two Soviet Bear Delta aircraft overflew the force. On successful completion of the trial a little later we finished one final round of the helicopter delivery service (HDS) before heading north to rendezvous with *Hermes*. As we steamed north, the group we had left in Ascension were ordered to race south.

For myself, it was another long day, not finishing until close on midnight. I had a huge pile of unpublished hydrographic data to review as everything of any possible relevance to the operation was rushed out of Taunton to us. Whilst we had been busying ourselves off Ascension, ten wives and their children met at Elizabeth Gotto's and it was at this gathering that they met the ship's link padre, the Reverend Bruce Neill.

Thursday, 15 April

After an overnight passage we slowed to calibrate our Type 182 noisemaker and then continued until two Sea King helicopters appeared. Shortly afterwards *Hermes*, *Broadsword*, *Alacrity* and *Yarmouth* came into sight. For the next two and a half hours, Sea King helicopters were busy transferring the Flag. We then headed back towards Ascension.

None of us knew how long we would be in the South Atlantic but reliefs were being prepared. *Bristol* and her group were due to reach Ascension on 20 May. All we knew was that we were proceeding south with *Hermes* as guide and ourselves stationed on Circle 5, a circular station 5,000 yards from the guide. We were to spend many days on Circle 5 and people were heard jokingly to remark, 'What did you do in the war, Daddy?' – 'I was on Circle 5'.

Friday, 16 April

At 0700 we closed to within 500 yards of *Hermes* for a firepower demonstration by Harriers including live cluster bombing, air-to-air missile firing and rocket firings. It was put on for the press rather than representing a genuine practice. On board we felt increasingly certain that diplomacy would fail and we just wanted to get on south and finish the job. We had heard that *Veinticinco De Mayo* and the cruiser *General Belgrano* had been at sea, although not straying far from port, but with two SSNs on station and a third only four days away, a military clash was a distinct possibility at any moment.

Air defence exercises were conducted with aircraft from *Hermes* attacking *Invincible* and vice versa. On arrival back at Ascension we made a close pass down the side of *Hermes* and showed them our recently made banners. The polite one, mimicking British Airways read, 'We will take good care of you – fly the flag!' The more candid one read, 'Don't go near South Georgia – the scrap merchants are still there!' Already the rust was showing through on *Hermes*.

Whilst at anchor, the ship's divers checked the hull as warlike precautions were taking place above the waterline. These included enhancing darken ship measures by placing masking tape over anything that might be visually compromising. By the time the diving team had secured, mail had arrived. I received another letter from Marianne and it was a great help to hear how well she was coping at home. She had accepted the reality of this horror, faced it and come to terms with it, sending cheerful letters to keep up my morale. I could not have wished for better support. This enabled me to concentrate on the task in hand but I wondered how my two young daughters were coping.

The world news continued its grim tone. We would be fighting in some of the most inhospitable waters at the most inhospitable time of the year. To cheer myself up I pondered upon how my counterpart in the Argentine Navy was feeling and consoled myself that he was up against the finest navy in the world, and that he must be feeling more than a little apprehensive. Likewise, I had heard that the Argentinian soldiers in the Falklands were underclothed and underfed, and so although Argentinian morale on the mainland was quite high and jingoism rife, the same could probably not be said for the conscripts who might have to fight.

Saturday, 17 April
At 0800 we were alongside the storeship RFA *Resource* with about 60 loads to come across forward and 150 loads aft. For the first couple of hours, everything went well, but shortly after 1000 the after rig became defective so that everything had to be shifted to the forward rig and it was 1230 before we eventually broke away. This was the biggest stores replenishment I had experienced to date. Holding *Glamorgan* alongside for four and a half hours without a break, where a moment's lapse of attention could swiftly spell disaster, was physically and mentally exhausting.

General Haig was on his way back to the UK after more shuttle diplomacy, leaving the Argentinian generals and their staffs to consider his latest proposals. These developments all pointed towards hopes of a peaceful settlement but in the meantime the Royal Navy continued to head south. Whilst we were conducting our replenishment a Soviet Bear aircraft overflew. We were fifty miles south of Ascension at the time, so with luck *Glamorgan* would be plotted as already en route towards the Falklands and this mis-information would probably be passed to Argentina. The crisis continued to deteriorate as the conditions laid down by Argentina were unlikely to be accepted by the UK. After dark, having fully re-fuelled, we heard that we would be heading south in the morning. One of the administrative preparations completed in Ascension was the issue of Geneva Convention Identity Cards. These we would use in theatre instead of our normal Royal Naval Identity Cards.

Chapter 3

Ascension to the Total Exclusion Zone

Sunday, 18 April

Mail was landed as we sailed from Ascension and I promised Marianne I would see *Glamorgan* back into Portsmouth. At 0945 the first action of the war took place. *Olmeda* sighted 'a periscope' whilst refuelling *Invincible* and *Yarmouth* while *Broadsword* 'detected Argentine submarine radar'; both *Alacrity* and *Invincible* 'heard cavitation'. *Invincible* broke away from *Olmeda* and *Yarmouth* continued her stern replenishment whilst course was reversed; *Alacrity* and *Broadsword* investigated the submarine contact until the Sea King helicopters took over and Admiral Woodward ordered all ships to clear the anchorage to the north. As it turned out *Broadsword*'s radar intercept was eventually assessed as breakthrough from the dummy load of her own radar, *Olmeda*'s 'periscope' was possibly a whale spouting, and the cavitation came from ships' noisemakers. False alerts had got everyone going and the enemy was everywhere; we had much to learn before we engaged a real enemy. We had wrecked the morning's programme when the nearest enemy was still 3,500 miles away. By 1630, Ascension was only just visible forty-five miles to the northwest; the sun set on the warmest day we would see for months and we were on our way.

Further south *Antrim*, now 400 miles from South Georgia, was to insert Special Boat Squadron personnel there as soon as possible. Intelligence informed us that most of the Argentine fleet was at sea, albeit outside the exclusion zone.

Monday, 19 April

Olmeda returned to Ascension for twelve hours to mend a leaky pipe. After topping up the logistic landing ships (LSLs) there with fresh water, she rejoined at 18 knots. To help her, our group reduced speed to 12 knots. Overnight formations were changed; we screened

Invincible while the *Hermes* group lay to the east. The two groups then practised air defence against each other's aircraft.

A mountain of signal traffic filled the ether and it was an effort to keep on top of it. The main communications office (MCO) extracted signals addressed to us from other broadcast traffic which officially was of no concern to *Glamorgan.* Having lost the Flag we did not 'officially' receive Flag traffic but they also extracted the Flag traffic from the teleprinter backrolls and put them in a special log for selected officers to read. That log rapidly became known as the 'Buzz Log'. It would be very relevant if we had to suddenly resume as Flagship.

We were instructed to be ready in all respects for war by 22 April, but we were not yet fully fighting fit, having lost the fuel pump to the starboard boiler, and we limped along behind *Invincible* whilst the engineers toiled below in the heat. Lieutenant Commander Paul Engeham wrote about our war preparations: 'The upper deck is painted in uniform grey colours (no bright red boats!). Much surplus equipment has either been ditched or stowed. This applies between decks too. Such luxuries as carpets, sailing dinghies, chair covers and the wardroom piano found early watery graves.' In the meantime, our mail, minus two bags, arrived from *Hermes* and with the mail came newspapers which contained favourable comment on our activities. Back home, Marianne visited the local Married Quarters' Warden, and tried to obtain address details of the local *Glamorgan* wives. He was unable to provide any information, quoting the Official Secrets Act by way of excuse.

We now learnt that the Argentinians might use Brazilian air bases and so wartime cruising state was to be adopted that night. This was a two-watch system based upon Greenwich Mean Time (GMT) in which we remained throughout the conflict. The watches covered midnight to 0700, 0700 to 1200, 1200 to 1700 and 1700 to midnight. On reaching the Falklands, sunrise would be at about 1100 and sunset at about 1900. The second watch would see in the dawn and the fourth watch would be settled in before sunset.

Not everyone changed watch at the same time, however. The bridge and ops room had their change-over time thirty minutes apart, fifteen minutes before and fifteen minutes after the nominal watch change-over. This not only staggered mealtime queues but it ensured that whilst the ops room crew were settling in, the bridge team were undisturbed. When the bridge watch was changing over, the ops room crew were already settled.

Rumours began to permeate through the ship suggesting that the landings were likely to be in both East and West Falkland. I guessed at Choiseul Sound and Low Bay for East Falkland and between Albermarle and Fox Bay in West Falkland; I was way off mark which demonstrates the problem faced by the Argentinians. With so many options available, where would we land? One rumour which turned out to be true was that the RAF were resurrecting their 'V' bombers to bomb Stanley airport.

Shortly before midnight we intercepted a signal concerning our future employment. On reaching the exclusion zone we were to blockade the Falklands, fighting off the enemy whenever he ventured into the exclusion zone and then escort the amphibious force inshore. *Spartan* was already in the exclusion zone reporting Argentine ship movements and suspected minelaying.

Tuesday, 20 April
Wars are run in accordance with strict rules as well as in compliance with the Geneva Convention. The Fleet was subject to rules of engagement and we received the rules in force during the afternoon. The political policy was to avoid provocation with the aim of a safe transit to the objective, being prepared, however, to meet force with force. The detailed rules were that, 'We could respond to aggression with tactful firmness and were to exhibit a determination to meet any escalation, though not to exceed it. When the enemy was about to engage we were to use minimum force to prevent the successful employment of his weapons. For self defence we could consider an attack on one unit to be an attack on all. The Commanding Officer had the inherent right to use such force in self defence to protect lives. We could harass the Argentinians to a similar extent. Maritime International Law was not to be broken unless it was necessary to achieve the aim. Shadowing and surveillance could be both overt and covert. The requirement to remain undetected need not have priority over other operational objectives. South of 35 degrees South the political policy was for any attempt by Argentine units to threaten progress of the mission to be met with sufficient action to ensure mission success.'

Detailed rules included authority to, 'Take such action against positively identified Argentine units as was necessary to achieve the military task. We could assume all conventional submarines detected to be Argentinian. We could warn off all enemy units which constituted a threat and attack any Argentine units which demonstrated hostile intent. We could assume that the first attack by an enemy was the first in a planned multiple attack.' These were quite robust rules.

During the day we received some unexpected mail from *Hermes*; unfortunately, it was outgoing mail which we had sent days ago.

Our fuel was down to 63 per cent which concerned me as within two days we expected heavy seas. *Olmeda* was not due to rendezvous with us for three days by which time I anticipated our fuel would be down to 30 per cent. With thirty-six ships requisitioned for the operation, fuel was going to be a logistic nightmare.

Wednesday, 21 April

We awoke to rain and sonar conditions improved as the weather dulled. We were now ordered to be ready for war by 2000 on Friday 23 April when we would come within range of Argentine air surveillance. Our preparations continued with shell being fused, crystals fitted to Seacat missiles and efflux deflector plates removed from the Seaslug magazine. Now, if one missile ignited in the magazine, the entire magazine was liable to explode.

Scuttling charges had been placed by John Holden and the locations he chose included the huge seawater main inlets in the machinery spaces. As John placed the charges, worried stokers looked on in the steam turbine room and John jokingly assured them that they were perfectly safe, provided that they were kept cool and dry – the bilges of the steam room were invariably hot and wet.

Morphine ampoules had been issued to officers and senior rates in case of casualties. The doctor instructed the Chief Shipwright on how to administer an injection using a saline solution and an orange as props. The Commander, Chris Gotto, was then volunteered as the patient in a televised practical demonstration. The doctor had the first go, no one noticing that his saline jab leaked blood until the Chief Shipwright approached for his attempt. It completely put him off and his hand was shaking as he inserted the needle.

Everyone was now carrying Day-Glo orange survival suits that fitted into a pouch about the size of a lifejacket. I attached mine to my lifejacket pouch (taped in the bottom of which were two packets of mints and a small chocolate bar). Together with anti-flash gear and respirator, we felt quite encumbered. With an eye open for the worst, I kept my unofficial 'survival bag' on a peg in the charthouse. It contained socks, a shirt with shoulder badges, trousers, beret and a submarine sweater. It also contained more chocolate, mints and a flask of fresh water.

At 1140 we experienced our first genuine encounter with the Argentinians. An unidentified aircraft was detected at 120 miles and closed the force from the north, an unexpected direction. *Hermes* launched a combat air patrol (CAP) to intercept and the aircraft was identified as an Argentine military Boeing 707 flying at 42,000ft. This was a surprise. Two hours later another unidentified aircraft closed from the south and CAP was launched again, this time identifying an RAF Nimrod. The pilot was none too politely informed that we were on a war footing and instructed to identify himself considerably further away in future if he wished to avoid being engaged. As a result of the Boeing incident, Seacat missiles were loaded onto the launchers.

At 1630, *Olmeda* joined and we replenished. The day also brought unwelcome rumours that Argentina was acquiring aircraft from Brazil and this indicated, worryingly, that countries were beginning to take sides. That evening, emissions were detected from possible tracker aircraft radar which could have come from aircraft embarked in *Veinticinco De Mayo*. A dawn strike was a possibility. The Argentinians knew our location and if they eliminated our carriers with a pre-emptive strike, the war would be over and victory theirs. However, in conducting such a strike they would be exposed to counter attack. Argentine submarines might also be homing in on us. We were assuming defence watches at 0200 and from then on evasive steering was to be the norm.

The regular long squeak of the Type 184 sonar could be heard constantly through the hull as it searched the water for trouble. The 182 noisemaker was streamed with peacetime noise settings and, since we were not up against Soviet torpedoes, our best defence would be high speed. Worried that the Soviets might be listening and recording, we never applied the wartime settings to the 182 from which the Russians might have been able to devise a countermeasure; it was considered better to make some sacrifices in this sideshow in the Falklands rather than jeopardize our chances in a possible global conflict.

Thursday, 22 April
At 0200 the ship assumed the second degree of readiness and defence watches. From then on, two anti-submarine Sea Kings were

permanently on task and one Sea Harrier CAP was at permanent readiness. It crossed my mind that aviation fuel might become a limiting factor, but for that matter, so might fresh water.

A few hours later the Argentinian Boeing was intercepted at fifty miles by the Harrier and escorted off. We lacked the rules of engagement to shoot it down. Tension further increased when *Yarmouth* detected tracker radar, and during the afternoon, action stations were piped and the ship was fully closed down in fifteen minutes. The 3in chaff launcher was loaded in two and a half minutes, albeit using rockets already on deck; the starboard Oerlikon was functioned and two rounds were fired from the 4.5in gun, which led to the discovery of a cartridge ejection problem with the left gun. Despite my warnings, we needlessly lost both rubber muzzle covers, which could have easily been removed before the guns were loaded. In time, rust might make us regret their loss. Willie was launched for trials to determine whether lock-on could be broken on the Type 901 Seaslug guidance beam radar. Broken lock was achieved only once.

Throughout the day our station was Circle 5 on *Invincible*, a station which was devised for 'County' class ships to provide area air defence for an aircraft carrier without danger of the Seaslug wrap-round boosters landing on the carrier.

It had been a glorious day with a beautiful sunset. Now 2,200 miles away from the Falklands, we had settled down to the defence watch routine. At 2100 *Glamorgan* and *Alacrity* were detached to investigate a surface contact 120 miles ahead, which was identified as a Panamanian freighter. This was more of an exercise than anything else and it highlighted some minor procedural problems with a departing surface action group. We also tried out our station-keeping lights. Two pairs of lights were rigged either side of the masts, controlled by a dimmer box on the bridge. When silent, these lights could be dimly illuminated for visual ranging on our consort using metre-based rangefinders. If silent and totally dark you can only be seen up to about five cables (1,000 yards). At 5,000 yards other aids were required.

Friday, 23 April

The Argentine Boeing returned, was detected by *Glamorgan*, and intercepted by the combat air patrol at fifty miles. The Argentinians provocatively shone a very bright light at the Harrier and it was irksome to let the enemy escape to fight another day. After the

Boeing departed, *Brilliant* was detached to join the South Georgia group to provide additional helicopter troop–lifting capacity. She was to rendezvous with the *Antrim* group just north of South Georgia on 24 April ready for a possible landing on the following day.

Breakfast was interrupted when *Broadsword* picked up a fast-moving sonar contact. It was briefly held by *Alacrity* and a magnetic anomaly detector (MAD) fitted on a Lynx helicopter. Sonar conditions were bad with the layer (a variable depth beneath which sonar signals are distorted) at 100 feet, below which it was virtually impossible to hold contact. The contact went deep and to this day we do not know whether it was an intruder or a false alarm.

At 1045, we detected the Boeing, now nicknamed the 'Burglar', at 190 miles. A combat air patrol was launched but the Argentinian turned away with the Harrier still fifty miles from interception. Chaff was laid for confusion. Once the excitement was over I updated my ship position plot. *Conqueror* was moving to the north-west side of the exclusion zone; *Spartan* was on patrol off Stanley and *Splendid* had been withdrawn from hunting for the carrier group. The majority of the amphibious group had reached Ascension. A stream of other ships were all heading towards the Falklands. In all, I had forty-eight British ships on my plot, with many more due to sail shortly.

At 1720 our group was ordered to fuel immediately and proceed south in readiness to support Operation Paraquat. Intelligence had reported that the Argentine submarine *Santa Fe* was in that vicinity and I suspected that other Argentine forces would also be on their way. Drawing the Argentine fleet beyond the range of their air support could be to our advantage and then, once we had recovered South Georgia, we could exert political pressure from a position of strength.

Operation Corporate suffered its first loss of life that evening when, at 1930, a Sea King helicopter suddenly ditched without a mayday. Zero visibility conditions and driving rain were difficult for visual single pilot flying, especially after a long and hard day. The helicopter may have had a radio altimeter failure and, with no visual horizon, the pilot hit the sea. He managed to escape and fire a couple of flares that were seen by Willie and *Broadsword*. We arrived on the scene simultaneously with *Broadsword* who was made scene of action commander and once the wreckage and the pilot had been found, we moved off to rejoin the replenishment group. The pilot was recovered but his aircrewman, Petty Officer Kevin Casey, probably not strapped in, died. Two flotation bags were on the surface, one attached to a tail wheel, so it was presumed that the helicopter had broken up and sunk. As we returned to *Olmeda* there was an air of sadness and feeling for the lost airman's next of kin.

By 2200 we had completed fuelling. Economical steaming, using only the steam turbines, consumed about 50 tons per day. Every time we went above 16 knots our fuel consumption started to rise significantly. We could make 25 knots on steam alone and at full power on steam our fuel consumption was about five tons per hour. If we had to use our four G6 gas turbines, they really soaked up the fuel. Normally consuming five tons per hour, flat out each G6 consumed six tons per hour. Fuelling policy was for ships to report daily if fuel capacity fell below 70 per cent. Once down to that figure, if practicable, ships would replenish that night whilst any air threat was reduced.

The replenishment complete, we continued towards South Georgia to join up with the *Sheffield* group and be poised to give support to Operation Paraquat.

Saturday, 24 April
The weather turned foul, forcing us to reduce speed and as it deteriorated further we slowed down even more in order to stow Willie in the hangar. As we were turning to do so, the severity of pitch was so great that Willie's wheels actually left the deck. It was only the nylon straps which kept the helicopter on board.

Reacting to the Argentinian deployments, Admiral Woodward sent *Conqueror* back to South Georgia to conduct anti-submarine operations; *Spartan* covered Port Stanley and *Splendid* was returning to the exclusion zone. *Onyx* would also shortly be in the South Atlantic. We pressed on at the best speed but I did not fully understand why we were going so fast as we would eventually have to wait for the tankers to catch up.

At 1600, the 'Burglar' was driven off by a combat air patrol. The new rules of engagement allowed the Harriers to fire ahead of the intruder but not to shoot it down, even if it ignored warnings. Three hours later we suffered a serious defect to our 992 radar which could not be fixed until receipt of spares and as it was possible that one of the Type 21 frigates had the necessary spares we signalled the Materials Control Officer (MATCONOFF) with our requirement.

MATCONOFF was designated to co-ordinate and control the use of spare parts throughout the Task Force but defence cuts had slimmed down the stores organisation. Within two hours we would cross latitude 35 degrees South and enter the war zone and we needed the 992 for surface and air search as well as target indication.

Sunday, 25 April

Dawn saw the start of Operation Paraquat at South Georgia. The fact that the shooting had started was depressing as it rather indicated that all hope of peace was finally gone. Events then started to go wrong. The recce party landed but had to be recovered due to severe weather conditions and the recovery took place in whiteout conditions resulting in a Wessex crashing. Fortunately, its crew managed to escape and Lieutenant Commander Ian Stanley, *Antrim*'s pilot, executed a very skillful recovery operation in abysmal flying conditions for which he was deservedly awarded the Distinguished Service Order.

Further unwelcome news was received from South Georgia when *Plymouth* and *Tidespring* were sighted by an Argentine Hercules aircraft. We would have been even less enthralled had we known that the *Santa Fe* had *Tidespring* in its sights but instead of attacking, the submarine continued on its mission of attempting to land reinforcements.

We knew that the element of surprise in South Georgia was now lost and we were feeling that the operation was not going too well when, suddenly, Paraquat turned for the better with news that an Argentine submarine had been attacked on the surface. *Endurance* reported the submarine hit in the fin by an AS12 missile and the *Santa Fe*, leaking oil, proceeded on the surface into Cumberland Bay. Further signals reported a gun battle in progress with *Brilliant* and the submarine which was now unable to dive having been damaged by a depth charge. Shortly afterwards the submarine was reported to be aground at Grytviken. With our troops ashore, a naval bombardment commenced in support.

At 1630 *Invincible* detected a 'riser' (sudden appearance of a surface radar echo, normally associated with a submarine's periscope). This was probably a whale and after yet more false alarms a Sea King conducted a very spirited action against the creature, dropping one depth charge and launching a Mark 46 torpedo. With one submarine accounted for at South Georgia and another in a very dubious condition, I very much doubted that the Argentinians, unsure of our position, would deploy one of their two remaining submarines into the middle of nowhere. However, if you have a firm sonar contact in a dangerous position you cannot take chances.

By 1730 we had received a full sitrep (situation report) from South Georgia. The *Santa Fe* was aground, listing, smoking and leaking oil alongside at King William Point, Grytviken, and damage assessment considered her to be unfit to dive. The significance of the loss of the *Santa Fe* was that *Conqueror* could now be released from South Georgia to return to the Falklands area. The main landing on South Georgia was to take place later that evening and pressure to surrender was to be put onto the Argentinians by the *Antrim* group.

Meanwhile, the carrier battle group was to close the Falklands to sanitize the maritime exclusion zone. I was conscious of the Argentine air threat and I wondered whether we had sufficient ships to overcome it. Obviously, our prime target would be Stanley airport because if we could deny that to the Argentinians then their mainland based aircraft would only have very limited time over the islands before lack of fuel forced them to return home.

With the Sea King action over, we replenished from *Appleleaf.* We normally conducted fast approaches with fast decelerations when coming alongside for replenishment to break through the interaction zones of the ships' pressure waves as quickly as possible. Replenishment speed was normally 12 knots. When approaching we would ring on 22 knots but when the bridge was more or less abreast the stern of the tanker, we would ring on 'stop', setting revolutions for 12 knots. The machinery control room would apply astern steam, acting as a brake, to bring the shafts to rest. When four knots above replenishment speed, 'half ahead' would be ordered at the ordered RAS speed. If overshooting, 'half ahead' was delayed and if undershooting 'half ahead' was ordered early. This took a seaman's eye and confidence and nine times out of ten you would end up nicely in position to pass the gear. Occasionally, as today, the unexpected happened. We had a down swell course and unfortunately 'caught the surf' just at the moment of 'Stop', and were nearly carried past the tanker. We had to hold the brakes on hard for a long time. Station keeping was very difficult in the swell but the evolution was completed without further untoward incident.

Sunday drew to a close with an American newsman on Tierra Del Fuego reporting that the Argentinians in South Georgia had surrendered.

Monday, 26 April

It was confirmed that South Georgia had been recaptured, news which the families received with mixed feelings. We had won this battle but now there was a war to be won. The capture of the *Santa Fe* and the fall of South Georgia brought a very useful intelligence haul which we were to exploit.

The afternoon's air defence exercise against Harriers from *Hermes* did not go well. There were problems with both 966 and 992 radars and target acquisition to the gunnery system was poor. As the evening progressed, the wind and sea increased and we could only make good 10 knots. Even at that speed we took heavy seas green over the bridge. We were now less than 1,000 miles from the exclusion zone and by dawn we would be within range of Argentine bombers, raising the air threat warning to yellow.

Tuesday, 27 April

During standard operator checks one 3in chaff rocket was fired in error, leaving us with sixty-three remaining. By midday *Glamorgan* was only making good eight knots in a Force 9 which was generating 30ft waves. The ship was creaking and groaning and we frequently buried our head. We could feel the vibration throughout the ship as the screws raced when they came out of the water.

We heard that *Antrim* was to escort *Tidespring* back to Ascension to land the prisoners whilst *Brilliant* and *Plymouth* would join us, leaving *Endurance* on station in South Georgia. *Glamorgan* had been nominated as the surface action group Commander and if the Argentinians came out to fight we would be in the thick of it.

Updated information arrived concerning our submarines. *Conqueror* was bound for an area northeast of the Falklands; *Spartan* was in the maritime exclusion zone (MEZ), and *Splendid* was looking for the *Veinticinco De Mayo* group. One Argentinian Type 42 destroyer had been located outside the exclusion zone by *Splendid* and we knew that the Argentinians were in three groups to the west. *General Belgrano* was in the southerly group and *Veinticinco De Mayo* in the northerly group.

At midday my narrative noted that we had been told to go and replenish (RAS). The next entry was three and a quarter hours later and read, 'RAS completed followed by a hot shower and a cup of hot coffee. It was a bastard!' The fo'c's'le was completely untenable and at 10 knots, steering was dangerously sluggish. We made a slow approach from the beam, edging closer until well within Coston line gun range. The first gun line, about the same size as a bathroom lightpull cord, was successfully passed and was attached by the tanker to a messenger, a 1in rope to which the heavier lines could be attached. The gun line parted when the messenger was only 2ft outboard of us. On the second attempt we did not bother with a telephone or distance line. There was no need for a distance line; we were either too close or too far apart as we bucked back and forth. Speed was the other problem. When either ship hit a milestone (large wave), it virtually came to a shuddering halt but the snag was that the two ships never hit a milestone at the same time so that either the tanker or ourselves suddenly raced ahead and had to kill speed. We then had to get the revs on at just the right moment to match fuelling stations. *Olmeda* was a large tanker, fully laden. Despite this, her bow frequently came clear of the water and you could see right under her keel for 50ft. No doubt she got a pretty good view of our sonar dome. At times during the exercise we came close to *Olmeda*, but never closer than 30ft. Though in calmer conditions we would close to about 100ft to pass the gear and then open out to about 160ft.

At 1700 useful intelligence came in detailing the movements of the submarine *San Luis*. She had been given a twenty-mile radius patrol area north of Macbride Head (Area Maria) and with any luck *Spartan* would be able to intercept. Intelligence also reported a minefield bearing 020 degrees to 200 degrees from Cape Pembroke Point out to a radius of twelve miles. This covered the approaches to Port Stanley but left a small area of water close inshore where we could get close enough to bombard the port and the airfield. It was tight, with little searoom, and would put us under the artillery pieces situated on the hills around Stanley. Having by now dried out from the replenishment, I set about drawing up my bombardment charts, marking the minefield and submarine patrol area.

Wednesday, 28 April
Overnight we received revised rules of engagement. The policy was now modified to escalate the situation and we were to enforce a total

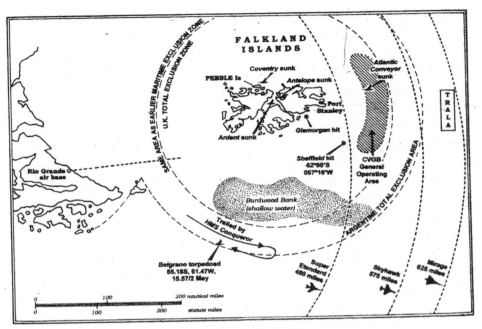

Theatre of Naval Conflict

exclusion zone (TEZ), establishing a blockade to prevent entry or exit of Argentine units, taking action as necessary to achieve the military task. We could attack designated targets with conventional weapons. Authority was granted to warn off commercial aircraft and merchant ships within the total exclusion zone and also to warn off all enemy units that constituted a threat. If merchant ships ignored warnings, force could be used. Authority was given to attack any submarine within twenty-five miles, and any ship or aircraft within forty miles which demonstrated hostile intent. We could assume that one attack by an Argentinian was the first of many and any threatening units could be attacked in order to prevent a pre-emptive attack. For self-defence purposes, an attack on one unit could be assumed to be an attack on all and the Commanding Officer had the inherent right to use such force in self-defence to protect his command and the lives of his crew. Maritime International Law was not to be broken unless it was necessary in order to achieve the aim.

The total exclusion zone would come into force at 1100 on 30 April and we would enter it shortly afterwards. Our first tasking was to bombard Stanley airfield and I commenced my preparations. We knew that howitzers were sited on Mount William and Sapper

Hill and that there were numerous concentrations of Argentinians around Stanley and the surrounding hills.

At 1700 we experienced our first serious incident. The 'Burglar's' radar was intercepted and a combat air patrol was immediately launched to intercept. *Invincible*, after an initial mis-report which caused a scare, reported a 'hostile' (confirmed enemy unit) west at 200 miles. People were very jumpy. The combat air patrol was held at eighty miles and chaff hotel (helicopter-launched chaff) was sown to confuse the 'Burglar's' picture. This was the first contact with the Argentinians for three days and the first relatively close to the Falklands.

Once the hubbub died down we replenished from *Appleleaf* and transfered outgoing mail, which was probably our last chance before the fighting started. *Appleleaf* was by now nearly empty and very buoyant and skittish. We tried the replenishment at 14 knots, taking the occasional green wave over the fo'c's'le, and nearly lost the Chief Boatswain's Mate over the side.

Thursday, 29 April
We entered the Furious Fifties where can be found some of the roughest seas in the world. I had seen a whale close to the ship, which probably explained the flurry of good firm sonar contacts in the morning which interrupted my bombardment preparations. The helicopter delivery service (HDS) that morning brought a photograph of the gridded map of the Port Stanley area and I was now able to transpose the grid onto the chart and draw up a visual bearing lattice to facilitate rapid and accurate fixing. Information on the minefield had also been refined.

In duels between ships and shore batteries, ships have come off second best. Shore batteries tended to be well dug in and if you missed a shore battery by 100ft no damage was done. A shell 100ft back from our turret, however, would drop down the funnel, so if we were to stand a fair chance of surviving, we would have to go in fast and steer evasively. I based the naval gunfire support gun-line on Wolf Rock and chose names for the five reference points after my daughters.

Shortly after sunset the 'Burglar' returned; he made only four sweeps on his radar. He was getting smart and less bold.

Friday, 30 April
The 'Burglar' returned in the morning but a combat air patrol was not launched. We were now just 250 miles from the total exclusion

zone and the Admiral wanted *Glamorgan* to 'tweak' the Argentinians with *Arrow* and *Alacrity*. We would be 100 miles ahead of everyone else without the protection of any Sea Dart ships and if the RAF failed to disable the runway at Stanley we would be terribly exposed to air attack.

That afternoon I was informed of a plan to bring down the 'Burglar'. *Glamorgan* was to be detached and when the 'Burglar' arrived, chaff would be laid. The hope was that the 'Burglar' might be lured within Seaslug range and we could get a quick shot at him. The only problem was that he never showed up.

The day saw peace talks finally break down. *Conqueror* was trailing *General Belgrano* and *Splendid* had latched onto three frigates, hoping they would lead her to *Veinticinco De Mayo*. *Spartan* was still after the *San Luis*. We had no information on the whereabouts of the other Argentine submarine. As a submarine countermeasure, I instructed the officer of the watch to ensure that the helmsman meandered 20 degrees either side of the set course. I also instructed the machinery control room to similarly meander the shaft revolutions by 20rpm, up on one shaft and down on the other and then vice versa. This would make obtaining a meaningful revolution count much more difficult.

As we covered the final miles towards the total exclusion zone tension was evident, though training gave us the courage to mask our fear. We were a well-knit team at the peak of our efficiency. As an escort, and thus expendable, we would find ourselves dispatched into harm's way and our very survival, and that of the Task Force, would depend to a greater or lesser degree upon how each individual performed. It is worth remembering that when *Glamorgan* sailed for the South Atlantic the average age on board was less than twenty; the youngest crew member, Junior Stores Assistant Hodges, was only sixteen and over half of the crew were teenagers. Mike Barrow and Brian Lister had their fiftieth birthdays during the deployment and were the oldest pair aboard. We all drew from their experience and calm resolution.

* * *

Whilst we prepared for the shooting our thoughts were also back with our families. On 26 April Bruce Neill had written the following letter to *Glamorgan*'s next of kin.

When the Falkland Islands Task Force was formed … it was felt that certain special arrangements should be made to help support the wives and families of the men in the ships. I am sure you already know about some of these. The purpose of this letter is to let you know that each of the ships in the Task Force has been allocated a link chaplain, and that I am the link chaplain for *Glamorgan*.

Also the whole of the greater Portsmouth area has been divided into sections with a chaplain allocated to each … A Task Force Information Centre has been set up in *Nelson*. The telephone is manned 24 hours a day. If you have any particular difficulty, or would like to feel a bit more involved, or would just like to phone for a chat, please don't hesitate to get in touch with us.

It was perhaps worse for the families than ourselves. We at least knew when we were in immediate danger and when we were relatively safe. The families, bombarded by jingoistic media, worried all the time. Judy Barrow was organising our families and setting up a comprehensive rear link support organisation which meant that we did not have to worry.

Judy, with the Commander's wife, Elizabeth Gotto, worked on a families' action plan. Confidentiality was uppermost in their minds as they compiled crew family lists. Before *Glamorgan* sailed from Portsmouth, Mike had given her an officers' list with details of wives, children and telephone contact details. These had been passed onto the officers' wives at a meeting held at Elizabeth Gotto's at the start of the crisis. Mike sent a further similar list of senior rates from Gibraltar.

Armed with these lists Judy and Elizabeth set to work. Following an invitation to lunch at one of the Portsmouth area naval establishments, Judy was seated next to her host. She explained what she and Elizabeth were trying to do and how a comprehensive list of the ship's company with next of kin details would be helpful. This request would have been turned down in peacetime but her influential host appreciated the significance and value of her request. Judy left the lunch with an address list of next of kin. With these, Judy, Elizabeth and Lynne Edleston typed out as many regional lists as necessary. Copies were then sent to next of kin who had contacted Judy or Elizabeth about the scheme.

The officers' wives met on 29 April for a *Glamorgan* picnic held at Rhian Raine's. They copied these geographically-based lists produced by Judy and Bruce Neill. Marianne was allocated fourteen wives living nearby in Gosport, and spent most of 30 April establishing personal contact. Other wives undertook similar activities in their areas. These wives and families fostered the *Glamorgan* spirit. The system worked by information received by Judy being passed on to the officers' wives who would then cascade the information to their respective groups. These groups would meet on a regular basis. Judy took it upon herself to maintain contact with the wives and families who lived out of naval areas and who were isolated. Thus the *Glamorgan* rear link organisation excelled. Other ships' families, noting such a difference in service, felt it necessary to complain, testament to Judy's work.

Further support was available from Fleet Chief Andrew Faulkner whom we had left behind in Portsmouth before sailing on 17 March. He was on call twenty-four hours a day and was more than willing to detail his son to cut wives' lawns. On the official side there was also a 'Falklands Helping Hand Centre' located in Gosport. These examples were representative of numerous other support groups that were formed all around the country. One should not underestimate their value, not only to the families concerned but also to ships' companies. In *Glamorgan* we were proud of how our families were supporting each other. So, with our families right behind us, *Glamorgan* went to war.

Chapter 4

The Longest Day

Saturday, 1 May

We gave up waiting for the 'Burglar' in the early hours and headed off to rejoin the carrier battle group. A skillet of chaff had been spilt in Willie's cab, contaminating everything and necessitating the helicopter's departure to *Hermes* for repairs. We temporarily received a Wessex from *Resource* which laid chaff to confuse the pass of a Soviet radar satellite.

At 0745, communications were established with the RAF Vulcan bomber Black Buck One after it had bombed Stanley airport. News of Black Buck's success spread throughout the ship and the Vulcan returned safely to Ascension. The attack must have come as an unpleasant surprise to the Argentinians, demonstrating our capability to deliver ordnance over huge distances, including mainland Argentina if required. Whilst the RAF were delighted with their achievement, photo reconnaissance showed that only one bomb had actually hit the runway: twenty had missed.

At 0819 we entered the total exclusion zone and the war zone. As the weather was fine, the Admiral decided we should replenish fuel before detaching inshore. At 1030, twelve Harriers were preparing to take off to bomb Stanley airport and Goose Green whilst we screened the main body in company with *Brilliant* and *Yarmouth*. People were understandably edgy. Almost immediately a helicopter obtained sonar contact and dropped two Mark 46 torpedoes. A whale and some blubber oil surfaced; two torpedoes had been expended on a false alarm. The next alert was genuine when two hostile aircraft were detected and intercepted by a combat air patrol at 100 miles. At 1040 the ship went to action stations for two Mirage aircraft 130 miles to the southwest. The anti-air warfare co-ordinator (AAWC) called air raid warning red (air attack imminent).

In films, when the action alarm sounds, everyone grabs their helmets and rushes to action stations. In reality, many people suddenly have an urge to urinate, even those who have only just been. Petty

Officer Balston recorded in his diary, 'Hell, here we go! Hands to action stations! On anti-flash, trousers tucked into socks, aircraft attack imminent. We move like lightening.' Two combat air patrols (CAP) were launched to intercept and two more to goalkeep. It was assessed that the Mirages had come from the mainland as a dawn CAP and being at the limit of their endurance, they would shortly be returning to base, probably before our Harrier strike arrived. Indeed, the two Mirage turned away a few minutes later.

At 1130 we detached with *Arrow* and *Alacrity* to bombard targets around Stanley. The 'Three Musketeers', as we were to become known, set off at 15 knots, leaving the rest of the carrier battle group to the east. We still had the borrowed Wessex embarked and by now Willie had returned. With space for one helicopter in the hangar, and one on the flight deck, flying operations were going to be complicated. Our feelings were summed up by Petty Officer Wiltshire, 'Christ, the Admiral is sending us in to the Falklands for NGS [naval gunfire support]. During daylight.'

Unknown to us, Northwood had similar reservations about sending us inshore in daylight but by the time Northwood had informed Admiral Woodward of their misgivings, we were almost there. It would have been too late to make recall worthwhile. Northwood, it seemed, did not consider escorts to be quite so expendable, especially a 'County' class destroyer.

Shortly afterwards, a combat air patrol intercepted two Mirage. One was 'seen carrying Exocet'. If true, the Mirage had to be a Super Etendard. If it was a Mirage then the 'Exocet' was probably an external fuel pod. Action stations was piped and chaff charlie (chaff delivered by a 4.5in shell for confusion) fired. One Mirage was seen to be on fire and a Harrier executed an optimistic victory roll overhead. Other reports indicated that the 'Mirage on fire' was, in fact, a Mirage launching a missile. Six minutes later *Invincible* locked onto a target at sixty miles and *Glamorgan* opened weapon arcs for Seaslug but within seconds 'hold fire' was called as the unknown was identified as a friendly combat air patrol returning. A potential blue-on-blue engagement had been avoided.

Just before midday, all of *Hermes*' Harriers returned safely from their bombing missions though one had a 20mm bullet hole through the tail. The helicopter delivery service arrived at midday as the action died down and we reverted to defence watches and had lunch. The wardroom galley was only being used for breakfast and so for the rest of the day everyone used the main galley, the officers eating with the senior rates in their dining hall. This was just one of the many minor administrative differences between peace and war.

At 1245 *Alacrity* sighted what she believed to be a torpedo. Action stations was piped and the 'torpedo' was also sighted by *Plymouth*. Since no submarine was actually present, these spurious sightings were signs of inexperience. Having conducted our torpedo countermeasures (TCM) we resumed towards the gun-line. *Alacrity* re-classified her torpedo as a unifoxer, a noisemaker towed astern to decoy homing torpedoes, though *Plymouth* and a helicopter continued to investigate a sonar contact. Whilst this was going on two contacts, believed to be Super Etendards, were detected closing at 170 miles but these contacts were again identified as returning combat air patrols. The same happened a few minutes later but just as chaff charlie was fired, Seaslug became defective and out ahead of the carriers we felt very exposed. Whilst this was going on, *Plymouth* obtained a positive sounder run and she attacked her contact twice with Mortar Mark 10. The two hostiles were soon within 120 miles and at 90 miles both *Invincible* and *Sheffield*'s Sea Dart systems acquired but the contacts turned away just outside missile range. *Invincible* then incorrectly reported a submarine. Gradually calm returned.

At 1317, there were a flurry of enemy reports and the ops room assessed that the radar intercepts were Mirage aircraft conducting combat air patrols over Stanley. When all hostiles were opening, we relaxed again from action stations for thirty minutes before the next raid. Seaslug was operational again. The raid went low and was lost to radar but CAP was dispatched to investigate.

At 1410 smoke was sighted rising from Port Stanley, a result of the morning's raids. Five minutes later more aircraft were detected and CAP was dispatched under *Glamorgan*'s control. The raid turned away before interception. It became evident that the enemy was trying to lure our combat air patrol towards Stanley over the anti-air artillery (AAA). It went quiet again until *Invincible* detected another pair of hostiles which were intercepted. Two further slow moving contacts to the west were assessed as either tactical direction aircraft or the Argentinian tanker tow line. This pattern of air activity continued throughout the day.

The Falkland Islands were now held on radar at forty miles and we were intercepting Argentinian Skyguard air warning radar coming from the Stanley area; they too would have intercepted our radar. We were now well within the range of Argentine Pucara aircraft, based on airstrips around the Islands, and they could come from anywhere with little or no warning. Shortly before 1530 the Falkland Islands hove into view and the ship closed up at action stations for bombardment, on which she was to remain until 2110 that night.

We were not the only units out on a limb. *Brilliant* and *Yarmouth*, with three Sea King helicopters, had been sent to Area Maria to search for *San Luis*. It must have come as an unpleasant surprise to *San Luis* to be suddenly descended upon by a dedicated anti-submarine warfare (ASW) group. *Brilliant*'s group attracted attention and at 1640 there was a CAP melee to the north of us, with missiles unsuccessfully being fired at the Harriers. Whilst this was going on *Alacrity* gained a sonar contact and Willie investigated, classifying the contact as marine life.

At 1704, a possible submarine was reported on the surface. It was on the bearing of Cape Pembroke Light and I suggested that it was the lighthouse. The contact was then reported as a possible conning tower with smoke. I once again reported to the ops room that there was also smoke on the bearing coming from fires ashore and that the reported contact was Cape Pembroke. It was not until 1748 that I convinced everyone. By then we had twenty-five miles to run to the bombardment start position; four hostiles were now just thirty-five miles away with a British combat air patrol intercepting. They were Daggers, Argentine versions of the French Mirage, which had been tasked against the Three Musketeers. CAP turned away and was engaged by the air defences around Stanley; as they retired, they laid down chaff to seduce surface to air missiles. Three Turbo Mentors closed, having been launched from Pebble Island to attack our supporting helicopters. They were intercepted by our CAP. Aeromacchis from Stanley were also tasked to attack our bombarding group but they never materialised.

By 1800 we were close to the minefield, in shallow water and some 100 miles ahead of the rest of the battle group. We recovered the 182 (torpedo decoy noisemaker) and streamed unifoxer in its place at short stay. The nearest known surface threat was the *Belgrano* group 320 miles to the southwest, being tailed by *Conqueror*. Argentine fast patrol boats (FPB) were somewhere in the Falklands, and, as we were close to shore, we could not discount an attack from them. As the air threat diminished, we prepared to bombard the airport.

Arrow and *Alacrity* were stationed on a line of bearing to the southwest at 1,000yd distances. Once we rounded the minefield and turned inbound towards Wolf Rock the Type 21 frigates, which had the Mark 8 gun with a maximum effective range of 21,000 yards, would be able to open fire as soon as we reached our maximum effective range which, for the Mark 6 gun, was 18,600 yards. The plan was for all three ships to open fire together.

At 1856, just as we were preparing to launch Willie, a periscope was sighted by the flight deck. I immediately turned the ship to put the contact on the other bow, the standard torpedo countermeasure, and we prepared to launch an anti-submarine torpedo down the bearing. Firm sonar contact was gained at 2,000 yards but we held fire pending classification, which a few minutes later was confirmed as sea life. Having discounted the flight deck's submarine, we turned back in and prepared to lay down our planned heavy bombardment.

Brian Lister, the Master Gunner, calmed us down. He was the only person on board who had seen real action before. Brian rubbed his hands together with a smile and said, 'I have not done this since Suez!' and the tension was immediately broken. Those around him had not heard his earlier remark in the wardroom: 'Well, this is a right pension trap!' And it could well have been so since, unknown to us, the Argentinians had dispatched twelve aircraft from the mainland to attack our bombardment group. These aircraft comprised of four Skyhawks, each carrying two 500lb bombs, with four Mirages providing top cover. Both of these groups flew out of Rio Gallegos. Four Daggers from Rio Grande completed the strike. All twelve reached the Falklands where they came under the controllers at Stanley who, in their confusion, directed the Skyhawks to the northeast of Stanley, mistaking a pair of CAP for ships! Two of the Mirage fighter pilots realised what was happening and dived on the Harriers but in the general melee neither side scored a success. Short of fuel, the strike returned to the mainland. Had the Stanley aircraft controllers been efficient, *Glamorgan*, *Arrow* and *Alacrity*, distracted by a non-existent submarine, would have faced a co-ordinated attack by eight aircraft with little searoom in which to manoeuvre.

A few minutes before we were in range of our target, I spotted a Skyvan flying low towards Goose Green. I passed the bearing to the ops room but, being busy with the air war, they were unable to allocate it to the Seaslug system - one very lucky Skyvan. Eventually, after all the excitement and false starts we were ready. All we now waited for was the executive signal from Mike Barrow to engage.

At 1923, before the order was given, *Arrow* opened fire. Given the chance to fire the opening bombardment shots of the war, we would have done the same and no rebuke was issued. *Arrow*'s range seemed to be a little short for I could see some shell splashes in the water just short of the Canache. At 1924, *Alacrity* engaged. We had to get closer to get within range and at 1925 *Glamorgan* opened fire at 18,000 yards. It was an impressive sight with all three ships firing together with huge battle ensigns flying from the yards. The shells were spread from Surf Bay to the coast by Yorke Point, fifty salvos from each of the three ships. We had provoked the enemy as directed.

Whilst the bombardment was in progress, *Alacrity*'s Lynx exchanged machine-gun fire with the Argentinian FPB *Islas Malvinas*, both units suffering slight damage with one Argentinian wounded. Willie was also engaged by two Tigercat missiles fired from the airfield but escaped unharmed. The shore batteries of the 3 Artillery Regiment replied ineffectively. Whilst we were bombarding, CAP, controlled by Lieutenant Commander Paul Raine our fighter controller, downed one Mirage.

At 1932, the initial bombardment was complete and all three ships were turned back to the southwest. It was intended that *Arrow* be first up to go back in and bombard selected targets. Eight minutes later the sky over Stanley erupted with a mass of AAA fire. I followed the flak with my eye and saw an aircraft fly into the middle of it. I thought it was a Harrier. Suddenly it seemed to almost stop in mid air, and flames erupted from the port side aft and then from both sides, before it started to plunge towards the sea. Just before it hit the sea, it turned on its side and I realised it was a Mirage; the Argentinians had just scored an own goal. It hit the water with a huge splash close to the shore by Rookery Point. The pilot, Captain Garcia Cuerva, failed to eject and, despite my jubilation, I felt a moment of sadness for the pilot and his next of kin. I picked up the main broadcast and informed the ship's company that the Argentinians had just shot down one of their own Mirages. Morale on board took a leap in the right direction, albeit not for long.

Ashore, John Smith, a Falkland Islander, had witnessed the incident from Stanley. He had also seen the Harriers bring down a

Mirage and a Canberra. These successes cheered the Islanders. Within two minutes of the red–on–red engagement, Lieutenant Owen Morgan, the Flight Deck Officer, reported three more Daggers which had just rounded Cape Pembroke, flying low at top speed.

Turning to starboard to retire from the bombardment left us running parallel to the edge of the minefield. Lieutenant Greg Gilchrist, the Principal Warfare Officer (PWO) in the ops room ordered the bridge to 'Come very hard left' to open weapon arcs for the port Seacat and the 4.5in gun, indicating the target to port Seacat.

I took one look at our position and ordered 'starboard 35', reporting to the ops room that a turn to port would have taken us into the minefield. Reversing the wheel put the target into the port Seacat system's blind arc and the starboard Seacat did not have time to acquire until very late, although one missile was fired. The sudden reversal in course spoilt the pilot's aim. Being an airforce pilot rather than a navy pilot, and unaccustomed to attacking ships, Captain Dimeglio did not allow sufficiently for ship movement.

The facts were that the centre Dagger came for us, attempting to strafe with shells and rockets. Just before the shell splashes reached the stern, the pilot took his finger off the trigger, releasing two 1,000lb parachute retarded bombs and a pair of rockets. As he pulled the stick up and flew over the top he attempted to strafe us again and a couple of shells bounced off the port Seacat director. As he overflew, the two other Daggers flew up either side below bridge level, firing at the two frigates which returned fire with their 20mm Oerlikons. The rockets whooshed close up each side and into the sea. The bombs dropped in the water either side of the quarterdeck and exploded with an almighty bang, lifting the stern 17ft and out of the water.

Eon Matthews, who was Air Picture Reporter (Force), saw all the aircraft movements on the radar and listened to air reports coming in. He watched as the raid closed, hearing the thunder of our guns and all the noises of the attack, but could not see its effects. He had felt the stern lift and immediately thought the worst.

Plumes of smoke were emitted from the after funnel as the gas turbines were flashed up, and as the aircraft departed, we managed to get in a few parting shots. *Arrow* and *Alacrity* also engaged their attackers. Seaslug acquired when the aircraft were outbound but no missile was fired. A couple of minutes later there was another large explosion and a big plume of smoke could be seen rising on the horizon in the vicinity of Lively Island. The explosion was not one of the attacking aircraft crashing since all returned safely to base. The most likely explanation was Argentina hitting one of their own ships. The fighter groups out of San Julian and Rio Gallegos put up twenty-four Skyhawk sorties and, of these, only one flight found a target. Fortunately for us, it was the merchant ship *Formosa* which had delivered a large cargo of military stores to Stanley and had sailed that morning. She was very lucky not to have been intercepted by our group but her luck ran out. She was south of East Falkland when she was bombed and strafed by the Skyhawks. Two bombs hit, one bouncing off and falling into the sea and the other not exploding. The explosion I heard was probably near misses exploding in the sea and the subsequent smoke resulted from the strafing. The *Formosa* made it back to Argentina believing that it had been attacked by Sea Harriers.

* * *

For all the ship's company, our bombardment of the shore had been a tense experience. Leading Steward Nigel Fielding witnessed the cannon fire and saw the jet drop its 1,000lb bombs. He was very shaken and had prayed for salvation. He also saw four air-to-surface rockets fired at the ship which only just missed. Petty Officer Wiltshire's graphic diary recounted,

> Hands to action stations - here we go, we creep past the minefield, Jesus, we must be mad! I am f — scared … We manoeuvre into position, the 4.5in bark their wrath over the targets, thump, thump, thump, we pump shell after shell into the airfield and gun emplacements. Fifty-four rounds of HE [high explosive] we send in, it must be murder, all that HE - men dying everywhere. We turn and make speed to leave the area. F — hell, here come the Argies, Mirage fighters coming from the Island, no radar picking them up, blind arcs, we cannot bring Seacat or Seaslug to bear. This is it, dagger, dagger, dagger - we hear the sound of cannon fire, whoosh missiles, the lot. Two loud bangs underneath the water. The Mirage fighter dropped its load and missed. *Arrow* was not so lucky, she took cannon fire on the superstructure and one man was wounded.

Midshipman Jones watched the attack from the gun direction platform (GDP). He saw the Dagger make a shallow dive and fire its cannon,

The shell splashes raced towards the stern but stopped just before they reached the transom. The pilot pulled back on the stick and the wings dropped off or at least everything on them! A pair of rockets were fired at us and a pair of 1,000lb bombs released. The rockets whooshed up the sides of the ship and, had we been beam on, most likely would have hit. As for the bombs, there was no way those bombs were going to miss until suddenly parachutes emerged at the back of the bombs, slowing them down. They plopped in either side of the quarter-deck and exploded.

Marine Phil Holding's action station was the 20mm Oerlikon. Marine Paul Dell and Junior Seaman 'Brum' were his loaders. Initially, they were just spectators of the bombardment. Phil witnessed the Argentinians shooting down their own Mirage, never forgetting the sight of it burning fiercely as it crashed into the sea. Shortly after the bombardment had been completed, air raid warning red was called on aircraft closing from astern. Phil swung his gun aft until it hit the safety stops and saw the Mirage. He opened fire on the third aircraft in the raid, emptying a complete magazine of sixty rounds. Phil was aware of the port Oerlikon engaging another aircraft. He recalled hearing the noise of the cannon shells and was a bit concerned about being shot in the back. He crouched over his gun, making himself as small as possible.

Lieutenant Commander Mike Walton, the Deputy Weapons Electrical Officer, was at the computer room display console where he kept in touch with the action. Mike saw two targets tracking west over the land. They turned south and the echoes closed the centre of the display. Mike tried desperately to alert the ops room but they were fully occupied both trying to lock onto the in-bound raid and in directing a Harrier onto another raid. Mike could see from the computer totes that the targets had not been allocated to any missile system but he lacked a command key to authorise an engagement locally. Thinking time had by then expired. The next thing he heard were two enormous bangs in rapid succession, and he felt the stern lift. Then he realised that *Glamorgan* had survived. 'Deo gratis' he muttered.

Sub-Lieutenant John Holden was in charge of the after section base, located aft. Suddenly, air raid warning red was called and shortly afterwards he heard the guns firing and a couple of whooshes. Then he felt the stern lift amid a pair of thunderous explosions as the pressure waves passed under the stern. Useful lessons emerged. John realised that damage control (DC) patrols had not been in contact with the section base. From then on they were to ring in every time they passed a DC telephone so that if anything happened their approximate location would be known by the section base.

Leading Marine Engineering Mechanic Taff Callaghan's action station was at the midships section base. He was unable to see the action but he had suddenly felt the stern lift. This was greeted by a section of white faces followed by a chorus of 'F — hell'. When things quietened down, Taff and Leading Marine Engineering Mechanic Roberts, both non–smokers, partook of a roll-up courtesy of Petty Officer Balston – the hazards of smoking seemed to have paled into insignificance when compared with bombing and strafing.

Chief Petty Officer Colin Phillips' action station was in the radar offices. He was in the 278 (height finding radar) office during the attack. Situated in the mainmast, the highest working space in the ship, he heard three loud whooshes followed by two heavy explosions which had made him fall down. On falling out from action stations he passed Lieutenant Commander Ian Forbes, the senior Anti-Air Warfare (AAW) Officer, who asked him, 'Do you now believe that we are going to war?' Until then, Colin had firmly believed that the politicians would reach a peaceful settlement.

In the forward section base, a young junior rating lay on the deck pounding the steel with his fists crying, 'I can't take any more!' He was steadied by the section base Senior Rate. Having been under constant threat of attack from above and below the surface for six hours the stress was beginning to show.

Despite being roughed up, no alarms rang on the bridge and the ship remained under control. Commander Chris Gotto appeared, checking for damage but, apart from our ashen faces and racing hearts, we had nothing to report. The only damage he found was minor splinter damage to the starboard Seacat director and a bent pillar in the tiller flat. During the attack, Chris had had an excellent view from the gun direction platform (GDP). He de-briefed the ship's company on the main broadcast. An immediate post action signal was made to the Flag, followed a day later by a more considered analysis of the enemy's tactics and errors, which had included attempts to aim different weapons at the same time. The signal gave clear warning that their anti-ship attacks were likely to be pressed home with determination and improve with experience. This signal does not appear to have been noticed at Northwood, amongst the flood of other signal traffic, but it should have been highlighted and drawn to the attention of all ships.

After the war, Argentine sources revealed the raid on the Three Musketeers had originally been tasked against the ASW group in Area Maria. On finding nothing other than one helicopter which they had let go, they closed Port Stanley only to discover the airport under heavy bombardment as our 150 shells rained in. It did not take them long to spot the culprits and Captain Dimeglio selected *Glamorgan* as his target, giving *Arrow* to his number two and *Alacrity* to his number three. The three aircraft came down to 1,000ft, rounded Cape Pembroke and closed at full speed in a shallow dive.

To observers, the huge explosions around *Glamorgan* and the column of yellow smoke from the gas turbines made it appear that she had suffered severe damage; and the sight of the ships retreating seemed to confirm this, but Mike Barrow had decided that we needed more sea room for effective air defence. We had all day so, rather than risking the group again, he elected to wait until dark to finish the job. As we retired, a sonar contact was gained and five minutes later a possible hostile aircraft was detected to the west. The sonar contact was classified as marine life, and the air threat reduced.

In his book *One Hundred Days*, Admiral Woodward criticised *Glamorgan* for being so close inshore, on the gun-line, whilst she was supposed to be providing air cover for the two frigates, but the briefing I had received was that we were to go inshore to bombard the Argentinians, and nothing was specified about providing air cover. Even if we had been tasked to provide such cover for the frigates, we could not have achieved it by being further to seawards because of the proximity of the minefield. The Admiral also mentioned that he had had to use a little 'needle' to encourage us to go back in again, but Mike Barrow had had a good appreciation of the immediate situation and recognised that we needed time to settle down before going back inshore.

After dark we reverted to defence watches to allow everyone to have supper. We listened to the world news based upon the Argentine version of events in which they claimed that no buildings had been struck but that three frigates had been hit and one heavily damaged. Inevitably, we wondered how our families would be reacting to that news. *Glamorgan* received a 'well done' from the bombardment control officer; our shells had been right on target. We also heard that *Invincible*'s CAP had downed one Argentinian Canberra and badly damaged another while we had lost no aircraft. At 2240 *Alacrity* was detached to bombard selected targets. *Arrow* was next up with *Glamorgan* due in at 0100.

Sunday, 2 May

The ship went to action stations at 0015. Our initial target was a troop concentration on Mount William. *Arrow* was still on the gun-line and at 0042 we observed her to come under heavy fire from the shore. Four minutes later a fast patrol boat was detected approaching at 30 knots and *Arrow* was detached to engage having just completed her bombardment runs and *Glamorgan* closed the gun-line.

We loosed off twenty-two salvos at the troops on Mount Longdon and as soon as the rounds were away we shifted target to a radar which ceased transmitting. At 0130 we laid down twenty rounds on another target before shifting to a gun emplacement; as we turned to starboard we almost lost Willie over the side. Ten minutes later we were illuminated by starshell and the shore batteries opened up on us. Though their fire was ineffective it was clear that the Argentinians were prepared to fire at us and that they were probably recording our movements; as a result I resolved never to follow the same track twice.

At 0211, we headed east to rejoin the carrier battle group and reverted to defence watches. On a light-hearted note, I had noticed that Cape Pembroke Light was not operating and I sent a signal to the Hydrographic Office, 'Cape Pembroke Light extinguished. *Glamorgan* not responsible!' Some years later, I told the story to Sir Rex Hunt at a Falklands dinner and he said he had known that *Glamorgan* was not responsible – he had disabled the light himself and it was extinguished for months.

So our first full day of fighting, and baptism of fire, came to an end. The bombardment had been a notable success, all runs having gone well with comprehensive preparation having been the key. We had survived 'The Longest Day' and lived to fight again and whilst most of the Task Force had yet to face direct attack, we had experienced it and were much steadier. The uninitiated were to remain jumpy for some time, but the Three Musketeers were rapidly blending into a dependable fighting unit upon whom the Admiral could trust.

Our activities on 1 May, bombarding Stanley in daylight, were to have serious consequences for *Glamorgan* later. Admiral Edgardo Otero had landed in Stanley on 26 April to become the Senior Naval Officer in the Islands and being on the receiving end of the bombardment he radioed Naval Headquarters in Argentina to demand action. He requested the deployment of fast patrol boats armed with torpedoes and though he was initially unsuccessful he did not give up. Instead, he contacted Captain Julio Perez, the engineer in charge of the Exocet workshops in Puerto Belgrano and floated the idea of launching a ship–launched Exocet from land. Perez made a detailed investigation and concluded that the task would be difficult but certainly possible. *Glamorgan*'s fate was put in train.

Chapter 5

General Belgrano and *Sheffield*

Within two hours of rejoining the carrier battle group, a surface search Harrier was illuminated by tracker and fire control radars. The Harrier investigated and located five surface contacts about 250 miles from the force. This could have been the Argentinian carrier group. Dawn came at 1030 and saw *Glamorgan* on Circle 5, with *Resource* the guide. Somewhere to the north was *Veinticinco De Mayo* which had successfully evaded our hunter killer submarine while the *General Belgrano* group was 160 miles to the south with our battle group in between.

The Admiral was conscious of *Glamorgan*'s achievement the previous year in the Arabian Sea when she had outwitted the American aircraft carrier *Coral Sea* whose surveillance capability was superior to our own. *Coral Sea* boasted that no ship could close within 200 miles undetected but this was to be disproved. Our embarked staff disguised us as a merchant ship and we approached at night, silently, with merchant ship lighting rigged. Challenged by light when we encountered the carrier's outer destroyer screen, I asked approval to put on my best Indian accent on VHF Channel 16 and purport to be the Indian merchant ship *Punjabi*. In response an American replied, 'This is an American warship, please disregard my light.' We passed the outer screen without further challenge. Shortly afterwards, *Coral Sea* was sighted at twenty miles and within Exocet range for our simulated firing. The inner screen then challenged us and, again, we successfully claimed to be the *Punjabi*, and then, as soon as our weapon arcs were open, we simulated firing four Exocet missiles at *Coral Sea* from a range of fifteen miles. Against all the odds we disproved *Coral Sea*'s claim. Admiral Woodward had been delighted and now recalled our success. If we could close undetected, so too might the Argentinians. With sixteen hours of darkness (320 miles at 20 knots) *General Belgrano* could close under cover of darkness. *Veinticinco De Mayo* was poised to launch air strikes from the north and, additionally, the Argentine Air Force had shown considerable resolve in attacking *Glamorgan*'s group on the gun-line. Heavy air attacks were anticipated.

By 1300 the group of contacts to the north had closed within the total exclusion zone. The SSNs were re-deployed to counter this threat, assessed as *Veinticinco De Mayo*, but no air raids materialised. It was only later we discovered that insufficient wind over the deck had prevented the carrier from launching her strike in a co-ordinated operation with *General Belgrano*. The operation had been cancelled.

After lunch, all was quiet and we replenished stores and ammunition from *Resource* and fuel from *Olmeda*. On completion, I took the opportunity for a spot of rest; after all, it was Sunday. The main body had tracked north for most of the day, accounting for the limited detection of air activity, turning at 1530 to head back towards the Islands. Three hours later we received orders to bombard the Stanley area. We felt this was risky since the Argentinians now knew where our gun-line was located. They had the opportunity to either extend their minefield or bring *San Luis* down from Area Maria to an area east of Choiseul Sound. As we closed the islands considerable air activity was detected.

We planned to fire 150 rounds at the airport whilst *Arrow* and *Alacrity* engaged other targets. We would all have to proceed inshore of the minefield which was a calculated risk and would limit our sea room and expose us to the shore batteries. To assist me during night bombardments, I had sellotaped a strip alongside the bridge radar display with the 2,023 times table which allowed me to convert nautical miles into thousands of yards for the gunners. Since we normally fired at between 16,000yds and 18,000yds, using 2,000yds per mile would introduce a 200yd error on the first shell. The Royal Artillery Liaison Officer Naval Gunfire Support (RALONGS) supplied lists of targets and was embarked for all of our inshore bombardments and was instrumental in ensuring that our rounds were effectively used in support of operations ashore. I very carefully selected initial firing positions as an error of 1 degree in bearing makes a lateral difference of 50ft at 1,000yds, something like 250yds at the ranges we were firing.

On 1 May the biggest limitation to our bombardment had been the lack of a gridded map; all we had was a photo of part of the target area with the grid superimposed. RALONGS now brought along an army gridded map and this enabled me to plot the grid onto my bombardment chart. Later, Taunton were to provide small-scale charts with 'grid ticks' which made life easier, but in the meantime I had to draw my own grid from scratch. With enough reference points it was a relatively simple matter to draw slightly curved grid lines on the chart equating to the straight grid lines on the army map. Naval charts used the mercator projection that was different from the Universal Transverse Mercator grid on army maps and so required the grid to be bent to fit the chart. Having completed my preparations I produced a target sheet which I photocopied and took to the ops room. Whilst there, I heard unconfirmed reports that a total of eleven Argentine aircraft had failed to return to their bases on 1 May. I then paid one of my regular visits to the machinery control room, armed with a chart, to let the lads below know what was happening.

We detached at 2015 and an hour later detected a surface contact at ten miles. We quickly discovered that it was a radar test balloon released by *Alacrity* for pre-action calibration of the ballistics. We relaxed for a moment and continued on our 25-knot dash inshore. We were due to reach the gun-line shortly before midnight and slowly apprehension mounted. Because the opposition would be expecting us, we had shifted our approach line and put our timing back. Our attack would also coincide with an insertion of the SAS to the north and we hoped to distract the enemy's attention from this activity. SAS had already been inserted ashore during the previous night. The night's bombardment was to concentrate on AAA sites as Black Buck, the RAF Vulcan bomber, was due in again that night. Our main concerns were mines, *San Luis*, Pucara aircraft, shore batteries and grounding in poorly charted waters. Since it was my task to select our track inshore, I would feel personally responsible if we hit a mine or encountered a submarine, and it weighed heavily upon my mind. Had I second guessed the enemy or had they second guessed me?

At 2300, all our preparations came to naught when we were ordered to cancel the bombardment and return to the carrier battle group. We suspected that the *Belgrano* group was closing. Shortly afterwards it was thought that three Argentinian corvettes were in the area. A Sea King, searching for *San Luis*, had overflown a vessel, believed to be a corvette. Forty minutes later, another Sea King was engaged by 20mm cannon fire from a surface contact in the same vicinity, and had to take swift evasive action. Since the corvettes were

:h Exocet I could understand the Admiral's desire to get us
the screen where he could have his surface action group
ngage this potential threat. The real reason for our recall,
however, emerged later. *Conqueror* had torpedoed *General Belgrano*.
The Admiral, still faced with a serious surface threat to the north,
wanted his escorts back; nor did he want to lose any ships that night
on operations inshore and subsequently lose or reduce the
psychological impact of sinking *Belgrano*.

Whilst we closed the carrier group, Lynx helicopters from
Coventry and *Glasgow* were ordered to attack the surface contacts.
Guided by the Sea King, *Coventry*'s Lynx fired two Sea Skua missiles
and then, after radar contact was lost, went in looking for survivors.
Both helicopters came under fire from what they believed to be a
second vessel and *Glasgow*'s Lynx fired two Sea Skua missiles at this
target, claiming further hits. *Coventry*'s Lynx's first missile had
actually hit *Alferez Sobral*, or rather its motor boat; the second missile
had passed close over the bridge. If the target had been a corvette
instead of the smaller patrol tug, both missiles would have hit. *Alferez
Sobral*'s 40mm cannon was still operational and it was fired towards
the helicopters when they closed. Both missiles from *Glasgow*'s Lynx
hit *Alferez Sobral* near the bridge but, despite heavy damage to the
upperworks, the hull remained intact and the engines still worked.
Lacking communications and compass, she limped away.

Monday, 3 May
By 0050 we held the main body on radar. *Broadsword*, *Yarmouth*,
Plymouth and *Coventry* appeared to be missing and we assumed that
they had been dispatched to the northwest to deal with the perceived
surface threat. At 0124, we received official confirmation that
Conqueror had torpedoed *Belgrano* which we announced on main
broadcast, and a cheer of relief could be heard throughout the ship.
Had *Belgrano* appeared, we were to be tasked to match our Exocet
and 4.5in guns against her Exocet and 6in guns. We would have been
out-gunned and have had to rely on superior skill to survive. To those
who believed that *Belgrano* should not have been sunk it is important
to remember that we were by then fully engaged with the enemy.
Glamorgan, *Arrow* and *Alacrity* had been bombed and strafed with
rockets and bombs the day before; the Royal Navy had already
engaged Argentinian aircraft, *San Luis* beneath the water, and
delivered bombs and bombardments ashore; other carrier group

units, apart from ourselves, had come under threat of air attack on 1 May. There was no doubt in anyone's mind that the shooting war started for real on 1 May and was in full swing when *Belgrano*, an immediate and serious threat, was sunk on 2 May.

Why were *Belgrano* and its two escorts patrolling in the vicinity of the Burdwood Bank on 2 May? They were there with hostile intent. Great Britain had made it clear that any Argentine units found within the total exclusion zone, and those outside the zone constituting a threat, were liable to attack. Whilst we were bombarding on 1 May, *Belgrano* was only 160 miles away and a real threat. The only reason why the pincer attack, by *Veinticinco De Mayo* from the north and *Belgrano* from the south, did not materialise was because there was insufficient wind for *Veinticinco De Mayo* to launch her attacking aircraft, and, of course, at the time we were not party to the cancellation of the Argentinian operation. The fact that *Belgrano* was steaming away from the carrier group when attacked was irrelevant; she could have reversed her course any time in the space of a couple of minutes. If *Conqueror* remained trailing, it was likely that contact, and the opportunity to attack, would be lost in the shallow water over Burdwood Bank. Whilst the Royal Navy was castigated for attacking *Belgrano* when she was steaming away, the Argentine Air Force was not criticised for attacking the Three Musketeers when they were steaming away from the Islands the day before. We were a threat, demonstrating ourselves as such when, a few hours later, we returned to bombard. The same principle applied to *Belgrano*.

After the war MPs asked to see *Conqueror*'s control room logs but these could not be produced, leading, inevitably, to accusations of conspiracy. There was never any conspiracy, however, to hide these from the Public Records Office. I sat on the Board of Inquiry which looked into the loss of these logs and it seems they were probably destroyed when a battered control room seat locker was removed during the submarine's subsequent refit. Had the logs been available, they would have contained little more than hourly course, speed and depth, and details of domestic routines. The control room narrative and contact evaluation plot were both available to the Board of Inquiry and from those records the entire action could be reconstructed in graphic detail.

At 0820, a surface search helicopter was dispatched to confirm the results of the night's action and look for survivors. At the time

Glamorgan was with the main body, heading south, the Admiral shifting position to keep the Argentinians guessing. At 1019, a liferaft, without occupants, was sighted by the flight deck crew and then, thirteen minutes later, another five-man liferaft was sighted, again with no occupants evident. No one bothered to call me or record the position at the time of sighting. Willie was then re-tasked to go to search for possible survivors. The base course had recently been shifted and visibility was poor which made the task difficult; Willie returned at 1240 after an unsuccessful search and the liferafts were assessed as kelp. If true, here was another waste of time, effort and fuel. How much score could we now place upon visual sightings?

I thought of the relatives of the casualties in *Belgrano* and of the downed Argentine aircraft, and imagined their suffering. These were hard times. War seemed to be such a waste. Although no one in the carrier group knew it, the Argentinians had suffered another loss on the afternoon of 3 May. Two Aeromacchis based in Stanley were tasked to investigate a ship contact to the east. The weather was poor and having found nothing, one misjudged his approach into Stanley airport, hit some offshore rocks and crashed into Cape Pembroke. The pilot was killed.

At 1810 a possible periscope was detected seven miles to the southeast. This was possibly another whale as the force had moved sixty miles south in the previous six hours and it was, therefore, most unlikely that a submarine had guessed exactly where we were heading. But we took no chances and, once clear of the area, the carrier group resumed course.

Learning that Black Buck would return again the following morning, I expected that we would once more be detached inshore to suppress the batteries around the airport. It seemed likely that last night's designated targets would remain on our list and if so, our plan would remain unchanged from that prepared for 2 May.

It had been a relatively quiet day until we received the night's tasking to create a diversion whilst more SAS were inserted into the south of the Islands. At 2055 the ship went to action stations when a Lockheed Neptune racket was detected to the southwest. It was suspected that this aircraft was giving tactical direction to a dusk raid. Two combat air patrols were launched with five more at five minutes notice for launch in *Hermes*. It was thought that the Neptune was about eighty miles away and had popped up for two sweeps before going back low. One Harrier obtained a single paint on its radar and placed itself between the contact and the land. The subsequent assessment of the Neptune was that it was searching for *Belgrano* survivors but it was actually providing targeting information for an Exocet raid that was planned for the next day.

At 2145, with the threat of an imminent raid, *Glamorgan* experienced a complete power failure. It was nine minutes before power was fully restored and all weapons systems were back on line. Two minutes later, power supplies dropped off again and it was twenty minutes before power was restored. The Harriers found nothing further and when it was completely dark the threat warning reverted to yellow. We reverted to defence watches.

Preying on my mind was the whereabouts of the Type 209 submarines. *San Luis* had been allocated Area Maria, but would it stay there once the position of the carrier group and the gun-line became apparent? Where was *Salta*? It would have been logical to deploy it further east in the hope of attacking the main body. I ensured that the officers of the watch maintained evasive steering. However, thoughts of the submarine threat were put aside when we heard that we were not to be deployed inshore. Commander-in-Chief, Fleet, directed that economy with shells was necessary due to logistical replenishment problems. I had mixed feelings, thinking that our plan was a good one with worthwhile targets.

Fighting a war created domestic problems. In order to get to action stations quickly, one tended to live in ones' clothes; fresh water consumption dropped significantly. As it was quiet that afternoon I chanced it and took a hot shower and I felt and smelt much better, but I hardly need have bothered because Marine Randall, while cleaning a Bren gun in the charthouse, rashly left an open tin of oil on the desk which ended up on the bunk all over the naval gunfire support maps. The charthouse now reeked of oil.

Tuesday, 4 May

We spent the night patrolling. *Brilliant* and *Coventry* both gained further sonar contacts which were assessed as whales. By 0745, we were 100 miles south-southeast of Stanley when Black Buck bombed Stanley airport again, killing two Argentinians but leaving the airstrip operational.

The Argentinians prepared thoroughly for their Exocet attacks, working with an Argentinian Type 42 to draw up the mission pattern for approaching undetected. The sorties were planned with one in-flight refuelling to avoid landing at Stanley. They were ready to strike as dawn broke over the carrier group with the weather set fair. My narrative recorded, 'things have been pretty quiet ... but we expect an air attack to develop this afternoon.' Within fifteen minutes of writing those words a pair of Exocet-carrying Super Etendards were en-route to attack us. A Neptune surveillance aircraft, which was detected by the carrier group, had already made contact with *Coventry*, *Glasgow* and *Sheffield* on the outer screen and with a Sea King returning from the SAS insertion. The attack mission was launched.

Lunch came and went without incident, and we remained unaware that the Neptune was passing updated positions to the approaching aircraft. At 1415, *Glamorgan* went to action stations following the interception of Super Etendard radar. There then followed the most shambolic three hours imaginable. Electrical interference had been causing spurious closing echoes to appear on radar. Unfortunately, one of these 'spurious echoes' was genuine. Having suffered many false alarms we awaited further confirmation before firing chaff.

The Argentine aircraft dropped to 70ft when 130 miles from target. A radio link with the Neptune confirmed the carrier group position and the aircraft turned in for attack. They popped up for a quick radar look without result and went back low again. A second pop-up look was made twenty-five miles further on giving an echo 30 degrees off the nose of the aircraft, which altered course and dropped back below 100ft. This pop-up was detected by the carrier group. At twenty-five miles the lead aircraft fired at *Sheffield*, followed by the second aircraft five seconds later.

At 1420, *Sheffield*, on picket duty, reported she was on fire with a 15ft hole in her side. She was twelve miles from us and I could see a cloud of yellowish smoke rising amidships. Five minutes later I saw two columns of smoke and *Sheffield* was asking for helicopter assistance. Barely a minute later, *Yarmouth* reported a missile overhead and shortly afterwards a splash was seen astern of *Alacrity*. Believing the force to be under further attack, *Glamorgan* fired chaff charlie and a full salvo of chaff delta, and turned down wind at wind speed to remain within the chaff pattern. A flash had been seen on the horizon, believed to be another missile launch. Chaff hotel was dropped by helicopters.

At 1440, we started to close *Sheffield*, whilst remaining within our allocated sector. Although we were unsure, it seemed likely that *Sheffield* had been hit by Exocet. At 1450, greater volumes of smoke were emerging and *Sheffield* requested assistance.

Glamorgan responded but was told to resume station due to the air threat from contacts at forty miles. *Arrow* and *Yarmouth* were dispatched to assist and at the same time, *Glasgow* reported a periscope. I recorded, 'We are under attack but we do not know what from ... Everyone is very jumpy!' *Glasgow* launched a torpedo at the 'submarine' before engaging the non-existent 'submarine' by gunfire. Thirty minutes into the incident, *Arrow* was alongside and *Yarmouth* close by while *Glamorgan* filled the resultant gap in the screen. An updated report indicated that *Sheffield* had suffered an underwater explosion close to the ops room. Confusion reigned. At 1508, the 'Burglar' was reported, suspected of directing a follow-up raid. *Glasgow* then claimed success with her torpedo but, the odds of such a perfectly timed co-ordinated attack were highly unlikely and, sure enough, six minutes later, *Glasgow* admitted there was no submarine. I wrote, 'There is a lot of confusion ... . A lot of valuable weapons are expended. The Burglar has been re-assessed as a Harrier.'

At 1528 *Arrow* reported a torpedo to the north. *Sheffield*, now twenty miles from us, was billowing smoke which started to blacken as the fires worsened. This was not a good sign. *Arrow*'s reported torpedo came to nothing only to be replaced by a possible Argentinian Type 42 destroyer plus another ship at eighty-five miles. A helicopter attack group (HAG) was dispatched, the main body turned away and *Glamorgan* and *Alacrity* detached as a surface action group. The 'enemy ships' turned out to be the Beauchene Islands and we resumed station. Almost immediately the 'submarine' was back. *Yarmouth* reported a torpedo and attacked with mortar whilst *Glasgow* gained sonar contact. Reports of torpedoes continued unabated and my narrative observed, 'Won't they be using electric torpedoes that leave no trail?' *Glamorgan*, already battle hardened, was more settled than other units experiencing their first action.

Arrow provided firemain for *Sheffield* which had managed to provide some lighting with emergency cable runs. The fires remained out of control forward but we hoped that *Sheffield* could be saved. Three hours after it all started, we eventually fell out from action stations. False alarms on torpedoes continued for another hour. At 1820, *Sheffield* abandoned ship and Captain Sam Salt was flown to *Hermes*. The Admiral initially ordered *Arrow* to observe *Sheffield* for one hour and then sink her by gunfire, then changing his mind by ordering *Arrow* and *Glasgow* to stand by as salvage was attempted.

Sheffield was eventually abandoned, and the Exocet attack had killed about twenty-five men.

Meanwhile, a Harrier attacking Goose Green had been hit by AAA fire over Fox Bay, crashing within three seconds, and killing the pilot. It was not all one-sided though, two Pucara being destroyed on the ground. The air war continued. At 1845, action stations was sounded in response to Hercules radar which we feared was directing another strike. Every time the action alarm sounded I felt that sickly feeling of fear in the pit of my stomach. At 1908, believing the Hercules was undertaking a stores run into Stanley we stood down. Church that evening was well attended but just as the padre started the service the action alarm sounded again and we rushed for the door; the padre's largest congregation for some time had disappeared.

Action stations was based upon a pop-up at eighty miles. A full salvo of chaff was fired and a flash and explosion were reported by *Glasgow* coming from the *Sheffield* hulk. At 2100, now fully dark, events calmed down and we reflected upon the day's events. Church resumed and I said a prayer for those killed, wounded and injured, and also for their families and friends. There was a subdued atmosphere on board. *Sheffield* had been our chummy ship having been in refit together in Portsmouth, sharing fuel together during sea trials and working up together. She had also relieved us on Armilla Patrol. We felt very disappointed that she had been crippled by a single hit without being able to defend herself. This really brought home the importance of damage control. Gone were the days when a ship could take a number of hits with little effect. Modern weapons were much more powerful.

In the darkness, the pained expressions on people's faces could not be seen but you knew what was going through their minds. The sombre atmosphere needed to be broken and it was reassuring to see people making a positive effort to bring back the smiles. The subject of smoking came up in the guise that each cigarette took fourteen minutes off your life. We debated how many minutes the action alarm took off our lives each time it sounded. This, and similar light-hearted conversations, helped us to think positively again.

We at least had the satisfaction of knowing that we had fired our guns in anger, damaging the Argentinians in the process. It must have been a very difficult time for *Sheffield*'s crew. They had not fired an offensive shot and I hoped that their team would feel that they had achieved something and not lose sight of the fact that for four days they had played a valuable role. Had *Sheffield* not been there, the Argentinians might have hit a carrier. Picket duty is a hazardous occupation. In taking the Exocet they had denied the enemy a high value unit.

A Sea King brought our contemplations to an end at 2225 with a sonar contact which came to nothing. The last combat air patrol returned and we maintained CAP deck alert overnight. In the distance *Sheffield* continued to burn, with the fires working their way aft. The Sea Dart and 4.5in magazines were still intact and she remained afloat. A bad day drew to a close.

Chapter 6

Settling Down

Wednesday, 5 May

Petty Officer Keith Balston had to allow himself twelve hours to think before he wrote,

> With my 'action man' kit I rush down to my action station, donning my anti–flash. The situation is not very clear. Reports are hitting us from every angle. *Sheffield* has been torpedoed. No, we are not sure! Now they are saying she has been hit by Exocet. *Glasgow* reports that she is being fired at by submarine, now *Yarmouth* is giving the same report. What the hell is happening?! We are all closed down now, frightened faces everywhere, a total fear with which you learn to live. It amazes me that people are not on the verge of panic. I believe the reason is that we do not know what the hell is happening or what the implications are; we just do our job.
>
> Clearer reports are coming in now. *Sheffield* was hit by Exocet ... Poor *Sheffield*. They did not know what hit them. What the hell is wrong with our radar? It is useless! We need air cover: early warning radar is what we need. The Gannet used to supply this ... when we were a Navy with Fleet Attack Carrier forces. Reports are coming in now, the *Sheffield* is burning like hell. *Arrow* has detached to help her – fires raging. The morale in the vicinity of me has dropped a mile, no more jubilant faces. This is for real! We have lost comrades in the *Sheffield* ... They abandon ship. She is finished, a burning wreck - done by that Exocet. The very word brings fear to us.

Those words were a fair reflection of how we felt, having taken a beating. It would take leadership and courage to rise above this disaster. The only welcome news for the Captain and myself came from CINCFLEET, 'Court Martial cancelled'. We were glad to have that distraction out the way.

Further air contacts and false alarms brought about the cancellation of our replenishment. This gave me an opportunity to read signals on the *Sheffield* incident. She had been in the process of going to action stations when hit. The missile explosion debris and fireball went through the ship, starting fires and smoke-logging her in twenty seconds. Whip damage broke the gas turbines, causing main machinery space fires and left the ship without firemain.

I used to dislike fog but now I welcomed the poor visibility that grounded enemy bombers and gave us a quiet day. Smoke was still billowing from *Sheffield*. Amongst those killed was David Balfour, a term mate of mine, and Petty Officer Cook Robert Fagan had also died. We had served together in *London* and his mother-in-law was a neighbour in Gosport. Other crew members had friends in *Sheffield* and their loss was deeply felt.

Various air contacts were detected during the afternoon, mostly friendly search helicopters. There was one worrying radar intercept and the Three Musketeers were dispatched to investigate but nothing was found. With nightfall, we eventually replenished, experiencing a few minor difficulties. Having been down to 50 per cent it was reassuring to be fully fuelled and Willie, a thirsty aircraft, was grateful for the twenty tons of Avcat.

Thursday, 6 May
For those who have not experienced war it is easy to overlook the minor personal discomforts that it imposes. All deadlights remained down and taped to ensure that no light escaped from within, also ensuring no daylight came in from outside. Mirrors were covered in sellotape to minimize the splintering effect if damaged but inconvenienced shavers. We slept partially to fully dressed; if the ship was in a high risk state when I was off watch, I would lie on my bunk fully dressed and kitted out. At night when at lower risk I felt able to reduce to socks and underclothes. If at medium risk at night my state of dress was half way in between. Daylight was always considered to be high risk. I normally showered at 2200, once it was dark. Likewise, my 'morning constitutional' was usually before dawn. I had no wish for the Argentinians to catch me with my pants down. On rising, cabins were fully secured for action, bedding lashed down and water left in washbasins. Despite drawing water for basins, on-board water consumption went down drastically and the laundry was crying out for business. Despite the discomforts of war, the civilians on board such as the Chinese laundrymen, tailor, and the 'ex-civilians' (the NAAFI staff) remained cheerful.

The day was profitable for me as I found a penny on the bridge deck, proving that the Boatswain's Mate had failed to clean the bridge properly and this earned him and the Officer of the Watch some advice. The light-hearted banter, however, soon turned serious. Communications were lost with two of the three Harriers conducting a photo recce over Stanley. At 1200 their endurance limit had been exceeded and our air capability was weakened.

At 1212 the warfare net sprang into life! '*Glamorgan, Arrow* and *Alacrity* form SAG to investigate contacts to the southwest!' Our response, 'Have gun, will travel!' and the Three Musketeers were off again. Neptune radar was also detected. Twelve minutes later there was still some confusion over the radar intercept and I hoped it was not a ploy to draw off some ships before an Argentinian air strike. Shortly afterwards, the intercept was re-assessed as shore radar. Revised intentions ordered us to open just to twenty miles from the main body. The other contact, at eighty miles, could either be a helicopter or fast patrol boat en route to investigate the *Sheffield* hulk. By 1240, we had the picket *Coventry* visual at seven miles. *Arrow* was three miles on our port beam and *Alacrity* three miles on our starboard beam. We were settling down nicely for our surface action group. Pleasantries were being exchanged by light, 'The Three Musketeers are off again!' 'All for one and one for all!' *Coventry* flashed 'Good luck, as always!'

Back in the Flagship, things were not going so smoothly. 'The general operations plot (GOP) is a bugger's muddle!' the Admiral raved. I pictured the poor unfortunate GOP operator in *Hermes* on the receiving end of the Admiral's wrath. The Flagship considered that the contact was in fact *Sheffield.* Whoever reported it as a fast moving contact certainly generated confusion. The awful truth about the missing Harriers then emerged. In reacting to the contact, two Harriers had dived through cloud to investigate and had, in all probability, collided. A poor report had resulted in a double own goal. I felt sick. The only consolation was that the Argentinians would not know and would assume the two Harriers had returned safely.

After lunch, thoughts turned to mail when we heard *Appleleaf* calling *Invincible*. We assessed *Appleleaf* would join within twelve hours. The other comfort was the return of fog which drove all threats down to yellow. I took the opportunity to calculate the current in case we should lose our electronic aids; all the time we were monitoring our environment and updating conditions. Our present downwind course was useful should a raid materialise requiring us to hide within our chaff delta pattern. All we needed to do was reduce speed by a couple of knots. We mentally rehearsed various scenarios so that should we come under attack our immediate reactions would be timely, correct and, with a little luck, serve us well.

Shortly before 1400 we detected an airborne track at only thirty-eight miles. Seaslug was immediately brought to yellow high. The contact split into two and identified as friendly helicopters just in time to avoid a blue-on-blue engagement. Seaslug reverted to yellow low, and calm was restored for a few hours. It was broken at 1800 with the pipe 'Hands to action stations. Air threat warning red. Five bogeys northwest at sixty miles!' Two sweeps of Hercules radar were detected and we believed we might be under a co-ordinated Exocet and conventional bombing attack. At 1809, aircraft were detected to the southeast and we fired chaff charlie. Within minutes an intercept was made. Whilst the rest of the force turned downwind at wind speed, we increased to 28 knots to put ourselves up threat of the main body. We were deliberately placing ourselves as 'duty target'. The threat came to nothing and we relaxed to yellow high, but two minutes later we were back at red with a contact at sixty miles. The activity was probably associated with a supply drop on the Falklands. Twenty minutes later, with no contacts within 200 miles we reverted to defence watches and were able to receive stores and mail.

Our responses were improving. Keith Balston recorded, 'Hands to action stations! I have got this to near perfection now. Anti-flash hood is now on before I reach the Senior Rates heads – most important this; if a fireball appears the head and face are very much exposed.' Darkness came, lowering the air threat and increasing the surface threat. Shortly afterwards we experienced another false alarm. We could not take any chances – a 'false alarm' might prove be genuine. An hour later air activity resumed. Seaslug was stood to and chaff charlie fired in response to a bogey at sixty miles. The aircraft, probably a Neptune passing tactical direction, loitered outside missile range. The weather was also playing tricks and generated false contacts while the turret developed a severe oil leak, preventing it from steadily following the director. Fighting a war without an operational turret was uncomfortable and the maintainers worked for ten hours through the night on repairs. These regular alarms were stressful. Leading Steward Nigel Fielding recorded in his diary at midnight, 'Went to bed at about 2250. Action stations were sounded at 2305. I have never dressed so fast in my life. The reason we closed up was a plane approaching at sixty miles from the force. It turned out to be a patrol plane. We fell out again from action stations at 2345. I will be a nervous wreck at the end of this .... Went to bed again!'

Back in the UK, Judy Barrow was keeping the families updated with factual information rather than press speculation. She wrote to them:

It has been very heart-warming to talk to some of you over the last few weeks. Thank you very much for your telephone calls, your support and encouragement. With the help of many *Glamorgan* wives, we have been organising 'snowball' gatherings of wives, families and fiancees. If you personally have not been contacted, I am sorry, but we are doing our best! Should you like to be in touch with others near you, please phone me or *Glamorgan* people in your area so that we can help.

Attached is a news signal that some of you may not have seen. Our reply has been recorded and should reach the ship next week. 'This is a message from *Glamorgan* families at home for everyone in the ship. Thank you for your welcome signal. This has been shared as widely as possible from Inverness to Plymouth, from Wales to Yorkshire and from Cheshire to Portsmouth. My reply brings you good wishes from all over the country. We wives are forming groups to keep in touch with each other and with fiancees and families. The back-up from friends and the Navy has been wonderful. Special love and greetings to all of you celebrating birthdays and anniversaries in May. We are all looking forward to your homecoming and to happy summer holidays. Love comes to you all from your families at home.' If another news signal is received, Padre Bruce Neill and I hope to post copies to all families as quickly as we are able. Hoping that it will not be too long before we all meet for our postponed families' day.

The attached news signal from *Glamorgan* read,

Many of you who may be anxious that you have not heard for a while from your favourite *Glamorgan* should rest assured that we are all very well and in good spirits. The problem is the lack of post boxes in this part of the world. We hope that the MoD radio mail systems will soon operate. We will let you know when it starts and you will then be able to send one thirty-word family-gram weekly. Please also keep writing letters because these reach us eventually and are much appreciated. After a brief spell of summer in the vicinity of Ascension Island, we are now cooler and will soon be much colder. When we shall all be home is uncertain, but we hope not to have to alter summer holiday plans.

BBC World Service broadcasts keep us in touch with news. Opportunities for your requests/messages to be transmitted are beginning to occur. Ask local stations. We much appreciate your support while we are away and eagerly look forward to our return. We are a long way from home and even after we turn round it will take a month to reach UK. However we still feel very close to you and you have all our love. Keep smiling and be patient.

Friday, 7 May
A further GLAMNEWS was sent,

We are well and working hard. Our preoccupation is watch-keeping for half of the 24 hours and in the remaining 12 we sleep, eat, wash, write our letters to you and respond to sudden alarms. The mail delivery has probably gone through its worst period of long delays as we received letters posted up to 20 April yesterday. We hope for more today. Our letters posted up to 30 April should reach you within the next week, our next will leave us in a couple of days and reach you about 26 May. We believe you got our GLAMgrams safely and quickly and there will be a similar service about 10 days hence. Unfortunately Familygrams from you are likely to be impossible in the foreseeable future due to operational signal traffic.

Most of our normal facilities including laundry are functioning but canteen stores are low - no more chocolate but still OK for beer. Food is rationed slightly but only enough to trim some of the larger waistlines. Beards abound. The attack on *Sheffield* will have worried you and we have lost some friends - we have learnt some lessons and will be taking extra care as a result. Weather has been kind and not too cold, but we envy you in the spring ... We are all thinking of you and problems our absence may have raised. If you have any difficulties, please ask for help; it is there for the asking and its effectiveness reassures us. Keep smiling and your chins up, our love to you all.

Back in the South Atlantic, *Appleleaf* joined and conducted a pump–over with *Olmeda*, though most people considered mail from home as the more important cargo. The BBC World News reported the loss of the two Sea Harriers and while I was in favour of accuracy in reports I also felt strongly that not everything needed to be reported so quickly. Likewise, reporting the *Sheffield* news before next of kin had been informed was terrible.

At 0830, I went to the ops room for a tactical update. We were just outside the total exclusion zone. The Admiral was avoiding regular patterns thus making it difficult for the Argentinians to predict our location. This was of limited value against the air threat, some value against the surface threat, and certainly important when considering the sub-surface threat. *Exeter*, the latest Type 42, was being hurried down to replace *Sheffield*.

All cease-fire prospects finally vanished overnight and we expected air activity to resume. Our only saving grace might be the weather; visibility remained low with similar conditions expected for the next couple of days. However, the weather was unkind to us for our masts were sticking out of the fog for all pilots, friendly or unfriendly, to see. It was also very cold, making life for the upper deck crews miserable and, at times, the fog was so thick that the bow was not visible from the bridge. To make matters worse we were experiencing super-refraction. The *Sheffield* hulk was held on radar at ninety-five miles whereas under normal conditions about eighteen miles maximum could be expected. This meant that the Argentinian shore radar probably held us.

On the fringe of the total exclusion zone, there was no wind and it was quiet. On deck, the only noise came from the compressed air venting from the aerial waveguides and the sounds of the radar aerials rotating. At 1045 combat air patrol activity was detected over the Islands which indicated that weather conditions on the mainland were suitable for flying. Conditions were less suitable for us, but we launched Willie for a three-hour anti-submarine back-to-back sortie; five minutes later he returned with a defective sonar. Just as he was landing, hostile aircraft closed. Chaff delta was fired but the raid was ridden off by Harriers. The flight deck could now concentrate upon Willie's sonar and an hour and twenty minutes later Willie was airborne. Meanwhile, *Hermes* was playing hide and seek with the fog banks, trying to keep out of the thickest fog to allow flying operations to proceed uninterrupted. Out of the fog

there was patchy high cloud and a shining sun. An air ⌐
Stanley was planned.

Forty minutes into his sortie, Willie returned with a hydraulic leak
on the rotor head. Another five minutes flying would have resulted in
the loss of all main hydraulics and Willie would have ditched.
Glamorgan had problems too. One of our naval compass stabilisers,
upon which weapons systems depended, failed.

News filtered up to the bridge that the off watch team were about
to watch a film in the wardroom and I made the mistake of going
down to relax and watch my first film for some time. As if *All Quiet
on the Western Front* was not depressing enough, every ten seconds
interference from the data link caused a loud 'burrrrrrrrp' to come
over the projector loudspeaker. It continually reminded one that
electronics were at war all around. After less than an hour, I was so
dispirited and tensed up by the film and link interference that I
returned to the bridge.

At 1620, what were thought to be air contacts started painting on
the radar at 150 miles. The Beauchene Islands were on that same
range and bearing and it quickly became evident that super-refraction
was strong. If surface contacts were possible at 150 miles then the
Argentinians knew precisely where we were. At least our turret was
back on line with its hydraulics fixed.

The Admiral was unable to launch the Stanley air strike and we
assumed we would be sent in to bombard. I began making preparations but left the charthouse when *Coventry* reported submarine
radar, quickly re-assessed as navigational radar, possibly a long way
off due to super-refraction. At 1800, rules of engagement were
changed allowing any Argentine units more than twelve miles from
the Argentine mainland to be attacked. I reviewed the plot. The SSNs
were operating west of the Falklands and whilst recording the surface
picture in the exclusion zone, the ship went to action stations. This
raid was assessed as a probe for Skyhawk bomb and rocket carriers.
By 1811, the link-received tracks of the raid were in to forty miles
though our own radar was still clear of air contacts. Fifteen minutes
later, with two combat air patrols launched, the ether was full of
Skyhawk and Mirage rackets. We fired off eight rounds of chaff delta
and two rounds of chaff charlie and darted in and out of fog. There
was a lot of confusion but the difference between 4 May and now was
that it was not accompanied by panic. The atmosphere was very tense
and I felt quite frightened, but did my best to hide my fear. Looking

around the bridge, it was clear that no one was enjoying the cruise. New unknowns were detected and it seemed that the air strike was having difficulty in localising the carrier battle group.

At 1836, Super Etendard radar was intercepted and more chaff was fired, but ten minutes later calm was restored. All rackets were now assessed as Falklands land based so we had wasted our limited stocks of chaff. But at such a high state of tension, mere mention of the word Etendard made the heart sink and, sure enough, two minutes later, another Etendard racket was reported, driving the air threat to red. More chaff was sown and the battle group reacted to a confirmed hostile. Ten minutes later we stood down from action stations. By now, after such a tense period, I was looking forward to the onset of darkness.

On review, the activity appeared to have been an escorted supply run to the Falklands. Ships were detecting atmospherics on their electronic intercept equipment and spurious radar contacts were common. These were given the nickname of 'running rabbits'. The difficulty was in differentiating between a 'running rabbit' and a hostile aircraft. At 2020 a Lynx helicopter obtained a submarine contact but the search came to nothing and we settled down to a quiet night on Circle 5.

Saturday, 8 May

Overnight, our 992 radar failed. At dawn the Three Musketeers and *Glasgow* were detached as a surface action group (SAG) to investigate two surface contacts. Since our 992 was non-operational, we were hauled off the SAG. We then heard that *Glasgow* had engaged with Sea Dart and then *Coventry* engaged with gunfire. The question in our ops room was 'Is it weather?' Ian Forbes, the senior Advanced Warfare Officer (AWO) said, 'It looks remarkably like cloud!' One minute later the Officer in tactical command assessed the contacts as anaprop (the result of atmospheric refraction). One Sea Dart missile, about a dozen rounds of 4.5in ammunition and more mental energy had been expended and, in addition, this 'non-action' was to delay the delivery of spares for our radar.

At 1125, back in defence watches, we had time for a quick lunch before replenishing from *Appleleaf*. Most of the mail arrived but four bags were missing. There was now a very fresh wind and a rising sea. As the weather broke, the Admiral wanted to regain the initiative. He instructed the Three Musketeers and *Brilliant* to deploy inshore that evening. *Brilliant* was to go to Falkland Sound, the Type 21 frigates to engage shore targets to the south, and we were to interdict any blockade runners along the north coast. Our tasking was hazardous, and knowing that *San Luis* was on patrol in Area Maria we would have to take the submarine threat very seriously. The ship's company, however, was growing in confidence all the time and I was not alone in recognising the strength of the team Mike Barrow had inspired. Petty Officer Wiltshire recorded, 'I find the professionalism in this ship second to none. The Commander is a tower of strength, he always looks so calm and collected, a fantastic person in a crisis. Morale seems to be increasing again after the *Sheffield* incident .... We are the backbone of this Task Force, better trained and better worked up than any. It is a privilege to be amongst such a smashing bunch of lads. *Glamorgan* is number one Musketeer!'

Weather conditions were ideal for air attack and a recce aircraft was ridden off by a combat air patrol. As the CAP headed back, an unknown was reported to the northeast. This turned out to be one of the CAP with a 180-degree compass failure who was guided back safely. A few minutes later jamming was experienced on the warfare net, although it lasted only a short while. We now eagerly awaited sunset, but the enemy appeared first at 1853 with the detection of a tracker aircraft, swiftly followed by other air contacts uncomfortably near at sixty miles, closing at ten miles a minute. A combat air patrol was scrambled.

At 1855 we detected further aircraft and the raid continued to build. CAP engaged but no aircraft closed within missile range of the carrier battle group, and then they turned tail when illuminated by fire control radar. The raid petered out and we reckoned that the activity was associated with another supply run. As darkness fell, all went quiet.

Chapter 7

Hitting Back

To avoid mutual interference, our night's mission inshore was cancelled. However, *Alacrity* was sent inshore, in the hope of catching Argentine fishing vessels previously spotted by a Harrier. *Coventry* and *Broadsword* patrolled off Stanley whilst helicopters conducted insertions into West Falkland; the rest of the carrier battle group remained 100 miles east of the Islands. An offensive posture was resumed, putting the airport within Sea Dart envelopes to prevent further re-supply. It was decided that *Yarmouth* should tow the *Sheffield* hulk east to South Georgia when she might be salvaged. Inshore, *Alacrity* bombarded positions around Stanley whilst *Brilliant* spent the night at 25 knots, searching Falkland Sound with helicopters but to no avail. However, *San Luis* fired a torpedo at a contact passing at 2,000 yards, without success, but proved the proximity of the submarine threat.

Sunday, 9 May
The air battle was still to be won. Harriers were doing well but the Admiral wanted to achieve further success with a '22/42 Combo', combining the long-range Sea Dart missile system of the Type 42 destroyer with the very effective close range Sea Wolf system of the Type 22 frigate. He hoped to achieve local air superiority around Stanley. We settled down to another day on picket duty whilst *Broadsword* and *Coventry* spent daylight close inshore. We expected some response to the night's activity inshore and the provocative sight of the 22/42 Combo off Pebble Island and, sure enough, the mainland air command dispatched eighteen Skyhawks to deal with the threat, though fourteen turned back due to bad weather. Of the remaining four, two turned for home when illuminated, one flew into cliffs and the other into the sea.

Despite the operational load on the signal broadcast, the Medical Officer in *Antrim*, en route to Ascension with the South Georgia prisoners, signalled CINCFLEET with his concerns at the shortage of fresh fruit and lack of roughage which would result in severe bowel disorders. Although not addressed, *Glamorgan* referred to *Antrim*'s signal, suggesting, 'Five air raids a day does the trick. Extra roughage is considered superfluous!' Our signal commenced a prolonged lavatorial exchange that eventually ended in Portsmouth in late July with *Glamorgan* sending, 'You have had the roughage, now enjoy the smoothage!'

The Argentine trawler *Narwhal*, believed to be fishing, had been warned to leave the exclusion zone a few days previously, but had ignored the warning. Suspicions grew and Harriers, sent to bomb the airport but unable to see their target due to low cloud, spotted *Narwhal* east of Stanley and attacked. One bomb hit, though it failed to explode having been set for high level attack on Stanley. *Narwhal*, still flying the Argentine flag, was strafed again an hour later and she was then boarded by the Special Boat Squadron and captured. Four Argentinians were wounded and we investigated the possibility of getting *Narwhal* under way but the unexploded 1,000lb bomb remained a problem.

Other air incidents included a Sea King helicopter, embarrassingly short of fuel, only just making it back to the carrier, whilst two Hercules aircraft, attempting a stores run to Stanley, were illuminated by *Coventry* and engaged at long range with a Sea Dart; a swift U-turn was all that saved them, and their stores returned to Argentina. An hour later *Coventry* reported splashing a Puma helicopter which had taken off from Stanley to assist *Narwhal* and it had the honour of being the first aircraft to be shot down by Sea Dart. Although the Mirage and Hercules had escaped, the loss of the Puma would be felt. The 22/42 Combo was proving to be a thorn in the side. After a good day's work, *Coventry* and *Broadsword* were relieved by *Brilliant* and *Glasgow* and with one Type 42 away from the screen we were placed on picket duty overnight.

It had been a quiet day for *Glamorgan* and Nigel Fielding had time to write, 'No action stations all day, even though I heard the klaxon going off sub-consciously several times.' The majority of the crew were consequently only on watch for just over twelve hours that day though some worked longer hours. There is no chance of a thirty-seven hour week when at war; we were averaging 115 hours – about sixteen hours per day.

Monday, 10 May

Fog came with the dawn finding us on anti-air warfare picket duty twelve miles up threat of the main body. Escorts were replenishing and the Combo was keeping Stanley under the Sea Dart umbrella. *Narwhal* was confirmed as a signals intelligence trawler which made her an extremely valuable capture and made us realise that we had under-estimated the enemy. With the unexploded bomb on board and making water, *Narwhal* was sunk by the SBS once all the useful information and equipment had been salvaged.

Now repaired, Willie conducted a test flight. No sooner was he dipping his sonar than he began gaining contacts, evaluated as marine life. The day was relatively quiet. At 1610, *Yarmouth* reported that *Sheffield*, experiencing worsening sea state, was now taking in water and listing and soon she sank. Overnight, whilst *Arrow* bombarded, *Alacrity* was to transit Falkland Sound acting as a 'fast minesweeper'. If she failed to emerge we could assume the Argentinians had mined the sound. Captain John Coward in *Brilliant*, a former submarine Commanding Officer, was concerned that the constant use of the Stanley gun-line would attract a submarine, something which had concerned me for a while. However, it later emerged that the Chilean Naval Attache had been told at a cocktail party that the Argentine intention was to hold back the Type 209 submarines so they could pose a permanent threat. At the time, however, I took no chances and ensured *Glamorgan* maintained evasive steering.

Although we had not been to action stations for a bit, half our Chinese laundry crew now decided they wished to leave the ship but their application was refused. *Regent* was due to join the following night and we hoped she had our missing mail. *Leeds Castle*, *Dumbarton Castle* and *Iris*, now at Ascension, were to be used as dispatch vessels so that mail and stores would arrive regularly. Thoughts drifted to home; I was missing my family and the day passed slowly.

Yarmouth rejoined at dusk and then, after dark, our replenishment from *Appleleaf* gave me a gentle reminder never to become complacent. Visibility was down to 100 yards and *Appleleaf* had just one small light on her stern which was much closer than expected and I later wrote, 'a substantial amount of starboard rudder was applied "pdq" (pretty damn quick) after sighting the light.'

Whilst we were replenishing, *Arrow* was having a close look along the north coast of East Falkland. The only ship she encountered was a jubilant *Alacrity* emerging from Falkland Sound where she had found no mines but had encountered a surface contact which she had engaged with her gun. After the bombardments of 1 May, the

Argentinians had ordered supply ships out of Stanley harbour and tried to hide them at dispersed locations in Falkland Sound. *Alacrity* detected *Isla De Los Estados* at six miles in pouring rain and after illuminating with starshell, had fired a dozen rounds to encourage the vessel to heave to. Taken completely by surprise, and believing she was under fire from her own side, she carried on so that *Alacrity* re-engaged and repeatedly hit her. When listing at 35 degrees, a petrol tank exploded and she sank with her engines still running, taking with her the 101 Anti-Aircraft Regiment's vehicles, 325,000 litres of helicopter fuel and radar generators. Fortunately for the Argentinians, they had already disembarked the Regiment's weapons and ammunition. This was the only surface action of the war. The local Argentine authorities did not know what had happened until two survivors were found five days later. The only clue had come from *Rio Carcarana* who heard a frantic radio call, 'Tell the bastards to stop firing'. Overconfident, the Argentinians assumed that Falkland Sound offered a safe haven.

Racing back at 30 knots, *Arrow* and *Alacrity* were unaware that they were being tracked by *San Luis* who then attacked *Alacrity*. The first torpedo, however, refused to fire and the guidance wire of the second parted. The torpedo never acquired its target; the frigates were soon gone and the opportunity missed.

Tuesday, 11 May

As dawn broke, the Argentine weather forecast warned of gales and we anticipated a stormy night. The broadcast of this gale warning indicated that their submarines were at sea. By midday, the wind was strong with seas to match, and three hours later it was gusting storm Force 10. By the time we detached at 2100 to escort *Regent* and *British Esk* to the relative safety of the main body, the gale had abated but the wind was still strong and the sea state remained very high. Conditions for the planned stores replenishment with *Regent* were marginal.

Wednesday, 12 May

During the night the action alarm sounded, ... and sounded, ... and sounded. There was a defect on the system rather than a genuine alarm. By 0300 we had located *British Esk* and *Regent* but aborted our attempt to replenish due to the extremely hazardous conditions and headed back towards the main body. The best speed we could make was 12 knots but even at that low speed we were shipping it green over the bridge.

In our absence, *Yarmouth* had inserted SBS into Port Salvador and it was clear that a significant number of insertions had now taken place. *Brilliant* and *Glasgow* were back on the Combo and we settled down to another day on the screen. By 1600, the weather had improved, permitting the Argentinians to mount a Skyhawk raid on the Combo. Two flights of four Skyhawks were sent against the ships and *Brilliant* engaged the first raid with Sea Wolf, taking down two aircraft in rapid succession, with a third flying into the debris and crashing into the sea. The fourth pilot managed to escape after failing to score a hit.

The second group of Skyhawks were extremely lucky in that the missile systems on both ships failed. *Brilliant*'s Sea Wolf re-set itself at the moment of firing due to a programming problem with this new missile system. The bomb released by Lieutenant Gavazzi hit the water just short of *Glasgow* without exploding, bounced and went right through the ship causing damage in the main machinery room. Lieutenant Gavazzi then took a prohibited route near Goose Green and was shot down and killed by his own side.

At 1710, *Hermes*'s planned Harrier strike was delayed as an enemy raid developed. We went to action stations and heard that *Glasgow* had been hit. More bad news followed. At 1729 'Pan, Pan, Pan' was called but the transmission was cut short. We only received, 'This is ...' as a Sea King went missing thirteen miles to the southwest. A rescue helicopter sighted a red flare and rescued the crew. At 1835, *Glasgow* reported another raid developing. *Hermes* launched two combat air patrols and the raid was turned away. We could now look forward to a quiet night on the screen.

As we slowly acquired air superiority we began to speculate as to where landings would take place. Would it be Choiseul Sound, Berkeley Sound, or perhaps Falkland Sound? There were many options but the prime objective was to retake Stanley. It was going to be difficult for the enemy to guess. As we waited, more ships continued to stream south in preparation for the landing.

Thursday, 13 May
Just as Mike Barrow was informing me that the landing was programmed for 20 May, Argentina was claiming to have seriously damaged two frigates and shot down a Sea King. In fact, only *Glasgow* had received significant damage. Other ships had problems,

Broadsword with her Sea Wolf and *Coventry* with her gun, but *Glamorgan* remained fully operational. Part of my morning routine was to collate the previous day's signals from the bridge log. One day's worth of signals was about two inches thick but records in wartime are vital and I made the effort to preserve as much as possible.

Hidden in a comforting blanket of fog, we refuelled from *Appleleaf* before stationing up-threat of the main body. Mike Barrow, leaving Chris Gotto temporarily in command, was flown to the Flagship for discussions with the Admiral. Due to the fog, *British Esk* delayed her pumpover to *Appleleaf* until mid-afternoon. *Regent* was twelve cables ahead of the pumpover. When it was our turn to replenish, I shaped course to intercept *Regent* but Chris Gotto, worried about the fog, did not want to cross ahead of the pumpover and so we made a detour of some ten extra miles.

Mail arrived with the stores but I was too busy to read it as I had to prepare the night's bombardment. The Hydrographer had produced a new metric chart of Pebble Island. I drew up the grid to cover the target area. Unfortunately, the chart only extended three miles north of Pebble Island. To overcome this difficulty I glued on and annotated a sheet of cartridge paper to extend the chart. Due to the distortions of the Mercator projection, this was not an entirely straightforward task. With the grid marked I constructed radar range grids, a visual bearing lattice and some parallel index lines on the extended portion of the chart. I plotted the designated targets and carefully selected pre-planned fire control positions. Precise chartwork was not assisted by the ship proceeding at 24 knots into heavy seas. Three hours after detaching, the mission was cancelled. There had been a delay in receiving intelligence from an SAS team, landed earlier by canoe. Whilst *Glasgow* was busy with repairs, we filled her picket station overnight.

Friday, 14 May

We remained on picket duty throughout the day but saw little activity, and then detached again for Pebble Island shortly before 1900. Our mission was to support the SAS who were to be landed to eliminate a radar site and any aircraft found on the airstrip. We could only make good 17 knots into a big sea and by 2000 a strong wind was generating even heavier seas. For the Harriers the strengthening wind was not a problem and they were tasked against Stanley airport. A 1,000lb bomb was dropped on the runway and another was set for air burst against soft targets. As they departed the pair were illuminated by fire control radar from two contacts off Port Stanley which confirmed that we had a potential surface threat to worry about as we closed the Islands.

We had been warned that the Argentinians had flown an Exocet battery out to Pebble Island. I laid off a course to keep us five miles clear of Area Maria before approaching the gun-line. Slack water was due at 0400, our given start time. Tidal stream data was very limited around the Falklands but it was vital to calculate it accurately for bombardment. Gradually, we were able to increase speed to 20 knots, pounding heavily with waves crashing on the bridge roof, the bridge windscreen wipers struggling to keep the windows clear. We were hoping to reach the turn-in point at midnight, leaving us sixty miles to run for the 0400 start. We had very little time in hand in these conditions, so we pushed the ship to the limit. As the gale intensified, 20 knots proved too much and we had to reduce to 18 knots. Our time in hand was rapidly being eroded away.

For this operation we had four members of the press embarked including BBC's Brian Hanrahan and ITV's Michael Nicholson. All four had grown accustomed to a smooth life in *Hermes* with occasional gentle movement and their stomachs were not prepared for a bucking destroyer. Despite their sickness, they did their job and quickly learnt what war in an escort was like. Even at 18 knots we continued to ship it green over the bridge, and the hammering onto the officers' cabin flat roof ensured that no one slept. We needed to be ready on the gun-line when the SAS called for fire as the Argentinians had 600 men on Pebble Island while D Squadron SAS had only forty-eight. *Glamorgan* evened the odds.

Just before we reached the final turn-in, we detected a radar contact at seventeen miles, too close for comfort, and weapons systems were stood to. Ten minutes later another radar contact was detected thirty miles to the north and assessed as one of the helicopters from *Hermes* delivering the SAS. The first contact was assessed as spurious and the second was actually a surface search helicopter from *Hermes*. Weapons systems were relaxed, and we pounded on.

Saturday, 15 May

Action stations was piped at 0330 when twelve miles from Pebble Island. The SAS had been successfully inserted and were yomping towards their objectives. We reached the gun-line at 0355, with just

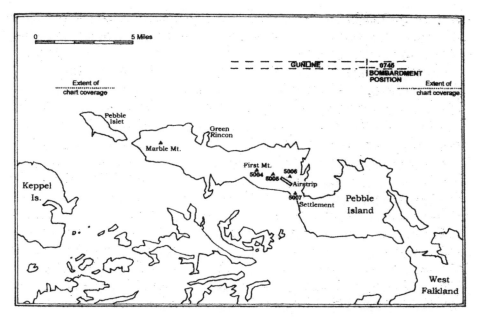

Pebble Island Bombardment

five minutes to spare, before settling down to refine the tidal stream whilst awaiting calls for fire. We could clearly see the land and the cloud was beginning to break up. As visibility improved we felt very exposed, especially as we had to 'cross the moon' a number of times. Anyone looking seawards from Pebble Island would have had a wonderful view of *Glamorgan* silhouetted against the skyline. I did not wish to dodge an Exocet fired from just a few miles. However, our duty was to sail into harm's way to support the SAS.

At 0430, when north of Green Rincon Point and nine miles from the airstrip, our maximum effective bombardment range, we reversed course. This was the furthest west any British surface warship had ventured in the war. We did not want to patrol too far away in case we received a sudden call for fire support from ashore. At 0515, we heard that nothing was expected to happen before 0630, so we continued patrolling. I became concerned since our orders were to leave the gun-line at 0700 and felt the SAS were cutting things fine. If we left late, should we cut across Area Maria and hope for the best? Whilst pondering upon what to recommend to Mike Barrow, the BBC was reporting that a major Soviet warship was in distress in the Baltic, which seemed to be a long way away; an entirely different world. Of more immediate interest, we learned that the submarine *Salta*'s patrol area had been shifted thirty miles northeast of Stanley. Were the Argentinians expecting a landing in Berkeley Sound?

Despite being in the lee of the shore, it was evident that the wind was increasing and I could see the hills on Pebble Island very clearly in the moonlight. We received an update from ashore. Instead of the radar, the SAS were going to deal with Pucaras on the airstrip first. With the ship's motion less severe, and the prospect of some action, the press emerged looking very pale. They favoured the gun direction platform which offered the best view and plenty of fresh air. They gathered with cameras and sound recorders at the ready.

At 0630 we were poised in position which we held for fifteen minutes. We had felt uncomfortable when patrolling at 12 knots but now we were literally a sitting duck. I informed the Captain that we only had fifteen minutes left on the gun-line. He asked to be kept informed of the moment we had to leave if by steaming at maximum speed, we were to be within ten miles of the carriers by sunrise.

We started manoeuvring in figures of eight, always turning towards the land so that weapon arcs for the 4.5in turret remained open. Any delay could cost lives and we had to remain at immediate notice for precision bombardment. All was quiet until 0705 when activity started ashore. Our first call for fire came, the target being an area of hillside occupied by the defenders. The spotter ashore passed the grid co-ordinates. At 0710, at a range of six miles, we loosed off twenty salvos. Five seconds before the first shell was due to land we passed 'stand-by' to the spotter ashore, then 'out' at the moment of impact. To the spotter's delight, twenty salvos landed right on target, catching the Argentinians in the open running for their guns. The effect was devastating and all of our preparations paid dividends. The Argentinians dived for cover as all hell was let loose around them. The Falkland Islanders in the settlement had a ring-side seat for a spectacular display and the SAS knew they had, in *Glamorgan*, a reliable friend offshore.

Cameras and tape recorders on the gun direction platform rolled. The spotter called for another fourteen rounds at fifteen second intervals to suppress the enemy. For the next three and a half minutes the night was shattered every fifteen seconds by the bark of our guns and we could clearly hear each shell disappearing into the distance while those ashore could clearly hear our shells whistling inbound. While the SAS knew where the shells were going to land the Argentinians felt them at first hand.

A new call for fire came through for the end of the airstrip. We fired a pair of high explosive salvos before six starshell were ordered, fired at thirty-second intervals. This kept the scene ashore illuminated and from the bridge we could see the activity. More high explosives and starshells followed. At 0742, we received another call for fire on a target two miles to the west. Whilst the settings were being applied I informed the Captain that it was time to go if he wanted to be within ten miles of the carriers at sunrise. Despite our orders, Mike Barrow elected to stay and complete the mission. He accepted that being late back would involve a risk both to *Glamorgan* and to the high value units which we would not be there to screen come the dawn.

The next call requested twenty salvos of high explosive direct action, 'fire for effect!' Starting with twenty salvos for effect, without ranging salvos, was not in the drill book. The SAS had assumed an accuracy of naval gunfire support significantly greater than the Fleet Standard, probably impressed by the accuracy of our first rounds fired half an hour previously. Fortunately for them, the Fleet Standard applied to the average ship and *Glamorgan* was in an altogether superior class. The Master Gunner and his team had calculated the ballistics correctly and the navigational preparation ensured that the initial range and bearing were accurate. The salvos landed right on target, with the SAS only 150 yards from our bursting shells. The Fleet Standard for the first shell required an accuracy of 200 yards. Single or double gun ranging gave the opposition time to take cover and react so the shock effect of twenty rounds landing in rapid succession without warning was enormous. The spotter shifted target, calling for another twenty rounds and *Glamorgan*'s guns thundered again. As soon as one shell left the barrel, another one went up the spout. Before all twenty had been dispatched 'Check, check check!' was ordered and 'both guns empty' reported from the turret. The gunnery drill was perfect. Check fire had been called as the SAS moved across a stream onto the airstrip. They suddenly reported 'enemy sighted' though this 'enemy' was quickly identified as penguins on the move.

The guns briefly fell silent until the radio crackled into life again, calling for 'twenty salvos, fire for effect!'. Our bombardment was being walked down the airstrip. The peace of the night was again disrupted. The press, with the smell of cordite in their nostrils, had forgotten their seasickness and were having a field day reporting the heaviest bombardment since Suez. When our guns were not firing their cameras recorded the ever-increasing glow ashore, evidence of Argentine equipment being destroyed. They would have been even more impressed had it been daylight when they could have seen the paint on the gun barrels blistering due to the heat of our intense and rapid fire. For the first time in my naval career, not constrained by peacetime economies, I was witnessing a 'hot gun' incident.

No sooner had our shells landed than the radio crackled again, giving a similar spotting correction for another twenty rounds. After six salvos the spotter called for us to check fire; our job was done and the last of the aircraft were in flames. 'Check, check, check!' came from Brian Lister as the check fire bells rang. The turret reported 'Both barrels half cock'. With 'hot guns', which could cook off any ammunition left in the barrels, safe bearing was called. The guns were trained to the north and cleared.

When we received 'Thank you, good shooting, good night', Mike Barrow ordered me to shape course for the carrier battle group. As we opened from the coast we learned that eleven aircraft had been destroyed and that the SAS were about to destroy the remaining three. Three further explosions followed. The ship quickly reached 22 knots whilst the gas turbines were being flashed up but under the lee of land we were riding quite comfortably. With the gas turbines on line we increased initially to 26 knots, working up to 29 knots, and, as their excitement waned, the press realised they were in for a rough ride and their nausea returned. At 0815, we fell out from action stations to allow for some sleep. Once again, this was a calculated risk. Many had been up all night and would be up again in a few hours for the rest of the day. They were exhausted and a balance had to be struck between remaining at the first degree of readiness and allowing watchkeepers some sleep. After losing fourteen aircraft, Argentina ought to have reacted against the attackers. They knew that an escort had been five miles off Pebble Island at 0800 and could not be east of Stanley until after 1030 at the very earliest. If they launched an early raid, they could catch us on our own, exhausted and vulnerable. We remained vigilant.

We kept clear of Area Maria, accepting the delay this would impose. As we opened from the coast, there was still a near gale blowing and the sea state was by now very high, with a heavy swell from the starboard quarter. The sea increased even more once we were clear of the Islands and the ship started to broach. The helmsman was facing forward trying to steer a course and he could not watch the sea aft and anticipate it by applying counter rudder before the effect was felt; we began to take course excursions of up to 60 degrees. The only answer was for me to give the helm positive rudder orders and I kept one eye on the gyro tape and one eye on the stern. The onset of dawn made it easier to judge the swell.

We detected the two Sea Kings returning to *Hermes* with the SAS and learned that whilst we were off Pebble Island, *Arrow* had entered Port Salvador for another SBS insertion. We finally reached the carrier battle group at 1230, having consumed 120 tons of fuel in our dash for safety. We were immediately assigned picket station for the day. The press, returned to *Hermes* by helicopter, had experienced everything; rough seas, high speeds, starshell, high explosive, fires and masses of tracer ashore, the sound of alarms and the crash of gunfire. Most important of all, they had witnessed a good result. The only British casualties that night were one member of the SAS with a wounded hand and another with concussion. The cost to the enemy included seven Pucaras that could have caused serious damage to the forthcoming amphibious landing.

Once back with the carrier group we updated our stateboards. Fuel was down to 65 per cent and we needed to replenish ammunition. We had a quiet day on the picket line and surprisingly, there was no Argentinian air activity. Harriers went back to Pebble Island to finish off the radar site and fuel dump.

Back at home, a *Glamorgan* families get-together at Rowner had been arranged by Reverend Neill and Judy Barrow. It was a great success and the mutual support it provided helped the families through this difficult period. Initial news of the Pebble Island raid was broadcast on television and radio that evening. When Mike Barrow's voice 'the voice of the Captain' came on air, Judy immediately recognised her husband and the news spread like wildfire amongst the *Glamorgan* rear link. This was the first positive information they had received of our whereabouts and it confirmed that we were giving a good account of ourselves; and now they had something to share. The name of the destroyer involved was not disclosed at the time though. In the following days the press filled in the details, only some of which were based upon fact. Thus the Pebble Island raid went down in history.

Chapter 8

The 'Tornado Express'

Sunday, 16 May

At 0630 we left our picket station to fuel from *Olmeda* in dark and difficult conditions and as we were disengaging from the tanker, *Alacrity* suddenly switched on her navigation lights. Neither bridge, nor ops room, nor lookouts knew she was only 600 yards away and all were on the receiving end of my wrath before we returned to our picket station.

The first indication of an air raid was often from our submarines, stationed up-threat of us. Using a satellite link their reports of the enemy would be broadcast to the carrier battle group via Northwood. Combat air patrols could then be scrambled and ships' crews warned. At 1300, a report came in that the Argentinians were mounting a raid on a naval unit north of the Falklands and that a pair of Super Etendards were on their way; but there was no naval unit north of the Falklands. We were the closest unit, on picket duty northwest of the main body. We remained on alert whilst the Super Etendards scanned an empty ocean until lack of fuel forced them to return. When sure that they were on their way home, we stood down. Attacks that did not materialise were almost as stressful as attacks that were pressed home.

At 1515 we gained a sonar contact and a Sea King, a Lynx and Willie were sent to prosecute. Intermittent contact was held by the helicopters and a depth charge dropped. This was a classic anti-submarine action that was well executed but ten minutes later the contact was assessed as marine life. We felt sorry for these whales but we could not afford to take chances.

We then started to prepare for Operation Tornado, the deception plan to be executed by *Glamorgan* alone. We had to convince the Argentinians that the landing was to take place south of Stanley. We were also tasked to harass positions around Stanley. The battle group attempted to further deceive Argentinian intelligence by allowing them to intercept false signal traffic. We detached at 1930 and raced inshore. Over the next week we spent every night charging around at high speed and *Glamorgan* became informally known as the 'Tornado Express'. We planned for a noisy night, firing 150 rounds between Stanley Common and Moody Valley, an area reportedly full of Argentinians, and at other targets south of Stanley. Willie was to be launched at midnight to drop flares and lay chaff whilst we bombarded. *Alacrity* and *Brilliant* were active in Falkland Sound and to avoid mutual interference, we had to put a lot of effort into planning these inshore operations.

Monday, 17 May

At midnight Willie was launched and half an hour later action stations piped. We maintained radar silence hoping to achieve some degree of surprise. We had experienced jamming before and needed to be crafty if we were to make effective use of our radars. As *Glamorgan* approached the gun-line, Type 1006 radar was switched from stand-by to transmit. The picture then started to fade and the Weapons Electrical Officer, Peter Galloway, was unjustly summoned to retune the set. The 1006 was taken off line whilst the maintainers went to work. We continued on, using 992 radar. Five minutes later, 1006 was back on line with a great picture, only to fade a few minutes later. The set was handed back to the maintainers. Peter Galloway soon reported there was nothing wrong. Then the penny dropped; the Argentinians were jamming us and we had to resort to intermittent transmissions on sector scan. Each time we overcame the Argentinian jamming, they became smarter and we had to keep one jump ahead. It was a battle we won. They failed to interrupt our activities and never degraded the accuracy of our bombardment.

Much went according to plan in the three hours we spent at action stations. During the bombardment we came under fire but this was rendered ineffective by our evasive steering. In the enclosed bridge we initially heard and saw nothing and it was the flight deck crew who informed us that shells were landing around the ship. This explained why the ops room were picking up tiny blips on the radar which were rapidly tracking in towards the centre of the displays. These blips were to become regular features.

One of our shells, directed at the bridge at Rock Point, hit something significant and caused a spectacular explosion. At one stage we were extremely close to Bertha's Beach within almost point blank range, and very conscious of the risk of our position. Willie came under fire from a fast patrol boat in East Cove and escaped unscathed but it was quite possible that other FPBs were lurking. It took courage to repeatedly fly into harm's way, never knowing exactly where the enemy had anti-aircraft facilities, but knowing that a low flying helicopter was a very attractive target for anyone with a gun or missile.

The very small Direction Island, a mile off the beach, gave a radar echo similar to a patrol boat. At one stage, the ops room were indicating Direction Island to the gunnery system, preparing for surface action. Inspection of the chart, followed by some effort convincing the ops room, spared Direction Island which would, of course, have been impossible to sink.

The final three shells, destined for East Cove, were cancelled due to an intermittent radar on Lively Island that might have been targetting us. Our final parting shot was one round of chaff which was intended to drift into Choiseul Sound on the wind to look like a boat insertion. There were a lot of people about for a Sunday night and we were pleased that they had observed our interest in the area; the deception plan would be working. At 0300, we stood down after firing 142 rounds and headed back towards the main body, arriving shortly before dawn.

With plenty of space in the magazines, shell rooms and fuel tanks, we prepared to replenish ammunition from *Resource*. Our preparations were interrupted at 1105 when the force went to action stations in response to a Harrier detecting low contacts to the west. These were soon assessed as weather and at 1120 we were alongside *Resource* passing the gear. Five minutes later the ship went back to action stations, conducting an emergency breakaway. The dreaded cry 'Handbrake' had been called, indicating Super Etendard to the southwest. The last place we wanted to be during an Exocet attack was alongside an ammunition ship. Once clear of *Resource* we fired two rounds of chaff charlie hoping that any Exocet firer would be confused by one of these blooms, and for fifteen minutes we waited, tense and alert. No missiles were detected, which was just as well as during this raid our Seaslug system chose the most inopportune moment to go defective and, with 992 also unserviceable, we were virtually defenceless. The maintainers worked flat out to get the systems back on line, the threat of an incoming Exocet providing an additional stimulus.

At 1142 a combat air patrol investigated a contact 130 miles to the west only to find once again that it was weather. Cloud banks were confusing the Harriers' radar. Shortly afterwards, with the genuine raid on its way home, we once again prepared to re-ammunition. Over the next hour and a quarter (lunchtime) we embarked 250 rounds of 4.5in shell and a similar number of cartridge. With ammunitioning completed, the replenishment crews could finish off what had been lunch.

The impending landings were the subject of much speculation. The Cabinet had been briefed to expect to lose at least six ships and the Defence Secretary had warned families to expect casualties. We rued the absence of mine countermeasures support as life on the gun-line would have been simplified if the minefields had been swept. Likewise, we missed heavy repair depot ships. Having them available in South Georgia would have given us greater flexibility and durability. *Stena Seaspread*, a North Sea oil rig support ship taken up from trade (STUFT), whose crew was augmented by members of the fleet maintenance team, was used as a substitute.

Visibility improved during the afternoon to such an extent that the Harriers could see the gas turbine ships' funnel smoke at ninety miles and it seemed that in not attacking us in such fine conditions, before the arrival of the amphibious force, the Argentinians were missing an opportunity.

Tuesday, 18 May

At midnight, as *Invincible* and *Brilliant* headed southwest past the Beauchene Islands, to launch Harrier attacks, *Glamorgan* was put in charge of the main body. This was the cover story for a Sea King to land SAS who were to stay to destroy the Super Etendards at their Argentine base. Surprise, however, was lost at the last minute, the raid aborted, and the Sea King landed on a beach in Chile where it was destroyed. At 0145, the carrier battle group lost another helicopter when it ditched. The crew were recovered and the helicopter sunk by gunfire. Meanwhile, *Hermes* sailed north to rendezvous with the amphibious force.

As dawn approached all was quiet and the opportunity was taken to fuel all escorts. As the RAS progressed, part of the amphibious group, the troopship *Canberra* and the hospital ship *Uganda*, arrived from Ascension. As we handed the main body back to *Hermes* we were pleased to have achieved an undisturbed day's fuelling, leaving the Admiral with his escorts well placed for the next few days. At 1800, we detached at speed to bombard targets around Lively Island and the approaches to Choiseul Sound, and we also hoped to surprise the Argentine fast patrol boat if it was still in East Cove.

Wednesday, 19 May
We went to action stations as we approached the coast. Alert for Argentinian jamming, we only switched on Type 1006 radar right at the last minute, but the Argentinians quickly found our frequencies though not quickly enough to disrupt our firings. Willie was launched for surface and anti-submarine search and to lay chaff in a small bay and watch for any reaction. Just before we opened fire into the bay, we were illuminated by shore radar. The Argentinians were well aware of our presence.

We spent the next few hours bombarding selected targets along the coast and all went well except for an unusual moment of bad drill in the turret when the cartridge loader on one gun failed to leave enough room for the shell to be loaded; they were too keen to keep up the rate of fire. The firing pulse was missed, and the target only received nine out of ten planned rounds. At 0500, the Argentinian batteries in the hills began to engage us with 105mm and 155mm howitzers. Our 4.5in shells weighed 56lbs while the 155mm howitzer shells weighed 100lbs and a single hit could cause us serious harm. They came close that night but we successfully dodged their fire by turning towards the last fall of shot assuming they would apply a spotting correction. Whilst our final rounds were going out, we recalled Willie. At 0530 we increased speed to retire and were followed by a forlorn trail of howitzer shells. Half an hour later, out of range of the batteries, we stood down after a good night's work with 112 rounds having been fired at ten different targets.

At 1130, we sighted the main body and reduced speed. In twenty-four hours, we had burnt 300 tons of fuel. We refuelled from *Olmeda* and then assumed goalkeeping station on *Regent* for four uneventful hours and a welcome chance for rest. Five minutes before we detached at 1800, *Alacrity* detected Skyhawk rackets. The force went to action stations and it seemed sensible to stay in goal next to the supply ship RFA *Regent* until the raid either materialised or went home. Ten minutes later, the unsuccessful Skyhawks retired and we were off again for shore bombardment. Each time we went back in, the risks increased as it was more difficult to ring the changes. This time I elected to conduct a reverse run. High speed would reduce the threat from submarine and shore batteries, though it would be disastrous if we struck a mine, but I hoped the signalled location of the minefield was accurate especially as I intended to run close to its border.

In Argentina, rumours abounded that the invasion was due on the night of 20 May and we anticipated that the shore batteries would aggressively oppose our intrusion. The responsibility of deciding which track and which tactic to employ played heavily upon my mind. When does one decide that the risk has escalated too far? The Captain always has ultimate responsibility and I wondered what he was feeling. I considered what the Argentine defenders might do and tried to second guess their tactics. The enemy was working on a solution to interdict the bombarding ships.

Thursday, 20 May
The plan for the night was agreed. We conducted high speed runs close inshore, maintaining evasive steering, successfully delivering 102 rounds of high explosive (HE). As we were turning away on completion, we watched a number of explosions and a large amount of tracer coming from the Port Fitzroy area. They were not firing at us but we were the only British unit in the area. The Argentinians, it had to be assumed, were anticipating imminent invasion and were very jumpy and we guessed that we had initiated a spirited red-on-red engagement.

Maintaining 24 knots, we watched the last few howitzer shells drop uselessly further astern before the Argentinians finally gave up. The enemy could not stand down until they were sure that we would not return again that night but our off watch crew could now return to their sleeping bags in air-conditioned comfort, the enemy gunners could only shelter in a cold and probably wet tent. However, comfort on board was not total; there was a strong wind blowing, with a matching sea state, and at 24 knots *Glamorgan* had an uncomfortable trip back to the main body.

On re-joining we were ordered to replenish ammunition from *Regent* whose rigs played up again. That was not the only problem. The base course of the Task Force was into the wind and with a near gale blowing, seas were breaking over *Glamorgan*'s fo'c's'le. To minimise the risk of casualties, we reduced to 10 knots, significantly lessening the amount of water coming over the bow. This speed made the steering very sluggish and it was nigh on impossible to hold the bow steady. Eventually, after over two hours of 100 per cent concentration, with salt-laden wind and water keeping fatigue at bay, *Regent*'s temperamental rigs won the day and the replenishment was aborted.

After lunch, the other defence watch provided the replenishment parties for fuelling from *Tidepool*. Having re-fuelled, we returned to *Regent* to try again. This time our two hours alongside were successful. We had to use the after rigs which created shiphandling problems, pulling the sterns together every time the weight came on the jackstay. Sometimes, the sterns of the two ships closed to less than 20ft. At other times the gap opened beyond 160ft. Distance was not the only problem: fore and aft mismatch generated some significant angles on the rigs. At the RAS dumps, loads crashed against the shot mats as they suddenly arrived more swiftly than desired, courtesy of the South Atlantic. The RAS dump was not a safe place of work and survival required skill, teamwork, alertness and luck. We had plenty of the first three but had been drawing on our barrel of luck rather deeply.

At 1700, completion of ammunitioning brought a brief but welcome respite for most of the crew who had been up for almost twenty-four hours, but we were due to detach again at 2000. I had no time for sleep as I had to draw up fresh charts. This time we were to bombard targets north of Berkeley Sound which would force us really close inshore between the coast and the area occupied by *San Luis*. A long night was in prospect as we planned to conduct two circuits instead of one, albeit at different targets.

'H' Hour for the amphibious landing was to be 0630 on 21 May in San Carlos Water. It was crucial that we drew attention away from that area. As soon as the enemy appreciated what was happening, we could expect massive airborne retaliation. The day would be finely poised. Winning the air war was crucial to the outcome. My diary recorded, 'Tomorrow will either be a day to remember or to forget. Many lives will be lost on both sides and that is the tragedy'. I then considered the implications for my family should I not return and these sentiments were reflected in many a heart. Outside the naval ports and army towns, life went on as normal. The Falklands War was just twenty minutes extra on the news. We were in a different world.

At 2000 we closed the islands. We were not the only ones inshore that night. However, we were alone in the Stanley area and would be trying to draw as much attention to ourselves as possible. We were expendable in the greater scheme of things where priority was to achieve a surprise landing in San Carlos.

Friday, 21 May - Mike Barrow's 50th Birthday

As Mike Barrow entered the ops room he was greeted with a rendition of 'Happy Birthday', a cake courtesy of the chefs and a bottle of bubbly courtesy of his wife. Celebrations did not last long, with action stations at 0130. Our first target was the ridge north of Magellan Cove. To reach it we would have to steam a mile off the clearly visible coast, virtually within rifle range, to lob shells over Mount Brisbane. At 0200, *Glamorgan*'s guns once more shattered the quiet of the night.

We were not being jammed which meant that the opposition had not expected us in this vicinity. I made full use of 1006, a rare luxury. Apart from firing HE and starshell, we also loaded the guns with chaff charlie, sowing three 'ships' in Berkeley Sound. We hoped these would convince the enemy that other ships were approaching the shore. After firing the chaff, we hauled out to port to avoid entering the minefield, concluding our first circuit.

Whilst the gunnery was in progress the MCO and ops room teams had been making a lot of transmissions to simulate activity; one of the PWOs even resorted to reading passages of the seamanship manual on secure voice. On the upper deck, scare charges were being dropped and Verey lights fired. In every possible way we were saying 'Hello! we are here!' The headquarters in Stanley must have received plenty of reports of activity off Berkeley Sound, an area which was high on their list of likely landing sites. Whilst they were busy working out what was afoot, we were busy racing back for our second circuit. In addition to the on-board activity, we had launched Willie before the start of the first circuit to also make as much noise as possible. Willie re-fuelled between laps and continued dropping charges, igniting flares, and transmitting on radio, radar and sonar.

At 0310, we re-commenced firing on Mount Brisbane. To reach some of our later targets, despite being very close inshore, we had to fire at 19,500 yards, the extreme range for our guns. On completion of our rounds we opened to the east, and re-embarked Willie. We wished the Argentinians an unpleasant night and hoped they would be completely surprised by the imminent landings. Once clear of immediate danger we reverted to defence watches. We were totally exhausted but I felt unable to leave the bridge until 0600 when we were clear of the mine and submarine threat. We had been on the go, day and night, for what had seemed ages. We hoped that we could now look forward to a period of lesser activity.

By 1000, we were back with the main body and Operation Tornado was over. It had been very successful, convincing the enemy that the amphibious attack would materialise on the east of East Falkland. In wrong footing the enemy it saved many lives in San Carlos, and made a marked contribution to the success of the landings.

Chapter 9

Invasion: Supporting the Landings

Dawn saw *Glamorgan* on picket duty. The landing was late in starting but the beaches had been secured. The troops ashore were surprised to find enemy guns pointing the wrong way - the deception plan had worked. The weather was ideal for flying and we expected heavy air raids; there was an urgent need to get Blowpipe and Rapier surface-to-air missile batteries established ashore. Although the troops and ships in San Carlos would attract the bombers, the carrier battle group, 130 miles further east, was vulnerable to Super Etendards. Therefore, we were called off picket duty and defensively stationed close to *Hermes*.

The air threat remained yellow until midday when *Argonaut*, in the amphibious operating area (AOA), reported Super Etendard radar. No raid materialised and Harriers returning from a bombing run downed a Chinook and destroyed two Pumas on the ground. A fourth helicopter remained undamaged. One Harrier was hit by small arms fire but landed safely.

At 1310 Mirages and Skyhawks were detected. Shortly afterwards *Antrim* held eight contacts. We remained alert although it was the AOA which was under attack. Suddenly the ops room reacted to an airborne radar intercept and we turned downwind to hide in our chaff delta cloud. *Argonaut* was reporting further unknowns and it was evident there was a very heavy raid on the AOA. The Harriers did their best to intercept but some aircraft got through, attacking the beachhead and ships in San Carlos Water. The first raid scored no hits but further raids swiftly followed. As we listened to the action taking place ashore we suddenly had problems of our own – a fire in one element of the data link in our computer control room. The burning cabinet was injected with carbon dioxide and it would be some time before the full extent of the damage was known. Despite distractions, we could not afford to let our guard slip. Submarines were a constant worry and a zig-zag plan was in force.

The sonar control room crew searched below the surface whilst the bridge, ops room and lookouts scanned sea, horizon and sky.

At 1336, a combat air patrol engaged a raid of Skyhawks. Two minutes later *Antrim* was bombed and strafed. An unexploded bomb damaged her Seaslug missile system before coming to rest in the after heads. We hoped that *Antrim* had sorted out her 'severe bowel disorders'. Having a ticking 1,000lb bomb next to the pans would cure any constipation.

The maintainers reported on our own fire. The search was now on for a replacement amplifier. We did not carry a spare on board and we hoped MATCONOFF would find one somewhere within the battle group. Meanwhile, the affected system remained unserviceable. Moments later the cry 'Bootlace' was called from the electronic warfare office on a Mirage aircraft. We prepared to defend ourselves but the enemy focused upon San Carlos with *Argonaut* the victim. Things did not seem to be going very well but on a strategic level, the Army were getting ashore despite our naval losses. The enemy too were suffering losses.

In the early afternoon Willie reported a surface contact ten miles north of *Glasgow*. An anxious five minutes passed before Willie's contact was assessed as a surface search helicopter. Heavy raids continued on the AOA throughout the afternoon and the Harriers were unable to intercept all the raids or force them to turn away though they did have some successes. Harriers also strafed an Argentine fast patrol boat which was abandoned, aground and on fire. Unfortunately, we lost an RAF Harrier though it was difficult to keep track of losses because of the confusion over claims. The battle was intense, as can be appreciated by the following fifteen-minute period recorded in my narrative,

'1748 Further unknowns approaching the AOA, being taken by CAP.
 1750 Low Bogeys attacking *Brilliant*. *Brilliant* hit! *Antrim* under attack from Skyhawk.
 1753 Two CAP splash two Mirages.
 1755 Two Mirages attacking *Brilliant*.
 1759 Three Skyhawks closing unknown callsign.
 1802 *Ardent* hit. Has fire forward. Oh God, this is beginning to go badly!'

Twenty minutes later *Ardent*, on fire, was reported as sinking by the stern. One of the attacking aircraft hit her mast and a second aircraft bombed the blazing ship. In *Brilliant*, the fighter controller was hit in the arm and one man hit in the stomach. It was with considerable relief that we greeted sunset at 2000. I set about preparing to fuel from *Olmeda* and ammunition from *Resource*.

The BBC world news claimed that Argentina had lost fourteen aircraft and two helicopters and that we had five ships damaged, two seriously. This worried the next of kin of all crews. We knew that we were safe but our families did not.

Shortly after 2030 we went alongside *Olmeda*. Ten minutes after connecting up, Mike Barrow came onto the bridge wing and said, 'Pilot, we have been ordered to go into San Carlos and replace *Antrim*'. My heart sank. I was absolutely exhausted as were the rest of the crew. I faced the prospect of spending most the night drawing up a new bombardment grid and navigational safety plans for the AOA. I knew that once we arrived we would spend most of the day at action stations. When not at action stations, being in confined waters, I would still be up keeping the ship off the rocks. Added to that the abject fear of being bombed and strafed all day. My personal morale sank to an all time low.

I could see Mike Barrow had similar worries. He knew we were in no fit condition, due to fatigue, to go inshore. He was also aware of our own weapons systems' limitations close inshore. A few minutes later Mike came back onto the bridge wing. I shall always remember his words, 'Pilot, how do you tell the Admiral that you do not think it is a good idea for *Glamorgan* to go into San Carlos without being thought of as a coward?' I thought he was being serious and hated myself for replying, 'You cannot, Sir, we have to go in'. I suppose it was my way of indicating that he would have my full support in following orders, whatever the cost.

I then spent the most miserable thirty minutes of my life. To this day I do not know whether Mike Barrow spoke with the Admiral and, if so, what was said. However, Captain Hugh Balfour in the brand new Type 42 *Exeter* was due to join before dawn and the Admiral made the very sensible decision to send *Exeter* rather than *Glamorgan* as a replacement for the battered *Antrim*. When Mike Barrow returned to the bridge wing and said, 'Relax! *Exeter* is relieving *Antrim*' a sense of overwhelming relief swept over me; common sense had prevailed.

After refuelling, we went alongside *Resource*. It was still very cold and like many others, I was gradually freezing. I was delighted when Mike Barrow offered to relieve me for ten minutes so I could thaw out over a cup of coffee. It worked wonders and I was soon back on the bridge wing, less cold and fully alert. Mike Barrow always thought of his crew and it was these little gestures which made him so popular.

Finally, we hauled away from *Resource* and headed back to Circle 5. It was the end of a long and hard fought day. Going through the signals I came across the following from the Admiral referring to Operation Tornado, 'I know how busy you have been every night and every day over the last week. Well done. Take a weekend!' It was a thoughtful signal but we would have to take the weekend as we found it - probably on Circle 5. However, at least we could hope for more time on defence watches and less time at action stations. We were all exhausted but well pleased with our achievements.

Saturday, 22 May

The previous day's action losses were worse than we thought. One of *Argonaut*'s bombs damaged her steam plant. The other bomb, which failed to explode, lay in her flooded Seacat magazine. She was very lucky. As the bomb entered the magazine, one of the Seacat missiles exploded. *Brilliant* and *Broadsword* suffered defective or damaged Sea Wolf mountings although *Broadsword* managed to recover hers overnight. *Antrim* lost one Seacat system together with her Seaslug. A Lynx helicopter and *Antrim*'s Wessex were also damaged.

After a successful bombardment operation, *Ardent* had been attacked by eleven aircraft. Having shot down two of her attackers, her gun was disabled. Whilst fighting her fires she was hit again, putting her Seacat out of action and leaving her defenceless. Further attacks followed, and she was hit fourteen times. With her stern blown off, she was abandoned and sank with the loss of twenty-two of her crew. They had acquitted themselves well but in the end were overwhelmed by numbers.

The Army had also suffered. Two helicopters were downed and a fully-loaded, troop-carrying Sea King crashed following a bird-strike. All twenty on board were killed. Heavy losses had never deflected the Royal Navy from its purpose and the Royal Marines and Army were now well established ashore, digging in and setting up anti-aircraft batteries. The Royal Navy was achieving its prime task. Supplies were being ferried ashore by helicopter, landing craft and mexifloat. The soldiers were happier now that they were on terra firma, instead of cooped up in ships.

Noon came and went as we awaited the first raid of the day. *Coventry* and *Brilliant* were lying in wait north of Pebble Island as a missile trap. The other amphibious ships and their escorts were close inshore around San Carlos. *Exeter*, *Ambuscade* and *Antelope* had joined overnight, the latter surviving a collision with *Tidepool* during replenishment.

Shortly after 1300, *Antrim*, *Canberra*, *Elk* and *Stromness* rejoined the carrier battle group from the AOA. As *Antrim* closed we could clearly see about six shell holes in her side underneath the hangar door. I was contemplating a cheerfully rude 'welcome back' signal, when Mike Barrow, ever the diplomat, signalled, 'Can we help?' Her reply was, 'You were right, brown bread and bran not required! Have plenty of bog rolls but reduced bog stations'. For our part, we had plenty of functional heads on board though paper was in short supply. We responded, 'Request the pleasure of your company for bog any day – bring own paper!' As *Antrim* proceeded, *Intrepid* reported Pucaras closing, and the raids began.

We were blessed with a peaceful afternoon and the welcome arrival of mail. Heavy Argentine air losses might have explained the apparent lack of air activity as they took stock. Had they been able to mount just one more major air raid the previous day it was doubtful whether the escorts could have prevented them from reaching the high value targets in San Carlos.

Late afternoon was a common time for an Argentinian air raid, so I returned to the bridge to cover the last few hours of daylight. Willie was now fitted with a radar reflector, similar to an overgrown biscuit tin, to seduce Exocet missiles. Should a threat come, Willie would station in an appropriate offset location up threat, hovering at 200ft. The theory was that Exocet would go for this target, harmlessly passing underneath and disappear into an empty ocean.

At 1755, *Coventry* detected an major incoming raid. The AOA went on alert and *Plymouth* reported being under attack. We remained uncertain of the outcome as we faced our own alert. At 1808 *Antrim* intercepted Drumbeat radar from a Tracker aircraft which was probably providing tactical direction for an, as yet, undetected raid. A few minutes later six hostiles were reported and *Glasgow* and *Glamorgan* intercepted Mirage radar. Combat air patrols were launched and further intercepts were made and yet more hostiles detected. CAP turned the raid away and the Mirage and Skyhawk aircraft retreated to base. Harriers have a limited endurance and it was vital not to launch them too early. For self protection, the carriers were well down threat and this further limited the full potential of the Harriers. We remained on alert until it began to get dark. The previous hour had been typical of how a raid built up and then faded away as seen from the battle group east of the Falklands. It was a different story for the AOA. They were usually in the thick of the action. It remained quiet until 2145 when an unidentified surface contact was detected thirty miles away, subsequently identified as *Norland* re-joining from the AOA.

Sunday, 23 May

Overnight, *Yarmouth* had a spot of luck, forcing *Monsunnen* aground whilst she was ferrying supplies to Port Stanley. (*Monsunnen* was a small coaster that used to be operated for the Falkland Islands Company and she was re-floated after the war to resume her normal business.) All was quiet in the carrier battle group although the relentless search for the enemy continued. Searching an empty ocean for hours on end was tedious and often boring, but our lives and the lives of our comrades depended upon vigilance.

As dawn broke on Argentine Air Force Day, we wondered what they might have in store for us as we patrolled Circle 5. Their propaganda was making excessive claims, exaggerating their progress and belittling our successes. Activity soon resumed with the first raid of many on the AOA. A combat air patrol splashed one Bell, one Puma and forced another Puma down. By my tally, 10 per cent of their entire air force had been lost. The charthouse tote was as follows:

Ship Losses

Santa Fe	submarine	sunk at Grytviken
A69	corvette	damaged at Grytviken
General Belgrano	cruiser	sunk off Tierra Del Fuego
Narwhal	ELINT trawler	sunk in TEZ
Monsunnen	supply ship	beached en route for Stanley
	FPB	sunk in TEZ
	FPB	beached in Choiseul Sound

Tug	sunk by helicopter missile in TEZ
Tug	damaged in TEZ

Aircraft losses

Helicopters		Fighter-bombers		Bombers		Utility	
Puma	9	Mirage	13	Canberra	2	Skyvan	2
Chinook	1	Skyhawk	11				
Bell	1	Pucara	10				
	11		**34**		**2**		**2**

Total 49

The raids on the AOA continued throughout the afternoon. The Combo off Pebble Island came under attack, *Broadsword* downing one Skyhawk. The carrier battle group also had its alerts. We fired chaff charlie and three rounds of chaff delta. For chaff delta to be fully effective we needed to fire a full pattern of sixteen rounds but *Glamorgan* had been built in the days before chaff delta and the chaff fit was an add-on, lacking full chaff magazine facilities. We only held enough rockets for four full patterns.

Damage reports started to come in from the AOA. One of the landing ships had suffered minor damage though worse news was to come later. We had pinned a lot of hope in Rapier but so far it had not proved very effective. We soon had our own problems with a series of false alarms intermingled with genuine alerts. With the possibility of an imminent Exocet attack, the Seaslug system went unserviceable and was not available for fifteen minutes, by which time any incoming raid would have come and gone. Argentinian Air Force Day was celebrated with a massive raid as the afternoon drew to a close. We had six combat air patrols in the area with more in transit. Battle reports flooded in. Rapier were claiming two Skyhawks, *Broadsword* one, CAP one which, counting one that hit *Antelope*'s mast, made five in total. In all the confusion, there was double counting of kills and when the assessments were completed later, the five Skyhawks downed were re-assessed as only three.

At 1834, just as Seaslug was reported fully operational, the last of the rackets was lost and it all went quiet. *Hermes* prepared to launch four bombers to keep the opposition awake and CAP returned reporting a ship had been hit in San Carlos. We waited for full battle damage assessments to filter through and at 2030, the Admiral assessed that the Argentinians had lost eight or nine Mirage/ Skyhawks. The Harriers had been successful in dealing with Argentinian helicopter pads and fuel dumps. More Harriers were in transit to bomb Stanley airport where there were signs that arrestor gear was being fitted for the recovery of Etendards and Navy Skyhawks. Our aim was to keep the airport out of commission.

We then learned that apart from downing one Skyhawk with her gun and another with her mast, *Antelope* had taken an unexploded bomb but did not appear to be badly damaged. Later, the tally for the day was revised to six Mirage, three Skyhawk, two Puma and one Bell. It was very difficult to verify claims.

I turned in at 2300 anticipating a relatively quiet night. Within minutes there was a loud explosion quickly followed by a second explosion. The action alarm sounded. When there is an unexplained explosion, you assume the worse and react as if under attack by the enemy. At first people believed that one of the ships had been torpedoed and countermeasures were initiated but within five minutes the explosions were explained. One of the RAF Harriers on a bombing run had lost power shortly after take-off, possibly due to a bird strike and the pilot had released his bomb to lighten his load. That had been the first explosion. Seconds later the Harrier ditched – the second explosion. Sadly, the pilot did not survive. I wrote, 'So Operation Corporate takes yet another life. How many more will it take before it ends? ... . The loss of another Harrier does not alter our resolve to see this job properly finished. We must "keep on keeping on".'

Monday, 24 May

Overnight, more support ships were ordered inshore to San Carlos, escorted by *Arrow* and *Alacrity*, to offload heavy equipment, tanks, armoured personnel carriers and other heavy weapons. We were ordered to replenish from *Olmeda* before first light. As we fell out from replenishment stations bad news filtered through the ship. *Antelope* had been abandoned. Whilst the Royal Engineers were trying to defuse the unexploded bomb, it had exploded and fires then spread out of control until they reached the Seacat magazine which had exploded in the most spectacular fashion. We had now lost three ships, *Sheffield*, *Ardent* and *Antelope*. *Argonaut* was sorely hit and *Glasgow* was being sent home for repairs.

Less that a year before John Nott, the Defence Secretary, had agreed to large cutbacks in the Navy including *Glamorgan*, *Fearless* and *Intrepid*. My narrative recorded with sarcasm that, 'Mr. Nott is getting his Navy cuts now!' We needed a balanced fleet and did not have one. Airborne early warning was one glaring gap in our inventory. The price of that gap was now being measured in lives lost and ships sunk.

Air raids on the AOA resumed with an attack on *Intrepid*. In the carrier battle group, the morning passed uneventfully. The AOA and Combo continued to attract air raids throughout the afternoon and some air activity was associated with an Argentine stores drop on West Falkland. There had also been other activity ashore. The SAS were inserted into Weddell Island to blow up ammunition dumps, and ground attack Harriers bombed minor airstrips to keep up pressure on the enemy.

The only incidents of note in the battle group were the safe return of a Harrier which had been in difficulty and *Invincible* reporting chilled water flooding in her ops room which was evacuated for safety reasons. It was just as well that all raids were outbound at the time but credit must be given to the air groups embarked in the carriers. *Hermes* had fourteen Harriers embarked and on this particular day, she had maintained ten airborne with two ready on deck throughout. At night, the pilots were able to get some rest but it was at this time that the maintenance teams worked flat out keeping the aircraft operational. The ability of the carriers to keep their aircraft flying was a crucial factor in winning the air war.

Battle damage assessments came in. First reports indicated three Mirage splashed and possibly one LSL hit. Half an hour later the score was ten aircraft downed though analysis after the war proved these claims to be exaggerated. Similarly, the Argentinians claimed many ships sunk and even after the war many in Argentina refused to believe that both carriers had emerged unscathed.

With everything quiet I left the bridge for a hot shower followed by half a pint of lager. There was no way one could relax in daylight, but nights on Circle 5 were much less tense than on the gun line. I never drank more than half a pint of lager in any one day. All I wanted was to take the edge off the tension without materially affecting my reactions. It was a good compromise and really did the trick when preceded by a shower.

Chapter 10

Coventry and *Atlantic Conveyor*

Tuesday, 25 May - Argentine National Day

Damage to *Sir Lancelot* included one unexploded bomb forward and a major fire from a bomb exploding aft. *Sir Galahad* took two unexploded bombs which had yet to be defused. Of *Argonaut*'s unexploded bombs, the one in her boiler room had been defused allowing her to flash up one of her boilers, but the other in her Seacat missile magazine remained live.

Amongst the Argentine air losses, one reportedly wore Peruvian markings. Intelligence suggested Peru had given Argentina twelve Mirages. Having failed to make effective use of their aircraft carrier, the Argentine Navy, however, made very effective use of their naval Skyhawks; the naval pilots were well trained in attacking ships and their skill was reflected in our ship losses.

During the afternoon, *Coventry* splashed two hostiles with Sea Dart and a Skyhawk was splashed in Falkland Sound; so far, today, things were going our way and the *Bristol* Group reinforcements were due tomorrow. At 1730 we received reports of raids outbound from Argentina. Whilst we waited for them, Harriers bombed Stanley Airport and, shortly afterwards, *Coventry* detected contacts at 165 miles. Replacement combat air patrols were launched from *Hermes*.

At 1759, *Glamorgan* went to action stations and moments later two Pucara were detected over Stanley. Ten minutes later we assessed that the aircraft detected by *Coventry* could have been tanking aircraft, indicating a possible Exocet raid coming in from any direction and so the jammer anti-Exocet Lynx was launched under *Exeter*'s control. At 1815 we heard over AAWC net, 'A bloody great raid is building'. Willie, with his radar decoy fitted, was at five minutes notice for launch. *Hermes* prepared to launch two more replacement combat air patrols.

The first inkling of bad news reached the bridge at 1828 with *Broadsword* reporting being under attack and *Coventry* requiring a tow. In *Coventry*, a bomb had entered the after engine room and a watchkeeper was able to report the damage before the bomb exploded. *Broadsword* had been lucky as one bomb came upwards through the ship's side and flightdeck, taking the nose off the Lynx helicopter before disappearing overboard. Six minutes later *Coventry* was in danger of capsizing. The Combo off Pebble Island, which had taken the heat off San Carlos, was effectively eliminated. 'What a disaster', I recorded. A term mate of mine, Glen Robinson-Moltke (the First Lieutenant of *Coventry*), did not survive.

As *Broadsword* was picking up survivors, the foundering *Coventry* capsized ten miles north of Pebble Island. Four combat air patrols remained overhead whilst the remaining survivors were rescued. Of the destroyers which had been deployed south with us, we were the only one not to have been sunk or suffered significant damage. It transpired that a raid had suddenly opened from Pebble Island. CAP, about to intercept, was hauled off by *Coventry*, who then turned the wrong way. She crossed between *Broadsword* and the raid, breaking lock and preventing Sea Wolf from firing.

As we contemplated this disaster, jamming was reported on a fighter control frequency. At 1943, *Atlantic Conveyor* reported being hit by Exocet. We had gone back to action stations at 1940 when *Ambuscade* reported Super Etendard radar. The aircraft unexpectedly struck from the northeast. On pop-up, the aircraft had detected two similar echoes. Unaware of the surface situation, the pilots fired at one of the echoes. This was *Ambuscade* who immediately fired chaff delta. Two missiles were seen to be launched and at least one was seduced by chaff but after flying through the chaff, the missile seeker head resumed its search, and detected *Atlantic Conveyor*. She had no chaff launchers to protect her and the missile hit. The analysis on the second missile was that it failed to lock on and ditched.

Alacrity was sent to assist *Atlantic Conveyor*, playing hoses onto her flight deck, laden with helicopters. Shortly afterwards, *Atlantic Conveyor* lost firemain and the fires spread out of control towards the cluster bombs. *Glamorgan*, eight miles away, could see masses of smoke rising from the stricken vessel and five helicopters were dispatched to evacuate the crew. *Atlantic Conveyor* had been particularly unlucky, having only just been brought forward to go inshore to disembark her cargo, and six Wessex, three Chinooks and large quantities of ammunition were lost, significantly impacting on operations ashore.

This particular attack stuck in the memory of *Glamorgan*'s Leading Engineering Mechanic Taff Callaghan. On closing up at action stations in the midships section base, his normal routine was to dress the two fearnought suitmen, Marine Engineering Mechanics Day and Petherick, then act as Breathing Apparatus Controller. Whilst tightening up Day's breathing apparatus harness, 'Brace! Brace! Brace!' was broadcast. Taff grabbed Day's shoulders and pushed him to the deck, following closely behind. It became immediately apparent to Taff they had picked the wrong spot. The Canteen Flat was being scrubbed out prior to action stations and Taff found himself lying in a soapy puddle. Petty Officer 'Pony' More was underneath the ice making machine and would not let Taff take refuge under it as well, saying light-heartedly, 'Sod off, I was here first!' Possession of a good shelter was definitely nine tenths of the law when something unpleasant was inbound. Whilst waiting for the expected hit, Taff thought, 'How is Mum going to react when she gets the news that I am twanging a harp? Ah well, at least she can sell the car!'

Once the alarm was over, 'Pony' emerged and detailed people off to finish scrubbing out! This was greeted with looks of incredulity. Imagine being asked by your offspring, 'What did you do in the war, Daddy?' 'Armed with a bucket, scrubber and cloth, I blitzed the Canteen Flat!' Shortly afterwards, the section base team heard that *Atlantic Conveyor* had been hit. 'Pony' confessed to his team that on hearing the pipe to 'brace' he mentally began counting, believing that the flight time of an Exocet was about twelve seconds. When he reached twenty, he was convinced it had missed. Taff said it was a pity 'Pony' did not share this information with his team beforehand. It was just as well that he did not. An Exocet, released from forty miles, has a four-minute flight time.

I recalled arriving on the bridge just before the attack. Ships were firing chaff and though *Glamorgan* was hemmed in we managed to fire four rounds of chaff delta and attempted to place ourselves up threat to protect the main body. *Atlantic Conveyor* then reported being hit and I could see heavy brown smoke rising from her super-structure. *Invincible* fired four Sea Dart and immediately after they disappeared into cloud I saw a flash in the sky, almost like lightening behind cloud. *Invincible* assessed this as a hit on a Super Etendard but her targets were subsequently analysed as chaff.

Darkness fell with the Argentinians having achieved considerable success on their National Day. We had only downed five Argentine aircraft. The action, however, was not over for everyone. As the Super Etendards could have landed at Stanley airfield to refuel, Harriers and *Glamorgan* were sent inshore to pound the airport, hoping to catch the strike aircraft on the ground. Peter Galloway came up with a brilliant suggestion to target the airport with the Seaslug telemetry round which remained on board. He calculated the rate to lower the 901 radar in elevation once the missile was gathered. Seaslug, a beam riding missile, would follow the beam. Provided I could give Peter advance target details, he believed we had a new bombardment vehicle with a twenty-mile range. Everyone was very enthusiastic.

Wednesday, 26 May
At 0300, the ship went to action stations and Skyguard tracked us in as we approached. Forty-five minutes later, I piped, '*Glamorgan* Airways announce the departure of their one-way flight to Stanley airfield!', and the first ever Seaslug in the bombardment mode was launched. Firing at 17,000yds allowed us to immediately engage with our 4.5in guns. Seaslug landed in spectacular fashion. Whereas a shell burst flashes for a split second, the Seaslug fireball, travelling at mach 2, held on for about two seconds, covering a wide area. Those on the airport would have had no warning, just a loud explosion and huge fireball. We then commenced the serious business of lobbing 150 shells in the wake of the Seaslug. Using spotting corrections we rapidly shifted targets around the airfield. We had prudently planned a very swift and efficient bombardment which was just as well as Seaslug stirred up a hornet's nest and about four shore batteries engaged us. Having completed our job, there was no point in trading shells with the batteries. Ashore, John Smith, a Falkland Islander, recorded, 'It was very noisy with a heavy and close bombardment. They seemed to be firing at two-second intervals. Occasional return fire from the land, but not a great deal; they must be too busy keeping their heads down!'

Steering evasively with an aggressive zig-zag, we retired seawards at speed. The enemy quickly found our range with their howitzers, dropping shells around us until we were ten miles from the coast but none found their mark. Once again we had pushed our luck and once again the enemy had come off second best. Sooner or later they might get lucky with one of the bombarding units. Once clear of imminent danger, we stood down and rejoined the carrier battle group who were delighted to hear of our success with Seaslug. Our rate of fire, however, had been reduced in the latter stages due to the slow run out of the left gun. This defect was traced to a bent loading tray and rectified.

Petty Officer Wiltshire recorded the night's action more colourfully! 'Whoosh, Seaslug fires in its surface to surface role, seconds later the 4.5in guns bark their wrath, thump, thump, thump, – a good rate of fire! Our intention is to flatten the goddam place … . The Argies must have … when they heard Seaslug coming overhead! Two tons of missile! I hope the … landed right in the middle of the runway.' In contrast, Weapons Electrical Mechanician Roger Tipton's account was factual without embellishment, 'We must have stirred up a hornet's nest, because they started firing back at us with all they have got. 0349 – under gunfire from ashore. 0352 – gunfire ceased. 0408 – under fire from ashore. 0410 – shells landing around us. 0419 – now out of range of shore guns.'

As dawn broke, all was quiet around the battle group. *Atlantic Conveyor* was still afloat and burning and off Pebble Island, the capsized *Coventry* was still afloat. She might have to be sunk by gunfire if she risked obstructing the approach to San Carlos. The enemy was mounting a series of air raids against San Carlos but combat air patrols were successful in breaking up these attacks. The last raid came shortly after 2000 and, ten minutes later, the amphibious operating area reverted to defence watches. In contrast to heavy losses yesterday, today was relatively quiet. CAP had dealt with the only really big raid and had shot down a Puma helicopter.

Atlantic Conveyor's fires were dying down and attempts were made to recover useable stores; at the same time the battle group took the opportunity in the lull to consolidate the tankers. A big replenishment programme was planned for overnight. We needed fuel badly as we were down to 50 per cent.

Free aerograms from home reached the group but *Glamorgan* had not yet received any. Our latest mail was postmarked 15 May but our families had not received anything since 30 April and had no idea how we were coping.

Thursday, 27 May

Delays extended our replenishment with *Olmeda* to three hours. However, it was the most pleasant replenishment we had conducted since our arrival in the exclusion zone with the night so quiet that it was easy to hear unfamiliar noises, one emanating from the 1006 aerial training motor. It failed shortly thereafter and our minimum detection range was reduced to three miles on 992. In fog, we would be blind to close contacts. After fuelling, we closed *Regent* without radar to replenish ammunition and stores. With just her stern light visible, I went onto the bridge wing to get a better view. There is an amazing difference between looking directly from outside and looking through the thick glass containing heating elements and whose transparency is further degraded by dried salt spray. On reaching the bridge wing, it was apparent that we were very much closer than it seemed from inside the bridge but after taking swift evasive action we safely stationed alongside. The replenishment took just over one hour for fourteen loads which included ammunition and two days worth of chocolate. Whilst we were busy replenishing, more supplies were being ferried into San Carlos. In addition to fuel and ammunition, landing pads were put ashore for the Harriers which would enhance their effective endurance as well as providing the flexibility of a 'spare deck' ashore.

In the carrier battle group the morning passed uneventfully while ashore consolidation of the bridgehead continued and the perimeter was slowly expanded. During the afternoon, air raids built up over the Falklands. Petty Officer Wiltshire recorded the afternoon's events.

Three Argie aircraft are shot down and a couple more splashed. We lost a Harrier today, shot down by ground fire but the pilot ejected safely … . Another was slightly damaged but got back safely. We have been detached to carry out another NGS … . Some news of *Atlantic Conveyor*; she had an explosion on board as a result of the fire spreading to ammunition and she broke in half. The bow section has sunk but we believe the stern section to be still afloat. Ashore the Commandos and Paras are now beginning to advance on the Argie positions …. The weather is still holding. *Brilliant* has gone to get repairs done to her Sea Wolf and Exocet.

Comparing narratives shows how information and knowledge within a ship was fractured. At that time, I knew nothing about *Atlantic Conveyor*'s fate but I was well aware of the night's plan inshore. My narrative for the afternoon recorded snippets heard on AAWC and COL plus my own input:

'1715   One GR3 bomber ditched and a second damaged returning to the carrier.

1950   Multiple A4 raid on the ground forces. Two A4s seen departing trailing smoke.

2015   CAP took out two and two smoking. Detaching with *Alacrity* and *Avenger* for harassing the Argies around Stanley. 100 rounds each from the Type 21s, 50 plus two Seaslug from us – warheads this time!'

These were two very different styles of record. The former was written reflecting upon the day's events while mine recorded events as they unfolded and there was often little opportunity to do more than scrawl a few hurried notes whilst trying to fight a war from the bridge.

By 2030 it was quiet and with *Alacrity* and *Avenger* in company we closed the gun-line.

Friday, 28 May

At 0145 action stations were sounded. Our approach was monitored and the electronic battle with Skyguard radar continued as usual. We were unaware of the surprise the Argentinians had planned. At 0230 we launched our first warshot Seaslug at Two Sisters ridge. Perhaps interference from Skyguard or another problem caused our first shot to be unsuccessful but the missile dropped out of the 901 beam and exploded spectacularly, shortly after boost separation. We then engaged troop concentrations with the 4.5in gun, with *Alacrity*'s Lynx spotting, and came under fire from shore batteries. A couple of 155mm shells fell within one ship's length but our luck held.

Captain Julio Perez had progressed with his project of dismantling a ship-launched Exocet installation and transferring it onto the islands for land launch. Armed with a test set and using a missile simulator he determined that firing could be achieved manually by feeding in the essential data using a rudimentary system. The Argentinians used a wheeled chassis for the Exocet, a large electricity generator (converted to fit into a Hercules) and a manual control panel put together with various spare components. The makeshift control panel had its limits. Course corrections could not be verified and at least twenty minutes was required between firings for capacitors to discharge; and the manual firing sequence lacked any safety devices. A targetting radar was needed and an infantry radar with a 30-kilometre range was utilized. It had other limitations requiring a number of conversions to be made and the homing head had to be set on a wide radar sweep.

The installation was airlifted to Stanley and due to peaty ground around Stanley, the heavy equipment could only be placed on roads or tracks. One such track, linking Eliza Cove with the town, was selected and the Exocet was set up at the Cove each evening and hidden in Stanley by day. The firing sector was limited by coastal features to a mere 15 degrees.

Oblivious to the threat at Eliza Cove as we turned to retire and deliver our parting gesture, we placed ourselves virtually broadside to the shore and Captain Perez and his team, eight miles away, attempted to fire Exocet but it failed to launch. We were an easy target, at point blank range. It would have been almost impossible to bring our gun to bear, since it was in surface mode, and Seacat would have had very little time to acquire. Captain Perez waited a long time to let the capacitors discharge before attempting a second firing.

Unaware of our lucky escape, we launched our second Seaslug at Moody Valley. The launch was spectacular and with a glaring flash and tremendous roar it raced off into the night. It rode the beam and the last we saw of the missile was its efflux disappearing behind the crest of the hills. A couple of seconds later the under sides of the clouds were illuminated as it impacted on Moody Valley. It was not until mid-July that we learned how successful that missile had been. It had exploded amidst parked helicopters, taking out six of them.

Alacrity was next up. She too was covered in shell bursts from shore batteries and so we immediately turned back in support, sending ten rounds into the gun positions near Kelp Point. This seemed to do the trick and *Alacrity* fired her rounds unscathed. *Avenger* followed whilst *Alacrity* suppressed the batteries to the north. Whilst this was happening we could see gun flashes from the battle raging around Goose Green. They were not the only lights we saw. For some inexplicable reason, at 0347, all the street lights in Stanley were illuminated but we never found out why! Finally, the night's mission over, the bombarding trio rejoined the carrier group out at sea.

Ashore, John Smith described our activities: 'Very heavy bombardment last night, the heaviest yet. Illuminants were being used. We were able to hear the whistle of shells going over the house and then see the bright flashes of the explosions through gaps in the black-outs.' To the west, the Army and Royal Marines made significant advances over difficult ground.

Captain Perez's second attempt to fire Exocet was at *Avenger*, but inverted polarity caused an error so that the missile flew close over the frigate's quarterdeck. In *Glamorgan*, we did not know an Exocet had been fired at *Avenger* that night and the news of the attack only filtered through some days later.

On rejoining, we replenished stores and ammunition from *Fort Austin*, again experiencing rig problems. Whilst we replenished we heard that *Plymouth* had been attacked by three Pucaras, one of which had been splashed. We also gleaned from the morning situation report (sitrep) that *Atlantic Conveyor*'s stern section had been taken in tow by *Irishman*. It was the tug's opinion that the remains of the ship were not worth salvaging. The sitrep also informed us the Army had reached Teal Inlet.

In the afternoon a storm blew up which curtailed air activity and the battle group was left untouched. Only one ineffective air attack was conducted on the land forces, the bombs being dropped at random in thick cloud. Rapier was fired in the blind mode and neither side could claim any confirmed successes.

Darwin had been captured and Goose Green surrounded by 2 Para which explained the pyrotechnics we had seen. However, this victory was tinged with sadness. Colonel H Jones, the Commanding Officer, and sixteen paratroopers were killed with thirty-two wounded. About 100 Argentine prisoners were captured, including some senior officers. We also received details of *Coventry*'s casualties: eighteen dead with five seriously wounded. *Glasgow* had left for repairs in the UK whilst *Sir Tristram*'s and *Argonaut*'s unexploded bombs were removed without further mishap. The Argentinians were claiming some sort of submarine success but the carrier battle group were totally unaware of having been attacked and, had anything been hit, the victims would have been the first to know.

Saturday, 29 May

Unusually, *Glamorgan* was allowed a quiet night on the screen. *Avenger* and *Ambuscade* dashed inshore for a few hours on the gun-line, returning unscathed. A period of E/F band radar silence was imposed for Black Buck to target radar sites with Shrike missiles but the sortie was cancelled until the following night.

Important though Darwin and Goose Green were, they were only a secondary objective. Stanley was the key and the Army and Royal Marines were now pushing east. The land forces' front line had moved forward to Douglas Station, occupied by 45 Commando, with 3 Para in Teal Inlet and 2 Para in Darwin. Overnight a Canberra had managed to bomb the troops at San Carlos and the Argentinians made another attempt to fire Exocet, though a component failed and no missile was fired. It was replaced with a component from a radio. The next time the Argentinians were to attempt a firing, it would be more successful.

In the air, we lost a Puma helicopter to a Pucara, but on the plus side another Pucara had itself been shot down. At 1545, as we were about to replenish from *Tidespring*, a report predicted a Super Etendard raid. Appropriate precautions were taken and we waited for the attack to develop. By 1630, with no attack materialising, we replenished. It went well and with full bunkers, if not completely full stomachs, we detached again for the gun-line. Willie, grounded by a rotor head defect, would not be available for spotting. I was running short of ideas on how to ring the changes.

As we moved inshore, confirmation was received of the capture of Darwin/Goose Green with 900 prisoners, including 120 wounded. The figures demonstrated the intensity of the fighting and the magnitude of 2 Para's victory. A Skyhawk and a Mirage had attacked the AOA at 1800. Rapier claimed the Skyhawk although this kill was not confirmed. We were half way inshore when the evening's sitrep arrived. *Argonaut*, rid of her unexploded bombs, would be coming out of San Carlos whilst we bombarded to the east and *Minerva* was going in to assume fighter controller duties.

Sunday, 30 May
We were on the gun-line at 0315 and were due to support the SAS. However, en route we were informed that Stanley Airport was littered with light aircraft and we were tasked to deal with them. On approaching the airport we came under heavy and accurate fire from the shore batteries; they were getting much better and, unknown to most of the crew below decks, shells were landing within 200 yards. The peace of the night was then shattered by a very loud bang as a 6in howitzer shell landed close aboard. Those below decks may not have known what it was, but they certainly heard it. I had not planned to start the zig-zag for another couple of miles but a very loud bang is an excellent starting pistol. I immediately changed course and speed and our fast zig-zag quickly shook off the howitzers. By using one pre-planned position in which the gunnery

fire control computer (the Box) could be started, and then using spotting corrections to shift targets in lieu of designating new targets to the system, I both saved time and had freedom of manoeuvre. Course and speed were constrained whilst setting up the Box which took about one minute each time, while a spotting correction could be applied in five seconds with no restrictions on manoeuvring. This enabled us to fire seventy-eight rounds, in salvos of six, in very rapid succession, in fact firing so rapidly that the paint on the barrels blistered.

The enemy continued to take exception to our activity but before they could find our range we were racing away from Stanley, keeping up a spirited zig-zag. When about eleven miles from the airport, we launched another Seaslug. The arrival of the missile was announced by a brilliant flash as the fireball erupted across the airfield. Having liberally spread shrapnel about as tasked, we retired gracefully to our designated gun-line to await the arrival of *Ambuscade* who arrived at 0345 and prepared to bombard around Stanley airfield. Whilst she went inshore, we engaged the gun emplacements on Sapper Hill to distract the opposition. In the process the right hoist jammed, so we were only firing from the left gun, but at least we could fire. Such are advantages of twin barrels. We quickly managed to clear the jam but it was a waste of time; *Ambuscade* only managed to get one round away before her gun broke down.

The Mark 8 gun in the newer ships was not as reliable as the older Mark 6 version which we carried but our gun had a further advantage when it came to bombardment. Whereas the Mark 8 would place shells in a very tight pattern, the Mark 6 tended to spread them about. When firing five or ten rounds, one wanted to blanket an area rather than land shells in the same place. The one big advantage of the Mark 8 was its greater effective range, some 3,000 yards more.

We reverted to enhanced defence stations as we waited on the gun-line. It gave people some chance to stand down as the night passed away. *Ambuscade* eventually laid down another eighty rounds on the airport to re-affirm the notion in Argentinian minds that Stanley Airport remained too dangerous to use. With no further calls for fire, we withdrew at 0730. The spotter had asked if we could remain until sunrise for more firings but we politely informed him that this was not possible because we left a large gap in the carrier screen which had to be filled by dawn.

Top: HMS *Glamorgan* off Portland in 1981. (MoD) *Above:* The launch of Seaslug, *Glamorgan*'s principal long-range anti-aircraft weapon. (MoD)

Canberra conducting a helicopter stores transfer with *Resource*. (Author's collection)

Typical conditions in the South Atlantic. The 4.5in turret has its barrels turned aft away from the weather; the Exocet launchers are in the foreground. (Author's collection)

Top: Bombarding Pebble Island airstrip with 4.5in shells. (Author's collection) *Above:* The 29-knot dash back from Pebble Island. The 20mm Oerlikon and 3in chaff delta launcher can be seen beneath the 'Scott' aerial. (Author's collection)

Top: Embarking ammunition, 4.5in cartridge, from *Resource* by heavy jackstay. (Author's collection)
Above: The scene at dawn as damage control teams complete the clearing up of the debris in the hangar after the Exocet attack on 12 June. (Author's collection)

Top: The devastated hangar area viewed from *Stena Seaspread* when she came alongside on 13 June. (Imperial War Museum) *Above:* At sunset we buried our dead, (Author's collection)

Opposite page, top: Fighting the elements. *Glamorgan* proceeding at slow speed into a Force 11 gale. (Author's collection) *Opposite page, bottom:* Our Wessex V 'XR', damaged by the storm. (Author's collection)
Above: The modified trailer used to launch the Exocet which hit *Glamorgan*. (Imperial War Museum) *Right:* The author in front of the turret in San Carlos after the ceasefire. The Exocet launchers are clearly visible above the turret. (Author's collection)

Top: A peaceful evening in San Carlos Water. (Author's collection) *Above:* The Falkland Islands memorial chapel at Pangbourne. (Author's collection)

John Smith described his land-based view: 'A very noisy night indeed. Naval bombardment ... continued without let-up for five hours. They seemed to be aiming at saturating the area between Moody Brook and the Airport. The occasional few shells passed over the house.' Whilst we had been keeping the enemy occupied, *Argonaut*, with only one operational boiler, cleared San Carlos and rejoined the battle group.

Meanwhile, the Argentinians had been improvising again, rolling bombs out of the back of a Hercules, transforming the long-range transport into a long-range bomber, and they bombed *British Wye*, but missed. The Hercules, with a range of 1,800 miles, suddenly put the auxiliaries in a dangerous position. Someone would now have to look after the undefended STUFT (ship taken up from trade).

We rejoined the the battle group at dawn, having breakfasted and completed our personal domestic routines. In a near gale, conditions looked unpleasant for a replenishment due that afternoon. *Olna* was yawing heavily, making it very difficult to hold distance and position though our crew, despite their fatigue, were becoming ever more proficient at replenishment in poor conditions. Upper deck drill was down to a slick art and made it look easy to the casual observer. In the machinery control room, rapid and accurate responses were made to changes in ordered revolutions. On the bridge, the helmsman maintained an accurate course. I ignored relative aspect, relying upon true bearings, monitoring the gap between the sterns when altering course, and closely watching the waves. We slowly climbed up them before racing down the other side with the two ships rarely in sync. Teamwork was everything and whilst replenishment was in progress, the warfare teams remained alert for the enemy.

On completion of fuelling, we were ordered to remain with the carrier battle group until 1730 before proceeding to the tug and repair area (TARA) to provide support and conduct some long-overdue maintenance on both machinery and men. The crew were, in a word, exhausted after a full month of high intensity activity by day and night. Most of our machinery was working but a number of significant defects needed urgent attention.

At 1730 we detached for the TARA. Five minutes later the dreaded cry 'Handbrake' came over the intercom. The ship went to action stations and we immediately reversed course to regain our original station on Circle 5. Chaff charlie and chaff delta were fired and chaos ensued as we hosepiped shells all over the Southern Ocean. The Argentinians had one last remaining air-launched Exocet carried by a Super Etendard which on this occasion was escorted by four Skyhawks. The approach was made from the east after flying around the theatre of operations to achieve surprise. They found an echo at pop-up in the expected spot and the pilot fired with the escorting fighters carrying on in just behind the missile. Two fighters were shot down.

From our perspective, we believed at the time that there were certainly two attacking aircraft and it was certain that one, and probably two, Exocet missiles had been fired, but, in fact, there was only ever one. A Lynx reported a smoke trail coming in our direction and we increased speed and pointed the threat. I sighted the smoke trail fine on the starboard bow and immediately turned the ship to point the smoke, informing the ops room of this sighting and that I had turned towards this threat. By estimating the missile's inclination and range, I determined that on its current course it would pass about half a mile away, but this was still in view of the missile's seeker head. If it detected us, it would turn towards us and probably hit. Racing up wind we were once again the expendable escort protecting the high value units.

As our speed increased our bows slammed into a milestone, shipping it green over the bridge. 'Where is it? Where is it?' screamed Greg Gilchrist the Principal Warfare Officer. 'I cannot see for the moment, the bridge is obscured by a goffer!' I replied. The view from the bridge windows was dark green! The green changed to white as the bridge window wipers strove to clear the water. Once the glass was clear I put my binoculars onto the threat bearing and trained slowly right. I saw nothing. If the missile was no longer in sight, fine on the bow, it meant that it was not coming for us and *Glamorgan*'s luck was holding. Greg Gilchrist was more pessimistic, piping 'Brace! Brace! Brace!' Throughout the ship, fully aware that we were under Exocet attack, people threw themselves to the deck, probably hoping that the missile would neither find them nor the Seaslug main missile magazine.

Even on the bridge people threw themselves to the deck. I immediately ordered them back to their feet and 'eyes outboard'. If the missile was still coming, the sooner we saw it the better. On the lower bridge Petty Officer Alan Carlisle threw himself onto the deck, closely followed by Martin Culverwell, the padre, who landed on top of Alan. Martin remarked, 'Alan, you will not get any nearer to God than you are now!' They both laughed and it helped ease the tension of the moment.

There are places to throw yourself on the deck, and places to avoid. In the transmitting station, one of the places to avoid is the gun foot push trigger. Unfortunately, one member of the transmitting station crew threw himself on the trigger and the firing pulse went to the gun which fired. At this stage I was not concerned since one of our standard drills was to hosepipe shells down the bearing. This was probably more for morale rather than any expectation that a shell splash would down the incoming missile.

In the turret, when the firing pulse came through, Petty Officer Allen, the captain of the gunhouse, ordered another shell in the breech. He knew the hosepipe drill; if a missile was coming our way, a new shell would replace the one just fired as soon as the gun had recovered from its recoil. The turret, still in local control and not auto, wandered to starboard as more shells were fired. We began firing towards the main body. Seeing the danger I pressed the check fire bell, piping, 'check, check, check!' In the transmitting station, the individual lying on the trigger did not realise that he was firing the gun while in the gunhouse, the continued firing pulse was reason enough to reload. High explosive shells continued to hosepipe to starboard, two falling short of an LSL (landing ship logistic). These shell splashes were reported by the gun direction platform as 'missile splashed' and this, and my continued exhortations to check fire, eventually had the desired effect and our smoking guns fell silent.

Petty Officer Keith Balston recorded,

Exocet heading for the ship, 'Brace, Brace, Brace'. Oh my God! We are done for. We are all lying spread-eagled on the deck waiting for the worst. Several minutes pass. Apparently chaff saved us, quick reaction from the ops room and by the bridge putting the missile on ship's head. The missile splashed into the sea. We are lucky once again.

Mechanician Roger Tipton similarly wrote,

Brace, Brace, Brace called!! ... .Thirty seconds had elapsed until the ship was released – it seemed like thirty years! I had not reached my action station and was caught amidships on the starboard side. My over-riding thought was that I was just about where the missile that had hit the *Sheffield* came through the starboard side. The call 'Brace, Brace, Brace' is only made when the ship is seconds away from being hit. It is supposed to give you a chance to get on the deck and hang onto something. The snag is, if one is below, one does not know what it is that is coming or where it is aimed. In this case we knew it was an Exocet, which made it worse for me as they go for the largest radar reflection, i.e. the middle of the ship!

Petty Officer Wiltshire summed up the action in his usual colourful style,

We came so close, it was ... frightening. These close shaves are making me feel very old! ... fell out from action stations. I zoom off to the mess, grab a tot glass and pour myself three stiff whiskies. 'Ah, that is much better, good old Grouse!' Everyone around me sighs with big relief.

There were other amusing incidents that occurred as a result of Greg Gilchrist's broadcast to brace. Shortly before the attack, Chief Petty Officer 'Hissing' Sid Scott was on his rounds checking the air conditioning plants and was out of earshot of the tannoy when 'Brace' was piped. He came nonchalantly round the corner into the junior ratings' dining hall to see all the section base crew braced in a big heap on the deck. His look of horror was only fleetingly caught as he managed to get to the bottom of the pile in one move.

Trying to establish what had actually happened in this spirited and confused action would take time. *Ambuscade* was justifiably credited for obtaining the initial detection of the Handbrake racket and the chaff countermeasures worked very well. It was a failure for Argentina who expended their last air-launched Exocet and a success for the carrier battle group who downed two Skyhawks. One Skyhawk had attempted to bomb *Avenger.* The bomb missed, hit the sea, and the splash brought down the releasing Skyhawk.

The whole incident from start to finish lasted five minutes. With the raid over, we once again detached for the relative safety of the tug and repair area. Our first task, replenishing stores from *Fort Austin,* took three hours. Five words - hail, gale, cold, dark and rough - summed up a foul replenishment.

Monday, 31 May
At 0100, I finally made my way below for some hot soup and a long overdue hot shower. My hands had become so cold that they had

stiffened up, making it difficult to write up the bridge narrative after breaking away. I pitied the upper deck crews who lacked the relative shelter of the bridge wing. They must have been frozen through.

Whilst gunnery and operations crews frequently receive the attention in a war situation, mention must be made of the unsung heroes. A warship has three priorities – to float, to move and to fight. The guns and operations teams execute the third of the three priorities, but it is the maintainers who keep the ship afloat and moving. The expensive noises we heard from the 1006 aerial was teeth being stripped off a cog wheel in the training motor. Engine Room Artificer Ralph Pratt manufactured a drive cog complete with teeth to get the radar back in operation. His technical skill with the limited onboard facilities merit particular mention. Nor must one overlook the supply department who were providing four square meals a day (even if the quantity was rationed) and spares for our equipment. Junior Stores Assistant Hodges was a member of this department – too young to vote but old enough to fight for his country.

Chapter 11

TRALA Manager

We hoped whilst in the Tug and Repair Area (TARA), that both ship and men would have a chance to recover. Whilst some watchkeeping posts were demanding, others only required people to remain awake and ready for an emergency. Petty Officer Dunn recalled how the many quieter hours on defence watches had been passed with Rubik's cube, *The Times* crossword, old copies of the *Portsmouth News* or playing cards. Some people passed the time making ashtrays from 4.5in cartridge cases. He also remembered when the NAAFI ran out of Mars Bars, the galley ran out of eggs and *Glamorgan* was seemingly the only ship without Task Force beer!

A major reason for our withdrawal to the TARA was the fact that we had nearly exhausted the southern hemisphere's stocks of shell and cartridge for the Mark 6 gun. Since the start of the operation we had fired 1,301 rounds. We had about 500 rounds left, 200 on the left gun and 300 on the right gun before barrel life reached zero. We actually had 800 rounds embarked so for a change it was barrels rather than magazine capacity which was the limiting factor. By withdrawing us for a few days, remaining stocks of ammunition were conserved so that we could support the final assault. There were larger stocks of Mark 8 ammunition. Expenditure had been limited by casualties and breakdowns.

The day passed without incident and, as we were not facing immediate danger for a while, faces were less strained and conversations less serious. We shut down one boiler for long overdue maintenance work in the steam turbine room and elsewhere. The port shaft was locked for bearing repairs and we were given forty-eight hours to complete our maintenance.

The TARA had now become the Tug, Repair and Logistic Area (TRALA). Changes in acronyms caused confusion as their definitions were sometimes slow to be fully disseminated. We drifted about, virtually hove to fifty miles from the western edge of TRALA central but whilst we were conducting our maintenance, the war continued. Black Buck made another attack whilst *Alacrity* and

Avenger kept pressure up with further bombardments on the airfield, radar sites and installations. They also softened up troop concentrations to make life easier for the Royal Marines and Army. We appreciated the risks faced by the gunships but were confident that *Alacrity*, one of the Three Musketeers and an old hand at the game of bombardment, would steer clear of trouble. They also had the advantage of being a smaller target than ourselves. Away from the action, we had to rely upon sitrep signals to keep us updated on progress ashore. From this source we learnt that a big push was planned on Mount Kent.

Tuesday, 1 June
Maintenance continued throughout the night and the new port shaft bearing required further investigation as excessive vibration was still transmitting along the shaft. The port boiler was back on line with all leaks repaired, but now the starboard boiler was shut down and was being allowed to cool in readiness for maintenance. Radar transmitters were being maintained and turret defects were being repaired. The South Atlantic climate was kind to neither man nor machinery but we were all determined to get the better of it.

In the amphibious operating area, activity remained relatively light. The land forces had advanced to within twelve miles of Stanley after fierce fighting on Mount Kent; *Cardiff*, *Ambuscade* and *Alacrity* had deployed close inshore to support the advance; Harrier strikes took place, and landing facilities for Harriers at Goose Green and San Carlos were nearly complete. The Harriers' Commanding Officer (CO), Sharkey Ward, achieved a notable success in splashing a Hercules, returning with barely a drop of fuel remaining. This attack contributed to his well deserved Distinguished Service Cross. Another Harrier splashed a Skyhawk. On the minus side, one Harrier experienced mechanical problems and ditched though the pilot ejected safely. We never knew how many Argentine aircraft were forced to ditch between the Falklands and the mainland where the pilots' chances of being rescued were very slim. The numbers on my tote of Argentine losses were steadily increasing and I had frequent visitors to the chart-house to study my record and see how the war was progressing. Further troops and supplies had been landed at San Carlos while at sea, the Argentine *Bahia Paraiso* was boarded by a Lynx to check its status as a hospital ship before it was allowed to enter Port Stanley; it then proceeded to the Red Cross Box to collect wounded prisoners of war. Although we were in an area of relatively low threat and all seemed to be going well I experienced, for some reason that I could not fathom, a period of high tension. Perhaps it was a reaction to not being under immediate threat; I was not used to such peace! There were now optimistic pointers as to the outcome of the war. The Argentinian air raids had noticeably diminished and the enemy were now using their Canberras at night. These veteran aircraft would be vulnerable and I expected their losses to mount. Having suffered huge losses in aircraft and pilots, their morale must have been under considerable strain and provided we maintained our resolve I was convinced the enemy would fold. More difficult to gauge was the strength of feeling in the UK. The public were enjoying the summer and were right behind us but once it was all over, it would take a month to get home and things might well have moved on. Would they welcome us? Some people thought that this war had instilled a new sense of purpose and pride in the country. I hoped so because out here it was rough and cold and life was very cheap and basic, with all the little comforts of shipboard life gone. We had taken five days of our thirty days leave allowance since the previous October and we were beginning to tire of our surroundings.

Our families were experiencing an equally stressful time. What upset me was the prospect of not getting back home before my eldest daughter, Katherine, started school. She was missing my influence at one of the most formative periods in her life. I also worried about my younger daughter, Sarah. Would she even remember me when I returned? I expected that, for a while at least, I would seem to her like a total stranger. There must have been many families experiencing similar worries.

I returned to the war and read the intelligence signals. There was an assessment that within the next week the Argentine fleet would come out to fight. One scenario was for a decoy group to the north to draw off the surface action groups whilst the *Bouchard* group came in from the south, in a similar manner to the *Belgrano* and *Veinticinco De Mayo* ploy. I did not fancy their chances but we had to maintain our surface search as the time and place of any attack remained of their choosing; we had to be ready to counter them.

Wednesday, 2 June

We were making good progress on our maintenance. The turret and hoist hydraulic leaks were repaired but the breech was badly corroded in places due to ingress of salt water. The vibration on the port shaft was traced to a cracked bearing housing support, attributed to the bombing on 1 May. Work on the starboard boiler was nearly complete so mechanically we were in much better shape.

The crew had also recovered a bit from battle stress and fatigue but it was not all rest for the operational teams. We still had plenty of work to do and the South Atlantic was no less forgiving, especially for replenishment. *Tidespring* was our tanker and she was nearly empty and being light was very unsteady in the heavy seas. We tried probe but the conditions were terrible and the probe disconnected three times as the two ships rolled in opposite directions. On one occasion, as the Petty Officer in charge at the fuelling point was heaving in on the preventer to re-mate the probe, the rig took charge. As the preventer suddenly became bar taut, he was thrown against the guard-rails and was very lucky not to have been thrown over the side. We persevered, completed our replenishment, and then settled back down to our maintenance.

By mid afternoon, the port shaft defects were completed and the 992 was back on line. More work was still required on the 1006 and the turret which could only be completed when we received the necessary spare parts. We ascertained that *Stena Seaspread* held some gauges that we needed and we awaited their delivery. Some spares, however, we could make ourselves, improvisation being the key. The engineers made a new phosphor bronze pin to replace the seized part in the breech mechanism which rectified the turret. Willie conducted a successful ground run, checking out repairs but as fast as a couple of defects were repaired, another cropped up somewhere else. However, we were fixing defects faster than they occurred and the pressure was coming off the maintainers.

Meanwhile, *Avenger* deployed inshore overnight to Pebble Island where a number of Pucara and other aircraft were reported. The enemy had obviously not learned the lesson from our raid in mid May. *Exeter* bombarded the Stanley area and at Goose Green the Paras were using the Argentinians for battlefield clearance. After a large booby-trap explosion killed a number of Argentinians, an Argentine officer informed the Paras where other booby-traps were located. Napalm was also found at Goose Green.

The Gurkhas and Welsh Guards had landed near Fitzroy and were advancing towards Stanley. The Argentinians now only held a perimeter to about twelve miles from the town and the Royal Marines reported that the enemy had made rapid departures from many

...ositions on the high ground around Mount Kent. They seemed to show little liking for isolated positions and left a lot of their kit behind; this was a sure sign of an enemy beginning to lose the will to fight. However, we believed they would defend Stanley more robustly and certainly they had managed to pull off some unpleasant surprises every time we seemed to have the measure of them. By sunset, I was again feeling distinctly uneasy. Shortly afterwards the TRALA was ordered to remain east of 052 degrees west and the carrier battle group was also withdrawing further east. Something was afoot, but what?

We headed towards *Fort Grange* for an enormous solids replenishment, which we hoped would include toilet paper and chocolate. We went up alongside at 2100, expecting to complete well before midnight. It was bitterly cold with pouring rain.

Thursday, 3 June

Unfortunately, the replenishment did not go nearly as swiftly as we had hoped and my narrative entry for 0530 summed it up.

> I have just spent six and a half hours out of the last seven on the port bridge wing in the pouring rain doing a RAS(S) with *Fort Grange*. It was her first RAS since refit, and was painfully slow. It was not helped by a hydraulic pipe which burst. This resulted in us breaking away for thirty minutes whilst she got it fixed. Although we disconnected we maintained RAS station abeam at about 250 feet. In the six and a half hours alongside all we managed to get was seventy loads! – one every five minutes! At least we received both mail and nutty – as well as eggs and fruit. Life is looking up a bit.
>
> The air temperature was close to freezing. We were more or less heading right into the wind, force 5-6. It was cold, rough and miserable! I had to concentrate every second of the time to hold *Glamorgan* alongside. The Captain took the con from me for about thirty minutes so that I could thaw out – but the creeping cold really got to me.

Once we had cleared up from the RAS, our main task was to organise the logistic ships. We called forward those needed inshore and distributed mail and small items of stores. With no flying to do, the Flight Commander, Gerry Hunt, was given the task of manager and he did a wonderful job of getting all the Merchant Ships (STUFT, ship taken up from trade) in the right place at the right time.

I appreciated that we were in a privileged position with regard to information about the war; the poor merchant ships had only the BBC World Service to rely on and out here reception was poor. They were starved of information. As I was no longer under pressure, I produced a daily TRALA Manager's newsletter, and tried, using the helicopter for delivery service, to get a copy to each of these ships on a daily basis, informing them of progress. Producing about thirty copies to give one per ship was hard work as we did not have the resources to produce multiple copies but the effort was worth it for the newsletters were much appreciated; for some it was the first news they had received. I included the tote of enemy losses as well as snippets from the 'buzz log' of signals traffic.

As the day progressed, the wind died away and wonderful fog blanketed the TRALA. Without the 1006, it was difficult to close ships for mail transfers. We lost contacts in the ground wave at about two miles on the 992. From then on in we relied upon dead reckoning and simple mathematics. This was fine when ships were proceeding at the speed they claimed. However, we experienced a problem with *Europic Ferry* while she was replenishing from *Tidespring* and broke away just as we were approaching her disengaged side. One could never relax. We caught up with *Intrepid* and *Tidespring* conducting a RAS and Vertrep (vertical replenishment by helicopter) and on the way learned that the Admiral wished *Glamorgan* to share *Olmeda*'s two hundredth replenishment since the start of Operation Corporate. Mike Barrow asked me to work out how many times we had replenished during the operation, excluding dozens of Vertreps, I calculated we had conducted a total of forty-two with a variety of warships and auxiliaries.

The helicopter mail run with *Argonaut* and *Stena Seaspread* was not completed until 2030. We then made our way back to the TRALA manager's office, a quiet patch of ocean in the middle of the TRALA, some thirty-five miles to the east. News came in of activity ashore and of a Shrike missile attack by Black Buck against shore radars. After the attack we knew that at least one surveillance radar was still working but we hoped that Black Buck had succeeded in taking out another surveillance radar and some AAA sites.

With life relatively quiet, we speculated on our return date to UK. *Glasgow* was on her way home for repairs and *Argonaut* would be going when she was fit enough to proceed. We did not begrudge their departure. Both ships had fought bravely. *Fort Austin* was also due to return shortly to top up with more stores. As for our future, the best indications were that we would sail from the exclusion zone on about 10 July.

Friday, 4 June

Our fourth day in the TRALA and with the merchant ships in good order another quiet day dawned. The Admiral, delighted with our organisation, asked us to continue the good work and to help us deploy stores around the Fleet, we were loaned a pair of Wessex which made a great difference.

Ashore, the advance continued. *Intrepid* and *Sir Tristram* moved into Bluff Cove to unload; three Argentine patrols were captured; 5 Infantry Brigade pressed forward and 8 Commando Battery, Royal Artillery, were moving into position. An insertion at Fox Bay was carried out by 2 Para and the settlements at Bluff Cove and Fitzroy were liberated. The Argentinians were rapidly being boxed in around Stanley.

At sea, *Onyx* was conducting an SAS insertion on West Falkland. An anti-fast patrol boat site was established on Centre Island, controlling Choiseul Sound. *Monsunnen* was at Goose Green and was being used by the Army for transporting stores. Poor visibility limited air activity on both sides and we heard that a Vulcan with refuelling problems had been forced to land in Brazil, but it was released and allowed to return home.

We were in company with *British Trent* and *Tidepool* as the helicopter delivery service (HDS) started and *Olmeda* reported a minor fire on board which did not, luckily, affect her replenishment programme. The other significant news, regarding land based Exocet, caused concern. Evidence of how much we, in *Glamorgan*, knew is summed up from my narrative and that of Petty Officer Wiltshire. He wrote:

> We believe that the Argies have set up Exocet at Pembroke Point. This will not allow us to carry out NGS [naval gunfire support] in that area ... We must find out exactly what they have got and where, and then proceed to take it out. If they have Exocet ashore this is going to make NGS a very hazardous pastime.

My recollection is that the signal with this report, or a follow-on signal, instructed ships to mark an Exocet danger area from 020 degrees clockwise to 220 degrees out to twenty miles from Cape

Pembroke Point Light. This left two possible safe bombardment areas to the northwest of the 220 degree line, one just south of East Island and the other tucked in close to the kelp south of Port Harriet. To reach these areas it was necessary to either transit the danger area or to cross areas charted as kelp. Bearing in mind Commander-in-Chief Fleet's unacceptable reaction to our entering a poorly charted bay in Oman, crossing charted kelp (on an even older chart) was not an option, especially as the caution on the chart warned that kelp was, 'a sign of danger and should be avoided'. We had been warned earlier that it was possible the Argentinians had Exocet ashore on Pebble Island and by 4 June we all believed that the Exocet was located close to Pembroke Point. This was the first specific warning we received as to its location.

That evening one of our compass stabiliser systems became defective as we hurried off to rendezvous with *Brilliant*'s Lynx to transfer some ordnance. At 2330 the surface threat was raised as three unidentified surface contacts closed from the west but when we investigated we were relieved to discover *Stromness*, *Fort Toronto* and *Iris* rather than an Argentine surface action group.

Saturday, 5 June

We heard that the Argentine destroyer *Hercules* had been keeping so close to the coast to avoid the SSNs that she ran aground. In 1981, we had been her liaison ship whilst we both conducted sea trials and she had spent some considerable time in Portsmouth where the sailors had happily fraternised with the locals. Petty Officer 'Alfonso' became very friendly with a young lady in Gosport. Now, at the beginning of June, the telephone rang and 'Dad' answered. It was 'Alfonso' for his daughter. Minutes later, his daughter came back into the lounge in tears and informed 'Dad' that she would never see 'Alfonso' again as his ship was on a suicide mission; the *Hercules* had been tasked to attack the carrier battle group (CVBG) hoping to be taken for a British Type 42. 'Dad' immediately phoned Naval Intelligence, which upset his daughter further, and the CVBG was fully alerted for a possible incursion. It was just as well that she ran aground and perhaps the daughter did see 'Alfonso' again. The night passed quietly and the majority of the CVBG were withdrawn to the eastern boundary of the exclusion zone. Those ashore started to make reference to the 'South African Navy', which was not entirely fair since if we lost a carrier we genuinely risked losing the war.

Intrepid and *Sir Tristram* remained in Bluff Cove where the Welsh Guards were due to disembark. *Sir Tristram* stayed longer than intended, delayed by a slow passage and the tardiness of the troops in disembarking. She lacked the air cover afforded to the amphibious operating area (AOA). *Exeter* with a Type 21 frigate was due inshore for bombardment support and to provide air cover for *Intrepid*. *Exeter*'s Lynx was sent in first with an enhanced radar target, travelling at slow speed to simulate a ship in the hope of drawing the Exocet. Nothing happened so *Exeter* positioned herself off the runway to interdict any supply run and, on land, Rapier batteries were moved forward to provide air defence for the advance on Stanley. The Argentinians mounted an air raid on Mount Kent in the morning but their bombs were well off target. As a pilot, it must have been uncomfortable to go in low knowing that Rapier was around but not knowing exactly where.

By mid afternoon, with stores stacked everywhere on the upper deck, *Glamorgan* looked more like an auxiliary than a warship. We were in company with *Canberra*, *Norland* and *Stromness* with about fifteen other merchant ships in the vicinity. The two borrowed Wessex helicopters were doing sterling work transferring stores as we organised the merchant ships for re-supply inshore. *Norland* was due inshore that night to embark more POWs, which would bring her total up to 1,300. She was then expected to be detached to Argentina or Uruguay to offload them. They might be home before us.

Alacrity, offered the opportunity, declined the idea that she return to the UK for, though we were all keen to go home, none of us wanted to do so until we had finished the job. *Arrow* was also determined to stay despite the split in her superstructure, caused by the ravages of the South Atlantic.

We eventually completed our transfers and closed the CVBG to disembark ordnance to *Fort Austin*. Mike Barrow took the opportunity to discuss TRALA management with the Admiral's staff who decided to keep us as TRALA manager for the next few days. No one minded.

Diving pay was becoming an issue of concern for Task Force divers. To qualify for this special service pay, divers had to spend a minimum of 120 minutes under water each quarter. Having been under way ever since Ascension and with the diving quarter due to end on 14 June, our diving team had yet to achieve this minimum requirement. Other Task Force divers were in a similar position and they were about to be financially penalised for going to war. My submission to waive the minimum diving requirement for this quarter was sensibly accepted.

Sunday, 6 June

We returned to the TRALA and fuelled from *Tidespring*, heading off for a transfer with *Europic Ferry* before returning to the TRALA manager's office. With a lower threat, we broke down into a four-watch routine allowing people more time off watch and permitting upper deck work to be progressed. On balance, we felt it worth taking the risk even though the 992 was still giving us problems with a faulty replacement part. We were therefore without both the 1006 and 992 and could do nothing about it until receipt of further spares.

Replacement Harriers had arrived from Ascension. Ashore, *Intrepid* managed to land only half her troops and equipment and the planned advance was delayed. However, pressure was maintained by *Cardiff*, *Yarmouth* and *Exeter* conducting heavy bombardments, while the Gurkhas and the first half of the Welsh Guards were landing with the rest of the latter due to land on 7 June. Probing had taken place and the noose was tightening. Every time we probed an Argentine position, they fell back.

Monday, 7 June

Argonaut and *Alacrity* were sent home whilst *Stena Seaspread* repaired *Arrow*. *Fort Austin* was due to return home shortly and we transferred the TRALA's outgoing mail to her. Without the support helicopters lost in *Atlantic Conveyor*, the main problem ashore was getting 5 Brigade and ammunition forward into battle. The Scots Guards landed to join 2 Para near Bluff Cove and it was hoped the Welsh Guards would land overnight from *Fearless*; the Gurkhas would follow after clearing North Lafonia of the enemy. The first LSL (landing ship logistic) was to enter Bluff Cove that night in support of the advance on Stanley. On the air side, the Harrier forward operating base at San Carlos was fully operational, improving our command of the air though shortage of Avcat remained a problem and, the day before, *Cardiff*'s Sea Dart had scored a blue on blue on an Army helicopter. At 1234 two Canberras closed San Carlos and one was downed by *Exeter*'s Sea Dart.

In the TRALA, whilst *Tidepool* was replenishing one of the merchant ships she suffered engine failure and before emergency breakaway could be completed, her rig was carried away. *British Trent* also damaged her astern rig whilst replenishing *Fort Austin* before the latter departed for the UK. These two incidents served to remind everyone of the hazardous nature of replenishing in the hostile environment of the South Atlantic.

Tuesday, 8 June

The 'Burglar' overflew *Argonaut* 400 miles to the north of us and was lucky it was *Argonaut* and not *Glamorgan* with our Seaslug; it was also lucky not to encounter the second pair of Harriers coming down from Ascension.

Inshore, bombardments continued whilst support ships came and went from San Carlos. The trawlers *Cordelia* and *Northella*, converted to minesweepers, arrived with their depot ship *Pict* to clear the minefields. The other maritime activity involved *Invincible* and *Brilliant* on Operation Canbelow, the forward combat air patrol tasked to interdict Argentine re-supply which was, in fact, the cover story for a secret SAS insertion into Argentina. *Cardiff* and *Yarmouth* were tasked against Mount Harriet, with *Arrow* bombarding the airport. *Onyx* remained on patrol in the vicinity of the Jasons.

Back in the TRALA we spent most of the day conducting transfers with only two incidents of note. The first was the detection of the two Harriers from Ascension. The second was a Flash signal from *Uganda*. An English voice was calling any British warship, with a request to call Port Stanley. Was the enemy beginning to crack?

At 1730 we heard that *Plymouth* had been bombed during a big raid. Half an hour later, without further news of *Plymouth*, we gleaned two Skyhawks were splashed. Although miles away from the current action, every time a ship was hit, tension grew and we felt for the victims. At 2200 we learned *Plymouth* had suffered splinter damage and minor fires. She had shot down one Skyhawk and damaged another. A second raid by four Mirages followed and all were splashed. We also heard Skyhawks had hit one LSL and one landing craft (utility) (LCU). The trouble with receiving snippets of information was that the full horror of the raids was yet to be appreciated. Mike Barrow, looking serious, remarked, 'We are not having a good day!' I updated the tote in the charthouse; Argentine air losses had reached 100.

The BBC World Service reported that a tanker, co-incidentally called *Hercules*, had been bombed and strafed 400 miles north of the

Falklands by an Argentine Hercules aircraft. The enemy hoped to hit a fuelling tanker used by our ships en route to and from Ascension. Unfortunately, *Hercules* was Liberian registered on US charter with an Italian crew and had no connection with the war. She was left listing and limping towards Brazil and *Hecla* was detached to assist. When full details became known, we learned that *Hercules*, after being bombed, had turned round and headed for Brazil. Three hours later she was called by an Argentine station using her own call-sign and told that if she did not steer for Argentina she would be attacked again. *Hercules* kept on towards Brazil and fifteen minutes later came under rocket attack from a Hercules. The first attack could have been put down to a case of mistaken identity, but there was no excuse for the second and the raid caused us to resume defence watches. It transpired that Argentina had unsuccessfully attempted a similar attack on a supply STUFT a week previously and had we known this, we would never have reverted to four watches!

* * *

One letter from *Glamorgan* was inadvertently published so it was time for some official news and Mike Barrow signalled 'GLAM-NEWS 8 June'. Judy Barrow put on a header '... from your favourite ship' and reproduced the signal for the wives and families. It read,

> Recently we have seen less action but have been able to catch up with maintenance, storing and sleep. We are now well fed and rested and shortages (including chocolate) have almost been solved. Weather is reasonable but getting colder.
>
> We are now protecting and assisting the many merchant and support ships on which the operation is so dependent. The ability of our troops in the Falklands to live and fight depends upon the weather, and on the availability of food, stores and ammunition. Our friends in the Welsh Guards are now ashore. We are doing all we can to smooth the soldiers' forward movement and counting our blessings. We are well insulated compared with the troops in their tents and trenches ....
>
> We were dismayed by erroneous press reports forecasting our early return due to damage from an unexploded bomb but glad to hear that they were immediately countered by the information centres. There is no definite news on our return date. It will depend upon progress

ashore and political decisions. Lieutenant Commander Engeham's inadvertently published letter gave a slightly embroidered view of our life. We are glad to say that the supply of fresh air has improved since he wrote his letter. We continue to receive messages of goodwill from the Governor of the Falklands, the Lord Mayor of Cardiff and Warrington supporters. This encouragement is most heartening and we hope you are getting all the help you need.

With mail delays, information for the families was a godsend; it gave them something to discuss and compare with other information gleaned.

Wednesday, 9 June

Before dawn we completed a transfer with *Regent* before detaching her to South Georgia. The latest signals were depressing. Yesterday, San Carlos came under heavy air attack and *Plymouth* was more seriously damaged than at first thought. She had received bomb damage to her gun, Mortar Mark 10 and associated magazine; another bomb had passed through her funnel and she was strafed. Both *Sir Tristram* and *Sir Galahad* were badly damaged in Bluff Cove and *Sir Galahad* was still burning and abandoned while *Sir Tristram* had an unexploded bomb on board. Although both LSLs had been largely de-stored, the Welsh Guards were still embarked when attacked and forty-five were killed, with many more badly burned, in *Sir Galahad*. Six Mirage and one Skyhawk were confirmed downed, with another four possibles.

After a number of transfers, we rendezvoused with a Hercules to receive an air-drop of eleven loads. With the nearest friendly airfield in Ascension, ships had two options to obtain essential spare parts, either by sea or by air drop. As the former would take weeks, stores were parachuted into the South Atlantic in large buoyant boxes. This took place in the rear areas. Until then we had been very much 'up threat' so this was our first chance to undertake the recovery of air-dropped stores. There was a strong wind with heavy seas and during the attempted recovery we realised that we had much to learn. It proved easier for me to place a 6,000-ton destroyer alongside a load than for a leading seaman to put a whaler alongside; it was too expensive for the Royal Navy to teach sailors the finer points of boatwork, and collecting large cardboard boxes attached to parachutes in the South Atlantic presented us with a real problem.

The recovery started slowly with the whaler wrapping the first parachute around its screw. The Gemini inflatable detached the parachute and attached some loads to *Brilliant*'s Lynx while the whaler, now underway again, assisted the swimmer to attach loads to our general-purpose davit after I had brought the ship alongside the load in the water. Together, it took just over three hours to recover all eleven loads. This was long enough but compared to *Andromeda*'s efforts, which went on for eighteen hours, we did quite well. With the upper deck littered with soggy cardboard boxes, we met up with *Andromeda* to distribute the stores. We also hoped to collect mail that afternoon but *St Edmund*, the postman, proceeded to South Georgia first and would not arrive until 15 June.

Ashore, the Gurkhas were advancing. Other units of 5 Brigade had captured Fitzroy and logistic support was well established for the final push on Stanley. The end was in sight.

Thursday, 10 June

After the air drop we returned to the manager's office to await daylight before the next round of transfers. After breakfast I updated my narrative, caught up on signals and collated the previous day's records. My narrative read, 'The Captain has aged terribly. He puts on a brave face. It is wonderful the way he keeps our spirits up but I can see the strain of it all on his face as he takes the responsibility for all of us.'

It was demoralising to hear that Argentina had possibly acquired twenty-four Mirage and twelve Skyhawk from Peru and Israel in addition to some Exocet missiles from Libya. If the Argentinians managed to re-arm, we could expect further ship losses. As for Pucara, there were none outside Argentina and a photo-reconnaissance of Stanley Airport revealed fourteen Pucara parked in the airport of which six were visibly damaged.

By midday, after further transfers, we proceeded for the next air drop which would contain fifteen loads plus two men, the relief CO for 2 Para and an SAS replacement. The boxes came first, then the live drop. The men were only in the water for two and a half minutes, the gemini recovering one and Willie the other. Flying operations for this recovery meant we steamed away from the containers. On completion of flying, we had to reverse course to look for the whaler and the soggy boxes.

With the air-dropped stores safely recovered, we closed *Tidepool* for RAS. She was completing a pump-over with *British Trent* and we anticipated a late night. Our quiet life came to an end when ordered to 'polish our guns' and be prepared for 300 rounds of bombardment on the nights of 11/12 June and 12/13 June. Having been stood down for a relatively extended period, we needed to check ourselves out once more. Just in case the enemy resorted to the use of gas, we programmed a citadel test in the morning.

At home, Bruce Neill forwarded Judy Barrow's newsletter to *Glamorgan* wives and families.

Greetings. It is now nine weeks and more since the Falkland Islands crisis began and you learned (or guessed) that the ship would not be returning to UK as planned. In that time a lot has happened. You have survived the initial shock of being thrust into a long and indefinite separation. You have learned to live with all the uncertainty and anxiety of a real combat situation. You have become 'families at war'. However, much life may go on as normal for those around you. It is certainly not 'normal' for you.

During these past weeks I have had contact with many wives, parents, children, fiancees and girl-friends of men of the Task Force. Some of you I have been able to meet personally, to others I have spoken on the phone. Also I have heard about many others second hand. From all these contacts one dominant impression emerges – you are coping, and coping very well, with a very difficult situation. We all have bad days when everything seems black, and we wonder if we can manage to keep going. We then pick ourselves up and get on with whatever needs to be done, and hope returns.

I want especially to thank all those of you who have been actively involved in organising contact groups or fundraising projects, or who have in any way done your bit to try and make sure that no Task Force family is left out or feels forgotten. I hear reports from all over the country of people getting together and that is good.

Friday, 11 June
Having found *Tidepool*, we waited until 0600 before going alongside and the whole evolution took ninety minutes. The amount of fuel taken on board since 2 April amounted to 5,647 tons. This equated to £1,129,400 for fuel for one ship alone. War did not come cheap.

We bade farewell to the TRALA and headed towards the action. I was very conscious that in our absence from the gun-line things had changed and the most worrying aspect was the alleged existence of the shore-based Exocet. My narrative read, 'Tonight we are off to the gun-line south of Stanley. Back to our old hunting ground! The odds are also increased. All attempts to "draw" the Exocet from Pembroke Point using helos to simulate ships have failed. Is it there?' Whereas we left the gun-line two weeks earlier as old hands, we were now akin to 'new boys' and would have to make sure that our preparations were complete in every way.

We rejoined the carrier battle group, transferring the drop stores before proceeding inshore. During the afternoon a defect developed on one of our gas turbines which was given high priority and quickly fixed.

Chapter 12

Taking the Hit

At 1700, *Glamorgan* detached at 26 knots with *Yarmouth* in company, hard pressed to make the gun-line by midnight when 45 Commando wanted us on station. We had yet to receive the night's target list and could not complete our pre-preparation for those few extra yards of accuracy. We would have to tuck ourselves close in under East Island and even considered nosing our way in amongst the kelp off Port Fitzroy which would be extremely risky, especially at night.

Muzzle velocity (MV) was a further complication. Having fired so many rounds, our MV was now very low. Every shell fired caused a drop in MV of about 3ft per second making our current maximum effective range under 17,000 yards. We were very conscious of the enemy's presence, including the reported Exocet threat and the 6in guns on Sapper Hill which outranged our own. Even the Padre remarked on the distinct rise in tension.

Ashore, a major advance was planned that night and we anticipated stiff resistance from the Argentinians. If they failed to halt this advance, they would lose the war. A hotline had been established between Stanley and San Carlos providing a method to effect a ceasefire or surrender.

The Captain's Secretary, Lieutenant David Tinker, passed my cabin as we raced inshore and stopped to chat. We both felt that the odds had increased since we were last on the gun-line. In planning to go very close in, we hoped that no one was sitting ashore with a machine-gun or anything bigger. A heavy machine-gun could cause significant damage to a thin-skinned warship, as the Royal Marines had demonstrated to *Guerrico* in South Georgia. I told David our intentions and he departed to prepare for a night at action stations. That was the last time I saw David alive.

Action stations was piped at 2315 as we approached the gun-line five miles south of the Exocet danger arc marked on the chart, before turning north to dash through the danger zone. Offshore rocks and kelp forced us to transit the zone before reaching comparative safety from Exocet. Close inshore, we would be a sitting duck for shore batteries but that was deemed the lesser of two evils.

Saturday, 12 June

By midnight we had crossed the Exocet danger zone and were on the gun-line awaiting the first call for fire. We conducted tidal stream checks for the gunnery system 400 yards off East Island and estimated that the stream was running at a foot per second. Communications were established with the spotter who reported being on the move. Whilst we waited, I refined the tidal stream before holding the ship just short of the planned box start position which would allow a speedy response to a call for fire.

Yarmouth arrived on station, one mile to the south of us, at 0020, followed by *Avenger*, two miles to the east, half an hour later. At 0115 we received our first provisional target information. Our target was just 300 yards short of our worn guns' maximum effective range. This was why we had selected a position so close to the coast. We lay stationary just one mile southwest of East Island. There was little wind and just over a half moon, making it a very pleasant night for anything except war. I could see the land clearly and we felt vulnerable. Kelp was also clearly visible 150yds away and we had very little sea room to the northwest of us.

The peace of the night was interrupted at 0120 when *Yarmouth* engaged her first target with twenty salvos. She hit the jackpot on a couple of occasions. Four minutes later our bombardment net became live with target information. As I worked out the calculations, the officer of the watch headed for the box start position. 'Twenty salvos, fire for effect' was called. It was pleasing that 45 Commando had such confidence in the accuracy of our first salvo that they never bothered with ranging salvos. Twenty salvos headed towards Two Sisters ridge, suppressing the enemy. Two minutes later, the spotter called for an adjustment. This was computed for the guns by our spotting disc operators in the ops room and the night sky was shattered once again as ten salvos were fired for effect, allowing the Royal Marines to continue their advance. *Yarmouth* was also firing. Five minutes later a new target was indicated and twenty salvos were duly delivered. *Glamorgan* and 45 Commando were working efficiently as a team.

More calls for fire followed before it went quiet for a while, indicating that the Royal Marines and the Army were advancing without significant resistance. Surprisingly, the shore batteries left us alone; perhaps they experienced trouble finding us tucked in so close to the coast. At 0213 we successfully engaged an ammunition dump which exploded and reports from ashore stated that our rounds had been most effective. *Yarmouth* continued engaging, firing about 100 rounds at Mount Harriet where the troops met stiff opposition. We waited in silence.

At 0315 the Argentinians put on a spectacular display for observers offshore. They were hosepiping hundreds of salvos into the sky, possibly having a go at the ships but they were way off target, wasting tons of ammunition. Four long-range mortars were then reported captured by 45 Commando. A few minutes later, amid much activity, I saw smoke rising from a large fire on Mount Harriet. We reverted from spectator to player at 0400 when our next call for fire came through. Five minutes later we were alerted that four Canberras might attack at 0430. Combat air patrols were airborne to counter this threat.

At 0520, 45 Commando reported taking the western ridge of Two Sisters, their first objective. I started to worry. Our orders were to be back with the carriers by dawn. If 45 Commando were only on the western ridge, they would need us for some considerable time and the minutes were ticking away. However, they were on the move, occasionally calling for further support. At 0600, a gun or mortar position was causing trouble and we laid down forty salvos which had the desired effect. That night we had fired 145 rounds – nearly four tons of high explosive delivered with telling accuracy.

The updated position of the carriers was then received. They had moved another fifty miles further east, for us an extra two hours steaming. There was no chance at all of reaching them by dawn, even if we sped right across the Exocet danger zone and the minefield. I informed Mike Barrow of the problem and he appreciated the dilemma, electing to remain until our job was done. It was most important to ensure 45 Commando succeeded. If we left them in the lurch, they would receive unnecessary casualties and the Royal Navy was not in the habit of leaving the Army and Royal Marines without support. They had justifiably come to trust us. Meanwhile, I was left to ponder our options once released by 45 Commando. With two totally conflicting requirements, I decided to compromise between being very late at minimum risk and being not so late with increased risk. I would head south until hull down from

Cape Pembroke Point and then alter 30 degrees to port to n
good 50 per cent of our speed towards the carriers whilst reducing
our speed away from danger by only 13 per cent.

Two Sisters was taken by 45 Commando at 0615, who then thanked
us for our support, saying they could now manage on their own.
'VMT (very many thanks) and good shooting' was their parting
message. I immediately ordered the gas turbines to be flashed up,
applied full rudder and increased speed to maximum on steam. With
60 degrees still to turn I eased the rudder to accelerate out of the turn
to save a few seconds. I steadied on south as we raced into the charted
Exocet danger zone. It was planned that *Avenger* stay on the gun-line
until 0830 and then to lie up in Albermarle harbour whilst we
returned with *Yarmouth* to the battle group.

Ashore in Stanley, John Smith recorded,

Last night was the most incredible, frightening one yet. Hundreds
of shells were fired, which screamed and whistled over the town for
hours on end - it is non-stop! They are still going on strong now. A
steady naval bombardment has been going on for some hours. We
could tell it was the Navy by the regular rhythm of their firing.

If it was terrifying for John Smith, for those on the receiving end it
must have been indescribably horrific.

As we raced away from the gun-line I kept my eyes glued to the
bridge 992 display. I paid special attention to the direction of Cape
Pembroke where intelligence had indicated Exocet might be located.
When nearly eighteen miles from Cape Pembroke Point, although
still in the charted danger zone, I made my planned alteration to port
to start making ground towards the carriers whilst still retiring
speedily towards the edge of the danger zone. I reasoned that, first,
we were now hull down from the coastline south of Port Harriet. Our
radar horizon was eleven miles and we were losing Cape Pembroke on
radar, hence a radar on Cape Pembroke would be losing us. Secondly,
if we were to be targetted from Cape Pembroke, they would have
already fired. We had been exposed for six minutes and as every
second passed their chances against us diminished. Thirdly,
remaining on south would keep us in the danger zone for another
nine minutes; altering 30 degrees to port would increase this by just
six minutes. Fourthly, the alteration to port would reduce our late
arrival back with the carriers by about fifteen minutes. Finally,

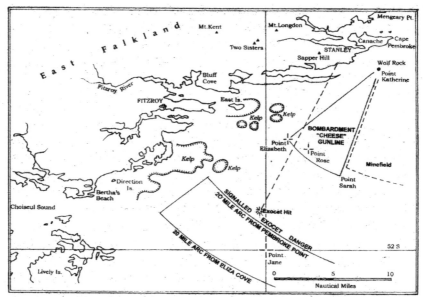

Taking the Hit

turning west once south of the kelp would only reduce our time in the danger zone by two minutes but would add fifteen minutes to the planned option.

Weighing up the pros and cons I calculated the risk was worth taking. There was one problem. All the mathematics used in the calculations were based upon Exocet being on Cape Pembroke whereas unknown to me, the Exocet launcher site was at Eliza Cove. So, an opportunity arose for Captain Perez when *Glamorgan* crossed the firing bearing fifteen miles down range. The charted Exocet danger zone was also flawed since it too was based upon Cape Pembroke Point. A twenty-mile circle based upon Eliza Cove extended it four miles further south. Thus, even if we had chosen the route of minimum charted risk, we would still have placed ourselves within range on the Exocet firing line from Eliza Cove.

Having altered to port, Mike Barrow instructed me not to come round any more as he had no desire to receive an Exocet. I told him that it was my intention to remain on the current course until clear of the danger area. He too was well aware that we were going to be significantly late back with the carriers who needed us back on screen as soon as possible. The stage was set for disaster.

The next event of significance came at 0630 when Commander Chris Gotto piped 'Fall out from action stations' and we reverted to defence watches, the second degree of readiness. As all the crew had been up for most of the night, I saw Chris's reasoning for standing people down as early as possible. Fatigue was another risk which had to be considered. Those falling out from action stations needed rest and food before closing up for another watch at 0800.

This change in state generated much activity. In the main steam turbine control room, Charge Chief Marine Engineering Artificer Michael Page had clutched in the gas turbines and the ship was steadily working up to 25 knots. Simultaneously he was de-isolating systems, returning them to a cruising state. In the operational spaces, noise levels increased as hand-overs started.

Petty Officer Alan (Clubs) Carlisle was Petty Officer of the Watch on Deck. He had been on the lower bridge and to him the night's battles had reminded him more of a fireworks display. On falling out from action stations, he relaxed and wished his little girl 'Happy Birthday' - she was twelve on 12 June 1982. He went below into 4 Mess where he met with Petty Officer 'Derby' Allen, the Captain of the Turret, who suggested going for breakfast in the galley. Fortunately, Alan's suggestion of taking a shower first prevailed and they remained forward. They were not the only ones who had considered visiting the galley. Sub-Lieutenant John Holden, the ship's Damage Control Officer, was in two minds as to whether to grab a cup of tea off the chefs in the galley or return to the wardroom for a soft drink before snatching half an hour of sleep. Fortunately for him, he elected for the latter and had just kicked off his boots in his cabin when he heard a thud.

I was conscious that we were not yet out of danger so I kept my eyes glued to the radar despite the large and spectacular fire-fight going on ashore. Mark Garratt, the second officer of the watch suddenly remarked, 'Wow! look at that ammunition dump going up!' as he spotted a bright illumination ashore. I moved my head from the 992 to have a look and my head was jerked back by the short lead headset that chained me to within a couple of feet of the display. I swore about still not having a long lead headset and put my head back into the hood of the bridge display. Had I seen the 'ammunition dump' going up, it might have alerted me to the fact that this was something else.

Unknown to me, there was a sudden lull in the fighting ashore as everyone's attention was caught by the very bright efflux coming from Eliza Cove. They followed it seawards until there was an equally dazzling flash in the distance followed by an ominous red glow. The flash was seen as far away as Darwin and Goose Green. Gradually, after a few minutes, the fighting ashore resumed. Whilst the Argentinians were elated by what they had seen, British troops wondered which ship had just drawn a very short straw. It was *Glamorgan*.

On board, Mark Garratt had not been the only crew member looking towards events at Eliza Cove. Leading Marine Engineering Mechanic Taff Callaghan, a member of the midships section base, had decided to get a breath of fresh air on the upper deck with Marine Engineering Mechanic 'Trevor' Brooking. They watched the tracer and fires burning ashore which were the result of the naval bombardments. It appeared to 'Trevor' that one of the fires was getting nearer. Taff told him that it was just his imagination and, having had their fresh air, the pair proceeded back down into the canteen flat. They had just passed through the flash doors outside the sickbay when they heard what they erroneously believed to be the 3in rockets being launched. Taff muttered, 'Why are we firing chaff?' The response was an almighty bang, and a shockwave visible in the cross passage.

Chief Petty Officers Geoff 'Pincher' Martin and Frank Pratt, with Leading Marine Engineering Mechanic Jan Peart, had also gone onto the flight deck for a breath of fresh air and a 'goof'. Whilst watching the land battle which was still in progress, Geoff noted that one light against the pitch black background seemed to stay in the air longer than the rest. The trio spoke about this particular light with such statements as, 'Bet it is a helo!' and 'It seems to be getting bigger!' They carried on the debate about the light for a few seconds before Geoff shouted, 'it is getting bigger, let's get the — out of here!!!' Frank led the race to the nearest door that would take the trio to relative safety within the ship's citadel. He was closely followed by Geoff and then Jan. They tore round the back of the hangar and up the starboard side, heading for the nearest door, some 15 metres from where they had originally been standing. Suddenly there was a cry from Jan. In the darkness he tripped over the Gemini dinghy. Frank and Geoff helped him to his feet and once again legged it towards shelter. Just as Frank reached the cross passage in front of the hangar, it lit up like a giant firework. Geoff was approximately two metres behind Frank, adjacent to the gas turbine engine air intake trunking. A massive fireball erupted out of the intake and Geoff instantly thought about the crew below, believing that they had probably just been wiped out. Survival instincts took over and after what seemed like a slow-motion dream sequence, all three made it to the door and relative shelter.

Seaman Barry Nixon had been exposed to the elements, high up atop the superstructure on the GDP as action lookout. He had an excellent view of proceedings. This was fine when ordnance was departing from *Glamorgan* but less appealing when we attracted the enemy's fire. He was one of the few to see the very close explosions of the incoming shells from the shore batteries. He was also one of the few to see the incoming missile explode.

With my head under the hood, I could see nothing other than the orange glow of the cathode ray tube. Just after 0636, on a bearing of 020 at just over eight miles, I noticed the faintest of small blips, about the size of echo given by an albatross. It was unusual, albeit not unknown, to detect birds at that range. Although it was not coming from Cape Pembroke, my heart jumped. At the next sweep of the radar it was gone and I breathed a sigh of relief but this was shattered one sweep later when, on the same bearing and closer in, a firm echo painted for the first time. In my heart of hearts I knew it was an Exocet. It could not have been a ship since we were steering away at high speed. No aircraft would fly over such a fire-fight ashore. It had to be a missile and I stared in disbelief. It was not what my tired mind wished to either see or register. I hoped that it would go away. It did not! At the next sweep, with the afterglow of the previous blip still painting, a second firm echo painted, closing on a steady bearing.

As my mind registered, 'Oh shit!', I called the ops room on command open line (COL, the intercom linking the ops room and outstations) and can very clearly remember the conversation that followed, 'Ops room, have you got that fast moving contact 020 at eight miles?' After a short pause, Greg Gilchrist the Principal Warfare Officer replied, 'It's a helicopter!' I replied, 'It is moving too bloody fast!' and he responded that it was an aircraft. I immediately ordered, 'Starboard 35!' The helmsman replied, 'Port 35', applying port rudder. I literally screamed, 'NO! STARBOARD 35!'

The Argentinians had set the missile with its seeker head radar on at launch. So why did the EW office not intercept this radar? The on watch anti-air warfare officer, Lieutenant Commander Hugh Edleston, later explained that our inclination at the time put the missile launch site in the 'reduced' segment for reception on the polar diagram, explaining why the EW office were unable to alert the ship.

I had thought about reminding the ops room to fire chaff. They were a very competent team who knew more about threat reactions than me but we had been targetted at a most inopportune moment having just fallen out from action stations and it took the ops room a few seconds to settle. The chaff delta launchers were in the process of being re-loaded, and were not available. Likewise, with the missile in to six miles, a little over thirty seconds from impact, we had no time to turn downwind at wind speed to hide in our chaff blooms. The turret was in its blind arcs for chaff charlie. Amid the turmoil of watch changes, and whilst reverting back to action stations, the ops room team were concentrating on indicating the target to the Seacat system. Each couple of sweeps I passed range and bearing of the incoming missile to the ops room and ominously, the bearing remained steady on 020 degrees as the orange blips on the radar 'kangaroo hopped' in towards the centre of the display. I also monitored the ship's head marker on each sweep in preparation for reversing the wheel to stop the turn at the critical moment. I concentrated very hard on the turn since I would need to reverse the wheel at precisely the right moment to steady on 190 degrees if we were to successfully bounce the missile off the ship's side; I had less than 5 degrees leeway for error. With full rudder at 25 knots, exactly how many degrees before 190 should I order 'Port 20'? Too soon and I would have to ease the rudder, thereby lengthening the time to turn and time was not on our side: too late and I risked the missile and its debris running the length of the Seaslug magazine. I was fully focused on applying reverse rudder at the precise moment and my mind failed to register that other lifesaving reactions had not taken place. No one had piped 'Brace, Brace, Brace!' Had I reminded the officer of the watch to make the pipe, more lives may have been saved, particularly in the galley. I was just concentrating too hard on the turn. Fatigue had slowed not only my brain but also that of others – no excuse, just the explanation of why we failed to get everything correct.

With the missile in to about two miles, I heard a scrabbling noise on COL as Mike Barrow donned his headset. He too had been in the process of handing over command to Chris Gotto. 'Where is it, Pilot, where is it?' he asked. I replied, 'I have lost it in the ground wave, last known bearing 025 at two miles!'

Leading Seaman Eon Matthews was on watch in the ops room as Force Air Picture Reporter. When stood down from action stations his job was to look at the long range air picture. However, as the ship was so close to land he was helping the Local Air Picture Reporter. He recalled, 'The bridge alerted everyone to a fast moving contact coming out from shore and then everything kicked in as years of training paid dividends'. The Air Picture Supervisor saw the contact and designated it to the ADAWS computer system. It was quickly appreciated that it was neither a helicopter nor a 155mm howitzer shell and assessed as Exocet. Both port and starboard Seacat systems locked onto the target and the contact was passed to the Missile Gun Director (Blind) to 'take'. He allocated it to port Seacat and got a missile away. Barry Nixon had heard the incoming threat allocated to the port Seacat and was half way up the ladder to the GDP when the Seacat was fired. He saw the missile heading out into the darkness. Unfortunately, the Seacat's dead range had not wound off before the missiles passed each other. The Exocet missile came on in and seconds later hit us before we had completed our evasive manoeuvre. The ops room crew felt the impact and were relieved that their compartment had not been hit. Barry Nixon on the GDP felt the hot blast of the explosion as it hit him full in the face.

On the bridge we heard a seemingly unremarkable thud, followed almost immediately by a 'whooomph' as the fuelled helicopter in the hangar erupted into flame. At about the same moment, the action alarm was sounded. To those closer to the explosion, it sounded equally as loud as a stun grenade and had a similar effect. People in the 'Rhondda Valley' (the main passageway running the length of the ship) some 150ft away from the explosion were blown off their feet. I did not see the flash, having my head buried in the display hood. I looked up as the bridge echoed to alarm bells. Night turned into day as 100ft flames towered above masthead height.

Remembering *Bismarck*, crippled with her rudder jammed, I yelled 'Midships, Revolutions 100!' I wanted to get as much rudder off as possible as the steering motors ran down, and reduce speed to 12 knots to minimise the stresses from the sea on the damaged section and to give the machinery spaces a chance to sort themselves out. 'There it is, about the hangar!' I responded to the Captain on COL, followed by 'Navigator off!' as I removed my constraining headset. I proceeded to the port side of the bridge, selected the starboard steering system and reset the compasses. I then pushed the alarm reset buttons. To my great relief all alarms fell silent. We had the ship under control. Although all the port systems were down, the starboard systems remained operational, reflecting good ship design. I ordered the helmsman to steady on 200 degrees.

When the missile had hit, the ship's head was passing 185 degrees, still under full rudder. Our precise position was 51°56.65S 058°00.8W. The turn caused the ship to heel by 14 degrees, lowering the ship's side just sufficiently for the missile to clip the spermwater, a 2in barrier at the deck edge which diverted water to the scuppers before it went over the side.

Perhaps the most vital lesson Captain Jas Briggs, in *Apollo*, had taught me was to use full rudder. As a cadet it had been instilled in me to limit rudder angle to 30 degrees since putting it against the stops carried the risk of jamming the rudder. This had been a problem in older classes of ship. Although the designers had long since overcome this difficulty, the habit of limiting the rudder to 30 degrees remained, and no-one questioned why. My natural instinct, both in an emergency and during manoeuvres, became 'Starboard 35' whilst just about everyone else still used 'Starboard 30'. Had I only used 30 degrees of rudder, the missile would have penetrated the ship's side and exploded in the Seaslug magazine, with horrendous consequences.

In turning, the intention was to present a very fine inclination to the missile to bounce it off the ship's side. Correct rudder was applied and with the missile now in to about six miles the ship started to turn. Perhaps it was the commotion of hand-overs on the bridge. Perhaps I did not speak clearly or slowly enough. Perhaps the helmsman was distracted. Charlie Wilson, the OOW had not noticed the helmsman's error. Most likely we were all dog tired and tired brains were working too slowly. For whatever reason, the initial application of incorrect rudder delayed our turn by five to ten seconds.

Had I ordered rudder immediately I saw the first faint echo, and had the helmsman immediately applied the correct rudder, we would have completed our evasive manoeuvre. Had I applied rudder before alerting the ops room, we may have completed the manoeuvre. In the many hours of soul-searching since, I have been over all the possible options, asking myself if I would have reacted differently. You cannot apply full rudder every time something paints on radar! With what was very limited information, and lacking any corroboration from either the GDP, the electronic warfare (EW) office or the ops room, two sweeps of a radar is not long to evaluate a tactical decision and come to a sound conclusion. From the moment the first faintest of echoes had appeared until starboard rudder began biting the water, twenty to twenty-five seconds had elapsed. Our speed of reaction was significantly quicker than *Sheffield*'s but not quick enough!

The missile skidded along the deck adjacent to the port Seacat launcher as the delayed action fuse ran down, punching a hole in the deck as it was being deflected upwards. About 12ft from the spermwater, when about 12in above the deck, the missile exploded, punching a 10ft by 15ft hole in the hangar deck and a 5ft by 4ft hole in the galley deck below. As the blast cone travelled forwards and downwards, the missile body sped on forwards and slightly upwards, penetrating the hangar door behind which, fuelled and armed, Willie was in the way and promptly blew up. The hangar roof was bowed and the concertina hangar door, which had been shut, became something akin to an untidy scrapyard, with debris strewn all over the hangar deck. Some of the debris was blown over the side sweeping the port Seacat launcher, with three missiles still on their pods, into the flight-deck netting. Shrapnel went everywhere, dealing death and destruction.

Within seconds, clouds of thick black acrid smoke were pouring out of the hole in the upper deck and what remained of the hangar. The fight to save *Glamorgan* began, but *Yarmouth* thought the fight was already over. On seeing the explosion she closed to pick up survivors but all she could see was a large cloud of smoke and she thought that we had been blown in half and sunk just like *Hood*. She later signalled that it was marvellous to see our bows erupt from the smoke cloud, 'still going like a bat out of hell'. We were still going but, unlike the bat, we were in our private hell and would remain there for some time to come.

The fact that the missile punched a hole in the upper deck as it was deflected upwards when heeling at 14 degrees indicated that at an angle of 15 degrees or more it would have entered the ship rather than be deflected. The principal lesson from this attack was to minimise the impact damage by taking an incoming Exocet missile at as close to a 10-degree inclination as possible, to bounce it off the ship's side. Bouncing the missile would cause the majority of the explosive force to vent to atmosphere. Equally important, the unspent fuel and remaining kinetic energy of the missile would continue on its way. falling into the sea. About 90 per cent of the missile's effectiveness would be lost and although one could expect a hole to be punched in the ship's side, damage would be localised and limited, within damage control capability. We had proved the theory of the countermeasure for Exocet which we devised back in April and it is applicable to other sea-skimming missiles. Had the hangar not been in the way, damage to *Glamorgan* would have been limited. As it was, we now had to prove our competence in damage control.

The prime strategy must always be to destroy or seduce incoming missiles. If these strategies fail, the bounce strategy was very much a last resort to minimise damage. To achieve the necessary manoeuvre in good time, quick thinking, and aggressive and precise shiphandling is required. Fuel economies necessitating a policy of economical steaming at a sedate pace offer little opportunity for aggressive shiphandling. Standards of bridgemanship are proportional to the training and experience invested in bridge teams.

Chapter 13

The Principal Lesson

The damage caused by the Exocet was extensive. The port Seacat launcher was blown overboard into the flight deck netting, and various communications and radar aerial systems, as well as the port Ship Torpedo Weapon System, suffered fire and shrapnel damage. The fires were not just limited to the vicinity of the damaged area. Radio aerials on the hangar roof were badly damaged and when the communicators attempted to transmit from the main communications office (MCO) this started a fire in equipment within the office, well away from the area of primary damage.

A large fire started immediately in the hangar, fed by Avcat and the magnesium alloy fabric of the helicopter. This fire spread rapidly into 'K' gas turbine generator space as the bulkhead between the hangar and 'K' had been bowed and split. What remained inside the hangar was rapidly consumed by fire and flames were sucked down the gas turbine room air intakes into the fans. The gas turbine room also suffered severe shrapnel damage, fire and flooding and the port auxiliary boiler, LI and L2 diesel generators were disabled. Numerous cables and pipe systems were fractured.

Part of the force of the explosion went through the hole in the upper deck into the main galley below where the servery bulkhead was flattened and unbonded formica shattered which inflicted very grievous wounds; the galley crew paid with their lives for the economy measure of not bonding the formica to plywood during the refit. The galley caught fire as burning fuel and debris descended from above and this fire rapidly spread into the Seacat transmitting station, putting Seacat out of action.

Part of the missile warhead penetrated the galley deck into M2 breaker room, destroying half of the breakers. Water from the hangar spray, fractured firemain, and later the firefighting water, drained through the holes in 01 deck and 1 deck, flooding the port passage on 2 deck to a depth of 4ft. The shock of the initial explosion caused the Grinnel automatic spray heads to shatter, flooding the Seaslug magazines. The magazine firemain was also damaged and added yet further to the flooding. Luckily, most of the lights stayed on. With 4ft of cold, dirty water on 2 deck, it was going to be difficult locating the Seaslug magazine drain control valves which were at deck level.

The 901 was severely damaged as was the Seacat transmitting station (TS) and director. In the Seaslug TS normal electrical supplies failed, losing power to the various components of that radar system, including the director spinners, metadynes and gathering aerial blowers. The system was shut down and an unsuccessful attempt was made to flash up again; shortly afterwards the TS was abandoned via the only remaining possible exit.

Glamorgan had lost three out of her five generators and was limited to the steam plant only, just 50 per cent of her power. There were no supplies from M2 section and Seaslug and Seacat missile systems were out of action. There was a potential fire risk from damaged cables and fuse panels while food preparation was severely limited. There was no citadel and no helicopter. Finally, many mess decks were now barely habitable.

Unlike *Sheffield* and *Atlantic Conveyor*, serious though the damage was, *Glamorgan* could still float and fight. The gunnery system remained fully operational to counter an air or surface threat, or to provide further bombardment. Our Exocet system was undamaged and could counter the surface threat, and we still had the starboard anti-submarine torpedo system to deal with the subsurface threat. Morale had been dealt a severe blow but there was never the slightest chance that we were going to give up and go home.

I heard numerous graphic accounts of the night's horrors which, for the sake of those who knew the victims, are not recorded here. The fact that thirteen died, despite the best efforts of the on-board medical team and medical support from other ships, is evidence enough of the horror. Everyone had a tale to tell. With so much activity taking place simultaneously throughout the ship, it would be impossible to recount the full story here. Likewise, at the time, no-one had the full picture and it is apposite to recount a selection of individual experiences to give an impression of what occurred and what was achieved that night, bearing in mind that many acts of courage passed unseen or unrecorded. Conversely, there were some light-hearted moments.

There was no doubt that, in falling out from action stations a few minutes prior to the hit, the ship had been caught with its pants down. At least one crew member was literally so caught. Seaman Sefton had just fought his way down through layers of clothing, overalls, lifejacket, anti-flash gear, and made himself comfortable on a pan in the forward heads when he heard something akin to a giant sledgehammer. He was trapped in the 'trap'! Initially, he had great difficulty in standing up as the ship was still heeling hard and his legs were lashed together with a collection of outer and underclothes around his ankles. He simply could not stop banging his head against the door in his struggle to don his kit, but the strange thing was that, at the time, he just could not stop himself from laughing at having literally been caught with his pants down. Within the very private confines of the heads, the comedy of the situation was real enough, but on escaping from there, all light-heartedness was eliminated; our situation was deadly serious.

Having returned to the midships section base from the upper deck, Leading Marine Engineering Mechanic Taff Callaghan and Marine Engineering Mechanic 'Trevor' Brooking heard screams coming from inside the electronic warfare office where the door and escape hatch had jammed. Those section base members at the corner of the cross passage on the port side saw the chaos in the galley and servery area and ran to help. Their first casualty was Chief Cook Moore who had been standing just forward of the galley by the catering office door when the missile hit. Fortunately he was behind the entry hole and ice cream machine. Nevertheless, he was thrown 20ft up the port passage and through the smoke doors. The flash and explosion left him dazed and blinded for two days with his face pockmarked with spatter wounds.

Taff then called for Marine Engineering Mechanics Day and Petherick. Rory Petherick was there but there was no sign of 'Happy' Day, so Taff donned a fearnought suit in 'Happy's' place as there was no-one else available except for young Marine Engineering Mechanic Carter who was suffering from shock. Taff handed his lifejacket and once-only suit belt to Marine Engineering Artificer 'Shakey' Braithwait, the Breathing Apparatus (BA) Controller, with the words, 'Shakey, keep hold of these for me; I think I might need them shortly'. Taff never realised how close his words came to being true.

As Taff was being dressed, his assistants were distracted by severely injured survivors being evacuated from the galley and he had to shout at them to snap them back into reality. Once dressed, Taff was ordered by Chippy Thomas to go into the galley via the starboard

or and ascertain whether or not it was still on fire. The port
is inaccessible due to the damage. He found six inches of 'free
surface' water already on the galley deck but, with only the
emergency lighting still on and the galley full of smoke, was able to
confirm that the fire in the galley was out.

Some time later, HQ1 then called for two fearnought suitmen to
assist with the hangar fire and so Taff and Rory Petherick proceded to
the upper deck. They were ordered onto the hangar roof to isolate the
severed hangar spray which was flooding compartments below
through the hole in the upper deck. The ship was taking on a
significant and increasing angle by this stage and the task proved too
difficult. With the guardrails gone, their night vision destroyed by the
fire, encumbered by their equipment and hampered by tangled
wreckage and smoke, there was a very real risk of the pair falling into
the fire. They then went down to the Seacat director deck and assisted
in fighting the hangar fire that was contained but still very much alive.
He recalled that 'ammunition was still exploding. The heat was
intense, even through fearnought suits and memories of time and
action merged into a blur'. He remembered going into the ship's
office at one point to find Jack Dusty suffering a brainstorm and
handing out new socks and steaming boots but he duly took advantage
of this early Christmas box as his own socks and boots were soaking
wet from wading through the galley.

Taff was then told by Marine Engineering Mechanician Gerry
Gerrard to take a break. He took off his fearnought suit and the
moment he sat down, he did not want to get up again. It was at this
moment that Marine Engineering Mechanic 'Spud' Yeomans
appeared. Taff thought of him as something of a cockney wide-boy in
the *Only Fools and Horses* mould; an 'Alright Spud?' enquiry was
greeted by a cheesy grin and a 'Yeah, alright Taff?' response and this
was a real lift for Taff. He thought that if 'Spud' survived the Exocet,
then so would the ship. At that moment, despite the 12–degree angle
on the ship, Taff was confident that *Glamorgan* would make it home;
he did not realise that the ship was in a state of loll and in real danger
of capsize.

The firefighting was still in progress when Taff returned to the
hangar to help. He vividly remembered seeing a body, obviously killed
instantly, lying half in and half out of the hangar office doorway. The
other thing which he recalled was the high pressure (HP) air storage
cylinder in the corner of the hangar steaming like a ticking bomb.

Several crew members were found dead in the hangar office and for decades Taff was wracked by guilt. He wrote, 'As fearnought suitmen, maybe Rory and I could have got there and pulled one or two out alive, and maybe there would not have been thirteen names on the *Glamorgan* memorial stone.' In fact, those who died in the hangar office died very quickly and Taff and Rory could not have saved them.

The other incident which Taff remembered clearly was his point blank refusal to eat a corned beef sandwich made by the Leading Regulator in the wardroom galley, believing it to be of Argentine origin. He had no reservations about eating ice cream delivered to the machinery control room later that afternoon by the chefs and he also recalled my visit there when I had said to him that next time I hoped I would remember to pipe 'Brace, Brace, Brace!' His response was that 'Hopefully, there wouldn't be a next time'.

Alan Carlisle was in 4 Mess with 'Derby' Allen when the 'bang' came. Simultaneously they both shouted, 'We've been hit!' They just knew, although it was impossible to describe the feeling. Derby raced back to the turret and Alan returned to the bridge. When he looked aft, the enormity of what had happened hit him. He saw smoke and flames billowing out from the superstructure on the port side. He then relayed messages from his vantage point on the bridge wing to keep the Captain informed as events developed.

He was deeply shocked when the first casualty was reported and the fact that the ship was listing heavily, almost dead in the water like a sitting duck, was equally disquietening. Once the initial chaos was over and the situation was under control, Alan left the bridge to assist in other areas and time seemed to pass very quickly. His Mess was being used as a first aid centre and it was there that he saw Steve Sillence, one of his soccer players, mortally wounded. Steve was talkative. Despite knowing that he was grievously wounded, he maintained a very stoical composure, even foretelling that there would be 'no more football for me!' Steve Sillence was the epitome of courage and Alan felt choked.

Petty Officer Dunn had just fallen out from the forward electrical repair party and was moving aft when he heard a tremendous bang. With water collecting in various compartments, the senior rate in charge of the after electrical repair party had been instructed by HQ1 to concentrate on pumping out. Petty Officer Dunn took charge of the other activities of the after repair party. He mustered what men he had and sent out patrols to get a sitrep before calling for more assistance from forward to rig lights in the galley and hangar so that the firefighters could see. By that stage, with the passageway above the gas turbine room flooded to about 3ft, he sent two men to find a submersible pump. The other pumping team were already rigging a pump in the Seacat hoist well. HQ1 then instructed him to run emergency cables to restore power to the after end of the ship. This proved impossible as the electrical connections were now underwater.

Ignoring the cold and wet, the firefighters only stopped to recharge their breathing apparatus and Petty Officer Dunn arranged an urn of tea for them but no-one wanted much relief; everyone wanted to get back and finish the job. By 1000, with the fires out and the water pumped from flooded compartments, damage control cables could be run to effect temporary repairs to the electrical supplies. There then came the job of clearing up and the grim task of recovering the bodies. The forward Petty Officers' mess was still being used as an operating theatre as Surgeon Lieutenant Gilbert worked on the wounded.

During his Naval Architecture examination at Manadon Naval Engineering College, John Holden had been given a 'County' 'Class Book' and a set of conditions that required a series of scenarios to be followed involving an imaginary 'County' class destroyer. The final scenario was a galley fire with water on 1 deck, 2 deck and 3 deck. The question was, 'What condition is the ship in? What action can you take? What would you recommend to the Command?' The staff answer was that the ship was approaching 'loll'. 'List' is a *stable* non-upright condition: loll is a *non-stable* non-upright condition. The answer was that there was next to nothing that could be done fast enough to recover the situation and the recommendation to the Command was to abandon ship. Without a quiet classroom and the best part of a day to consider what to do, he and his DC team faced a similar situation in *Glamorgan* and, achieving the near impossible, played a significant role in saving the ship.

John, hearing a distant 'crump', sensed the serious implications and ran towards 3 section base. As he passed the casualties he mentally blanked out what he saw. Finding his way obstructed by fire he returned to ensure that the midships section base was taking action before moving down the rapidly flooding 2 deck port passage. With the ship beginning to list, he described the scene in the Junior Rates dining hall as a tableau from hell, illuminated by the smoky red glow from the fire in the galley and drenched by water flooding in through the blast hole.

John took charge of the after section base and ensured that the situation was being reported to HQ1, the prime damage control centre. As more people arrived, he got them dressed in fearnought suits to tackle the galley fire and to search for any more casualties. As this was going on, the first aid team were working on the casualty in the dining hall who, although apparently unmarked, died shortly thereafter. Damage control teams had a dilemma – should they attend to casualties who were their shipmates, colleagues and friends, or should they attend to the ship? Human or steel – what was the priority? For some, the chosen priority was to strive to keep the ship afloat and the fact that this was the right decision did little to alleviate the soul searching in the years to come. Those involved with damage control and casualties remained deeply affected by their experiences.

John's priority was to address the steadily worsening situation of the ship herself. He asked the communications number to contact HQ1 to find out the extent of the evidently increasing angle on the ship. The HQ1 clinometer showed 12 degrees. There was flooding across the galley, across the dining halls, along 1 deck, 2 deck and 3 deck port from midships to 3R flat aft. This was almost identical to the scenario in the Manadon examination paper and John stood in turmoil – had the heavy list already degenerated into a loll condition? The logical option was to abandon the section base since there was little hope of controlling the situation but, to John and many others, giving up was not an option.

John's ingenuity and improvisation helped save the day. He noticed that sacks of potatoes were stacked along the passageway and recognising their value as substitutes for sandbags, he directed his men to construct a dwarf bulkhead forward to aft through the accessible part of the galley and forward to aft through the dining halls. Having succeeded with one dwarf bulkhead down the centre-line, he then ordered two more to be built to divide the width of the free surface of water by a factor of four. This greatly improved stability and converted the dangerous condition of loll into the stable condition of list.

He then sought approval from Commander 'E' to flood the three centreline ballast tanks to provide more weight low down in the ship and further increase the metacentric height and, consequently, the stability of the ship. What John did not know until years later was that

ıad compromised and only partly filled the ballast tanks. With
ght, this was a mistake because instead of increasing the
metacentric height, the free surface left in the *half*-filled ballast tanks
actually decreased it. It has to be remembered though that this was
new territory for everyone; we had never exercised this scenario.
Decisions were taken in the heat of action when so much was
happening; we did not have the luxury of a comfortable armchair and
all the time in the world, all the facts and no pressure to make quick
decisions. So, though we got most things right, some mistakes were
made but teamwork and initiative minimised the consquences of
individual mistakes.

John and his team had to repeatedly re-enter the devastated galley
in response to reports of fires and missing persons. Lieutenant Alan
Watt, the Deputy Supply Officer, noted how cooly and calmy John
was handling the crisis. Mention must also be made of the fearnought
suitman who, although absolutely exhausted and with his cylinders
nigh on empty, still volunteered to re-enter the galley. After the
section base teams had succeeded in bringing the situation below
decks under control, John went up to the flight deck to see what was
happening there and to get some fresh air. He described the hangar
area as, 'a scene from hell as firefighting teams still battled from both
ends to bring the fire under control'.

Surgeon Lieutenant John Gilbert was the ship's Medical Officer.
Hitherto, he and his team had had little to do. This was his moment
of truth. He recalled that there were four main kinds of injury. These
were blast, which was very destructive; flash, which mainly affected
the eyes; spatter, a classical hot explosive injury inflicting little
scorched speckles; and lacerations, predominantly from the
unbonded formica which had lined the galley. The first aid teams and
the Medical Department, particularly Petty Officer Medical Assistant
Westerman, did as much as could be expected on the day and nobody
died who had half a chance. Even Leading Cook Sillence made it as
far as *Invincible*. All the well rehearsed routines played a part, for
example lifting casualties in Neil-Robertson stretchers up through
hatches and across the devastated decks. It was uncomfortable
standing on an increasingly angled deck down in 4 Mess,
remembering what had happened to *Coventry* only a couple of weeks
before. All in all from a medical perspective everything worked as it
was supposed to. Eventualities had been allowed for and the best was
made of a bad job by a good team.

Once clear of the coast and out of immediate danger from the enemy, spare hands in the Ops Room were released for firefighting duties. Eon Matthews was tasked to don a fearnought suit to boundary cool around the galley fire. His comment of 'Boundary cool in a fearnought! That is a first!' seemed redundant as soon as he reached the galley and saw the effect that the missile had made. Having completed the boundary cooling task, he returned to the 'Rhondda Valley' (the main passageway running the length of the ship) to await further tasking. The Navigating Officer's Yeoman, Norman 'Scouse' Richardson, and Eon were later sent to the hangar to assist with the firefighting. On arrival, they were told to follow a hose, which was charged, and carry on firefighting in the hangar upper office. Eon found the end of the hose lying by a body and tried not to think of what he had just seen as he directed the hose into the upper office. As he began to climb the ladder, something fell on him and he fell on his back onto the deck. Weighted down by his breathing apparatus and encumbered by his fearnought suit, he felt like a tortoise. 'Scouse' Richardson helped him to his feet and with the fire out and their job done, they returned to the upper deck.

In the steam turbine control room, the controlling machinery space, Michael Page responded quickly to the damage. Although the steam plant continued to function, some of the control room lights had failed, one diesel generator had stopped and the other had shed its load though he managed to restore load to the latter in local control. In the gas turbine room it was a very different story. It filled rapidly with smoke and all indications to the engines were lost. HQ1 decided to steam drench the gas turbine room, believing it to be on fire, but this was countermanded by Michael when it became apparent that smoke was being ingested from above. The gas turbine engines were successfully shut down and declutched from the steam plant and, as a precautionary measure, the gas turbine room bilges were filled with 5ft of foam. The ship's speed dropped and the systems de-isolated a few minutes earlier were rapidly realigned. Once Michael and his team had stabilised the situation in the gas turbine room their main concern was safeguarding precious high pressure air, primarily for breathing apparatus supplies, since all high pressure air systems in the hangar had been destroyed.

As the angle and the risk of capsizing increased, Michael recalled discussing the possibility of losing top weight and whether the boats should be cut away. With over twenty people in the machinery control room he wondered if they would all get through the manhole in time should the ship start to capsize. The subsequent successful efforts of the damage control teams in reducing the list was a relief to everyone, particularly those on watch in the bowels of the ship.

Chief Petty Officer Colin Phillips was in his mess and was next in the queue for hot water for his cup of coffee when all the lights went out. As he raced back to his action station in the mainmast, Chief Cook Moore came stumbling towards him with blood all over his face. Colin summoned first aiders for Moore before going up to the 966 radar office. It was full of smoke and nothing was working. On the 966/278 radar office switchboard he selected the alternate supply and managed to restore all equipment except for the 966 aerial. This kept blowing fuses and was obviously damaged. Mechanician Tarpey came up to the office to assist and Colin decided to make sure that the aerial was still with the ship. He climbed up inside the mast and opened the very small hatch at the top to view the aerial and the fire in the hangar. The aerial had suffered some minor shrapnel damage but was basically intact. Opening the hatch helped to clear the smoke from the radar offices and Colin managed to get the aerial rotating with the help of some masking tape on the aerial starter box.

Leading Marine Engineering Mechanic Francis Ryle emerged from his messdeck to hear from Marine Engineering Mechanic Rene Cope that the galley had been hit. Francis immediately returned to the section base where Chippy Harding instructed him to take two stokers with a submersible pump to help out aft. Assisted by Marine Engineering Mechanics 'Shep' Woollard and 'Slug' Everall, he took the pump towards the damage through fully clipped doors. On arrival at the gear room flat, clips were being frantically hammered back on as fast as the trio could release them. The 'clip dance' only ended when Marine Engineering Mechanic McGlinchey shouted through the bulkhead hose connection to find an alternative route to 2 Deck passageway via 1 Deck.

There was about 5ft of water on 2 Deck as they began lowering the pump down the ladder. Petty Officer Tom Medcalf, a big chap, appeared at the foot of the ladder to receive the pump and he was up to his chest in icy water. Swimming in his wake, still wearing his glasses, all steamed up and lips blue, was Marine Engineering Mechanic Taff Whitton, at 5ft 3ins probably the smallest member of the ship's company. Francis asked Taff if he was alright. In his strong Welsh accent, heavy with sarcasm, Taff replied, 'Course I am. Freezing my f— b— off!' This raised a needed smile and pumping quickly started.

With the ship now over at 12 degrees and in danger of capsizing, Commander Jim Butterfield, in HQ1, was having a nightmare. Several feet of water had suddenly appeared in the gear room bilge without any report of damage in that vicinity, but, as a result, the list had significantly eased. What subsequently emerged was that Taff had had the presence of mind to remove the foam tube caps to the gear room and gas turbine room, thereby lowering tons of water from 2 deck. If any single action during the damage control phase saved the ship, this was it. It was not until 2001 that details of Taff Whitton's action became known, too late for him to be given official recognition. Finding the foam tubes in the dark under feet of dirty icy water was testament to his ship knowledge, ingenuity and courage.

Petty Officer Mike Wiltshire was mustering the midship's section base team when he was thrown to the ground by the blast. When he collected his senses he ordered the section base team to carry out a blanket search of the midships section. As he proceeded to the fuel working space, he heard the pipe, 'Fire! Fire! Fire! - fire in the galley!' Seconds later another pipe, 'Fire! Fire! Fire! - fire in the hangar!' This was followed by reports of further fires in the machinery spaces. Many of these subsequent reports were false, being made in response to smoke being drawn into compartments through the ventilation supply fans. It took a while to determine the extent of the damage and all the time he felt the angle on the ship increasing. He realised the dilemma. The firefighters were sinking the ship with their firefighting water, but if they did not cool the fire it would spread and eventually reach a magazine. As HQ1 was organising pumping out, he prepared to do the opposite and ballast Number 3 tank.

* * *

Events remain deeply engraved in my memory. Immediately after the hit, with the ship navigationally under control, I said to Mark Garratt, 'Go to the hangar and get a sitrep'. I then had second thoughts, feeling that perhaps more experience might be necessary and I handed the ship over to Lieutenant Charlie Wilson, the officer of the watch. As I opened the citadel air lock, the full extent of the fire was immediately apparent. Flames in excess of 100ft high were erupting from the hangar, the port Seacat director was on fire and flames stretched half way up the port waist. Nothing but smoke and flames could be seen aft of the Seacat director.

I leapt down to the port waist, coming across a couple of junior ratings standing by an unreeled hose connected to the firemain but lacking a nozzle. I ordered one rating to 'switch the ruddy thing on and find a nozzle!' I dragged the other rating with me and charged the flames. In my mind was the necessity to reach the port Seacat launcher before the three remaining missiles cooked off but I did not share my thoughts.

Despite lacking a nozzle, the flames along the port waist were easily extinguished. Without a nozzle, the hose had a short range and there was no alternative but to get close. Here was one night when I did not mind the cold. Having sorted out the port waist, we then tackled the burning port Seacat director which was full of shrapnel holes. The director fire was rapidly extinguished and if the Seacat aimer was still in the director, at least he would no longer be cooking. He was one of the injured survivors and I never discovered how long he had remained in his smashed and burning director.

As we approached the hangar area, magnesium and aviation fuel were not so readily extinguished but we continued to fight our way aft into the smoke to get to the Seacat launcher. I suddenly realised that not all the smoke was coming out of the hangar; a large column was erupting from where the upper deck used to be but where there was now a large hole. One more step and I would have joined 3 section base team in the remains of the galley.

Having narrowly avoided falling through the hole. I saw the Seacat launcher lying in the netting over the side with three missiles still on their pods. The launcher was in no danger from the flames so I altered my firefighting priority to the hangar area. I could see the helicopter rotor head lying on the deck just inboard of the gas turbine intakes, surrounded by fire. By this stage, I had come to the end of my hose and I called for another section of hose. The firemain was briefly switched off to fit the extra section, but I was still without a nozzle. I then advanced towards the rotor head, playing the water onto the gas turbine intakes, quickly extinguishing the flames which were being sucked into the intakes and down into the gas room.

Chris Gotto then arrived and, seeing we had no nozzles, quickly rectified the situation. I decided this was an opportune moment to return to the bridge to give them a sitrep and handed my hose to Radio Operator Roberts. I reported what I had seen and explained that no-one else was taking charge of the hangar fire; I also pleaded for more hands before donning an Aquarius diving set from underneath the bridge and returned to the hangar.

When I arrived, no-one seemed interested in getting close to the fire. I grabbed back my hose and drove a 'salient' through the fire towards the rotor head. Someone shouted 'get back!' and the reason suddenly became apparent. Small arms ammunition was cooking off in the hangar and bullets were flying around. I thought of Marianne and decided that she would be livid if she knew what I was doing. It was then anger took over from common sense. I muttered 'Sod it!' and went forward into the flames, going for the rotor head. I decided if bullets were coming in my direction a few feet would not make much difference and the rotor head would afford some degree of protection from the radiated heat and bullets.

I had the Aquarius face mask on loosely and when the smoke became too much I grabbed the mouthpiece for a gulp of fresh air. I knew there would be no opportunity to re-charge the set and I had to make it last, using it only when absolutely necessary. Shortly after I reached the rotor head, the nozzles arrived, so I retreated, had the firemain temporarily switched off to fit the nozzle and then advanced back into the salient to the rotor head. From there I could reach all parts of the hangar and the nozzle made a real difference.

My main concerns were: 'Was the helicopter loaded with a Mark 11 depth charge? and if so, if it cooked off, would it blow me over the side? Would the HP air reservoir on the hangar bulkhead explode with similar effect? With all the firefighting water draining down the hole in the deck, giving the ship a significant list, how much longer could we pour water on this inferno?' There was little I could do about my concerns other than extinguish the fire as quickly as possible. I attacked the fire for about 90 per cent of the time, boundary cooling bulkheads for about 10 per cent of the time. Adjacent compartments included the Seacat ready-use magazine and 'K' generator space which were two more good reasons for keeping the bulkheads cool! I also played my hose through the vent into the blazing upper hangar office. I did not believe anyone was still alive in the hangar office but had I known the truth, I would have attempted to reach the office much sooner. One of the hangar crew, who had been killed instantly, was lying half in, half out of the hangar office doorway. He lay there with a grin on his face and my troubled mind kept asking, 'Why on earth are you grinning, don't you know you are dead?' I still see that face today, and it still haunts me.

Having reached the rotor head, I quietly shuddered every time there was an ammunition flare-up in the hangar. It was at about this time I received a jet of charged hose in the small of my back. It went right through my pullover and shirt, giving me an unexpectedly cold shock! I swore, 'There are enough — flames to point at without pointing that — hose at me!' The culprit was Alan Watt. His hose had caught on some debris and he had turned around to free it. In the process his aim was unguided and I was the victim. I was not cold for long, however; the flames on three sides quickly saw to that. I then became aware the salient was being extended and the flames on the inboard side were being driven back. Roberts then joined me at the rotor head, looking rather worried. To break the tension I turned and said, 'So much for the eight-week turnaround! It will take Portsmouth Dockyard a damn site longer to fix this lot!' Suddenly a broad grin came on his face as he realised that if we put this fire out we would have earned a one-way ticket to the UK. He got stuck in with a will. (The eight-week turnaround in UK was to comprise of two weeks leave each watch, a couple of weeks trials followed by two weeks at Portland before returning to the South Atlantic.)

The extra hands I had requested arrived - both of them. However, not knowing the situation below, I could not pester for more people to help with our 'little' fire. Smoke was still pouring out of the hole and water pouring into it. They obviously had major problems below. With Roberts in an ideal position to attack the seat of the fire, I went to the ops room to give an updated sitrep. At this stage the ship was over at 12 degrees. That required an awful lot of water for a 6,000-ton ship. We rigged a plank of timber to divert some of the water over the side rather than down the hole. I was warned that we might soon have to stop pouring water on the fire. Things were obviously critical.

A few minutes after I rejoined Roberts at the rotor head, I noticed that the list had eased. I also noticed that the fire seemed to be less intense so we advanced further and for the first time started to make real progress. I called on some other firefighters to assist

Roberts with the words 'Kill it', before attempting to get into the hangar office.

It was the junk from the explosion rather than the flames which made progress to the hangar office slow. Dragging my hose with me I made it, carefully stepping over the body in the doorway. I was then amazed by a voice asking, 'Give us a hand'. There on the deck lay Aircraft Engineering Mechanician John Kelly, still alive. Of those in the hangar office when the missile hit, Air Engineering Artificer Ian Tait had been extremely lucky. Despite his dazed state, he managed to open the escape hatch and exit to the starboard waist. John Kelly received a fractured leg and only survived because Ian passed back his own respirator for John to use. John, unable to move, lay on the hangar office deck for two and a half hours, cooled by the fractured firemain spraying water onto the hangar office bulkhead. Not realising his leg was fractured in the blast, I thought he had managed to get to the hangar office shortly before me and had tripped over. I honestly did not believe anyone could have survived for the best part of three hours in that hell hole. I said to him, 'Hang on a minute, I am just going to put the fire out!' John must have thought I was a hard bastard, telling him to hang on a little while longer.

There were two problem areas: the upper hangar office where all the helicopter documentation was on fire and the compartment forward of the hangar office. Through the shrapnel holes, I could see flames. There was a mound of clothing at the forward end of the hangar office upon which I climbed to get my hose through the shrapnel holes. I knew what the mound of clothing really was but blanked it out of my mind. The only subject upon which I allowed myself to focus was the fire. Reflection would come later. I managed to beat down both fires but this generated a lot of smoke which drove me back. I went back to the hangar office door, saw Lieutenant Allen Hardcastle and called for a first aid party for John Kelly and support to kill the fire. Allen was a fellow diver and a person whom I could trust. Coughing and spluttering from the smoke, I again returned to the ops room to inform the Captain we had effectively won the battle with the hangar fire. Seeing my exhausted state, he said, 'Well done, go to bed!'

Not wishing to give up until the fire was truly out, I disobeyed him and went back to the hangar. I got a team onto the hangar roof to deal with the smoke from the obstinate hangar upper office. The fire in the hangar itself was now out and Allen dispatched a couple of fearnought suitmen to deal with the hangar upper office. Encumbered with their kit they had difficulties and Allen sent one of the diving team in, without breathing apparatus, to kill the fire. I returned to the ops room with the news that, apart from some smouldering paper in the hangar upper office, the fire was out. Mike Barrow then threatened me with court martial if I did not retire to bed. He wanted me fresh for later in the day. I took the hint.

Exhausted, arms aching, wheezing from smoke inhalation, I went to my cabin, stripped off my wet clothes, put on clean clothes and slumped on my bunk, my mind a turmoil. Sheer exhaustion won, and I slept for an hour. Others had to carry on. Petty Officer Wiltshire recalled not having any perception of time but it did not seem long before the ship was upright and making good speed on steam. With the fires extinguished below decks he remembered going up top to assist in extinguishing the fire in the hangar office. Once that fire was out, he saw the casualties. Eight alone were killed in the flight, along with his messmate and good friend Fred Adcock.

When I awoke, the ship was upright, making 22 knots, and dawn was breaking. I went to the bridge to check all was well before making my way to the hangar. The scene was very different from when I left. The rotor head and most of the debris had been ditched overboard. Lying on the hangar deck and embedded in the bulkheads around the hangar were hundreds of spent bullets. I picked up a handful, my mind going back to the 'crackling' in the fire a few hours earlier. We were lucky that no-one had been seriously hurt. A wisp of smoke was still drifting from the hangar upper office; the aviation paperwork was extremely stubborn.

I walked up the port waist where the dead were laid out in canvas. Steaming boots were protruding from one canvas shroud ensuring that the full impact was not 'out of sight, out of mind'. It was an extremely upsetting sight and, for the first time, I cried. Reaction was setting in. More tears were to flow, and go on flowing, on a very regular basis in the years that followed. During the fire I managed to block out all the personal feelings which were now beginning to emerge.

When I got back to the wardroom I enquired about casualties. Lieutenant Commander Ian Forbes said he thought the total was about seventeen, with three very seriously injured. He added, 'Tinks got it'. I recalled the long conversation I had with David Tinker just a few short hours previously.

Mixed with these feelings of deep sorrow was one of qualified elation. We had defeated the great ogre of Exocet. We had proved to the world that a ship could take an Exocet hit and survive in fighting condition. I witnessed a determined attitude to keep going and the feeling that it would take more than the night's disaster to crack us. We aimed to be back in business as soon as possible.

Having not eaten since the evening before, I went to the wardroom galley and was offered one of the Leading Regulator's now famous corned beef wedges. Feeling better, I went aft to see if I could replace my anti-flash gear. As I passed through the canteen flat there were cries of 'gangway!' Leading Cook Sillence was being taken to the flight deck to be airlifted to *Invincible*. The unbonded formica in the galley had inflicted horrific injuries upon him and he was not expected to survive. As the stretcher was lifted up the ladder there were quiet words of encouragement. The night's battle was not over. The wounded casualties were still fighting.

I returned to the bridge. There were some glum faces and I tried to change the mood to something more positive. Although we had suffered grievous losses, our achievement of survival was something about which to be proud. Unfortunately my buoyant facade was misinterpreted by some who felt that I had no feelings for those who had suffered. If only they knew the inner turmoil that I was suppressing.

* * *

Barry Nixon had watched the desperate battle to save the ship from the gun direction platform, manning the communications to the ops room. When he was eventually stood down he was shocked by what he saw in the aftermath of the attack but worse was to come. He was detailed off to assist with the clear-up and this included dealing with fallen comrades. John Holden had been tasked by the Commander to continue work in the galley to check for missing crew members. He took Petty Officer Marine Engineering Mechanic More and a couple of junior rates with him, including Barry, for this unpleasant task which took most of the afternoon.

They were not, however, the only ones who had to deal with the casualties. Alan Carlisle, along with Petty Officers Dave Cowan, Derby Allen and John Utley were asked by Chief Petty Officer Dennis Wing to assist with the dead. All four volunteered. The horror of war does not stop when you are hit. That is when the physical scars are received. Clearing up in the cold light of day leaves psychological scars that are not always readily apparent to another observer. Those scars go on hurting the mind and that hurt can be easily triggered by an insensitive comment.

As Dennis needed more volunteers, Alan went into 1 and 2 Mess. Still reeling with shock from the night's tragedy, none of the young men were willing to help. Alan became angry and perhaps said things that he should not have said. The only training you can have in losing shipmates is to experience it and the shock of the night's events was affecting every member of the crew, albeit in different ways.

Alan returned to the port waist and breathed in the sweet smell, the unforgettable fragrance of death. It is a smell once experienced that you never forget. By this stage most of the dead had been carefully placed in canvas. Alan remembered looking in Fred Adcock's bag. They had become good friends. After that, his memories of events became confused for a while, but his worst experience was yet to come. He was ordered to assist Surgeon Lieutenant Gilbert in identifying the bodies so that death certificates could be issued. Alan agreed to do it because he knew them all by face whereas the doctor did not. The President of 4 Mess gave Alan a tot of rum to fortify him in this psychologically arduous and unpleasant duty, and Alan had doubts about how he would cope when identifying the bodies, but when the time came, he managed the task. The tears would follow later.

Alan respected the courage of John Gilbert as he worked alone on the starboard waist in the late afternoon, opening the canavases and individually certifying death. It had to be done, even though it was stating the obvious. With the official certification complete, John had a quiet moment with all the dead. Alan never really asked John how he felt, but imagined that during the night he must have experienced hell.

By 1745 we were transferring our air drop stores to the carrier battle group. The bodies of our dead were laid out on the starboard side of the flight deck. Leading Cook Sillence died during the day in *Invincible* and his body was returned to us for burial with his comrades. We did not have enough ensigns of our own for each of the dead and requested additional ensigns from other ships. As was the custom, farewell messages were written on the canvas shrouds as comrades paid their respects to their 'oppos'. Many of the crew were still numb with shock. The cooks, stewards and flight survivors were understandably taking it particularly badly. The forthcoming weeks would be hard for them and the joy of returning home would be marred by feelings for lost comrades. I felt, as I recorded in my log,

> Not too bad at the moment. I have tried to cheer people up, but in private I must admit to shedding tears for those who died, in particular David Tinker. The most upsetting part is seeing them lying on the upper deck. They do not even get a proper coffin; lashed in canvas, weighted by a 4.5 inch shell. What a way to go. It is a very sad day, the price of war. My arms ache from the physical efforts of the night and my chest is sore from smoke.

Sunset was approaching and with it the burial service. With the fallen prepared for committal from the quarterdeck, everyone cleaned themselves up. I, and everyone else who was able to do so, had changed into our best uniforms for the funeral which was made somehow all the more poignant by the weather conditions. It was a glorious sunset with partial cloud generating vivid colours and the setting sun gave a glow to the sky; there was a gentle swell and virtually no wind. We were also on our own, the rest of the Task Force ships being far away, and valued our privacy. I went to the bridge and instructed the Officer of the Watch to heave to at sunset and record the ship's precise position which was 51°50.5′S 053°31.2′W.

As the sun set, a short service was held on the flight deck. After the last post had been played on a bugle by a young Marine Engineering Mechanic (Electrical) who had only learned it that day, the bodies were slipped over the side from the quarterdeck. It was absolutely still apart from splash … splash … splash … splash … of our comrades. It seemed to go on and on and tears filled my eyes. Although my head was bowed I could see other men crying. It was a sad and most moving moment and it was not an easy task for Martin Culverwell, but he performed the committal ceremony very well; it was a service which none of us would forget.

As darkness fell, emotions were mixed. Petty Officer Wiltshire wrote:

> Sadly at 1930, we buried our dead at sea, thirteen in all. Many wounded were also transferred to *Hermes* and *Invincible*. I thought, 'Oh God, please can we go home! I cannot go through this again. How much more can we take?' I would rather not mention some of the horrible tasks that I carried out with others. It is distressing to

write about it and is best forgotten but today I am proud to say I served with the finest men that could be brought together: Teamwork, courage and hard work saved *Glamorgan*.'

There was much truth in his last sentence.

That evening John Holden spent some time with the Chinese crew, part of his division. He then visited the Petty Officers' mess. They were understandably very upset at the loss of their messmates. John went to bed dreading having to go back into the galley the following morning.

John, like many others, went over the action, analysing it. He kept a record of draught marks and displacement and from these he was able to calculate the stability of the ship. From the incident boards he had a record of the extent of the free surface. Using that data he spent several hours in peace and quiet with all of his stability books, reworking the stability calculations. He could not see how the ship managed to stay upright and he reckoned that she was caught on the very limit of stability. He thought that perhaps what had made the difference was that the port Seacat launcher had been blown over the side, and with it most of the hangar door. Other 'topweight' in the hangar had gone up in flames. To him, there was no escaping the fact that it was a very close run thing. Had he known what Taff Whitton had achieved and taken that into account, he would have understood what, or rather who, had made the difference.

Reflecting afterwards, Taff Callaghan felt that he had taken the easy option and with the benefit of hindsight would have acted differently. He wrote:

> None of us had previous experience of being hit by a missile, especially at night. It is a most frightening and traumatic experience. We had very limited information – just the horrors presented before our eyes. We did not know how close the ship was to either blowing up or sinking. We had been up all night at action stations and were both physically and mentally exhausted. People did their best – they were, after all, human and not machines.

Eventually, everyone had a chance for rest. When Taff Callaghan finally went to bed he realised that he had slept for only a single hour during the previous thirty-nine hours. Many others had been awake and on their feet for similar periods.

Having buried our dead, we had to put this tragedy behind us, repair the ship as best we could and clean up the mess which had spread everywhere. We had been instructed to proceed to *Stena Seaspread* for three days to 'get fixed' and then take over again as TRALA Manager. The ship's own technical officers considered the damage to be more serious. Lieutenant Commander Mike Walton felt we would need a week with *Stena Seaspread* before being sent home. We might be able to get a couple of gas turbines going but one diesel generator and 'K' generator were certainly lost. Mechanically and electrically, we were in a delicate state. We made our way towards *Stena Seaspread* while Mike Barrow warned us to be particularly vigilant overnight since the damage could well start electrical fires or weakened structures could fail. Late that evening, I had a good look around for signs of impending trouble but the damage control teams had done an excellent job and the night passed without incident.

In London, preparations were underway for the trooping of the colour at the Queen's Birthday Parade in Horseguards. The celebrations were soured after lunch when Sir John Nott showed the following signal to Margaret Thatcher, 'HMS *Glamorgan* struck by suspected Exocet missile. Large fire in vicinity of hangar and in gas turbine and gear room. Power still available. Ship making 10 knots to the South.' It was not an auspicious start to the day and as more details filtered through, it was Sir John who had to break the bad news to the public on television later that day.

It was not only the ship and the crew who suffered from the hit – it affected the families too and is vividly recorded in their letters. Marianne wrote to me on 14 June.

Where do I start? I just do not know what to say. The news of *Glamorgan*'s hit was broadcast yesterday evening. With all the phone calls and visitors I just did not have a chance to write to you. It is probably best that I have had a day to think about it before writing. You must all be feeling absolutely devastated and I think you had some sort of premonition. In one of your last letters you said you felt that *Glamorgan*'s good luck could not last much longer; how right you were. It came as a terrible shock, but how pleased we were that next-of-kin could be informed before the news was broadcast publicly.

This morning, those wives from the wardroom who could manage it met at Judy Barrow's. We were shown the list of those who died and those who were injured so that if any wives who lived in our areas had been involved we could offer to help in any way. I am just so very thankful that you are safe. Let's hope that *Glamorgan* is not put into any more risk; I just pray that you are all sent home. You have certainly done your share out in the South Atlantic and have paid heavily for doing it.

I had always imagined how happy I would be seeing *Glamorgan* enter Portsmouth harbour. Even though I will be happy, there will be a part of me crying for those men who are not returning with the ship. The whole occasion will be tinged with sadness. It is all too horrible and I wish I could just wipe out 1982 and that we could all start 1983 in happier circumstances than at present. I will remember the spring and summer of '82 for the rest of my life, and I am sure you will too.

When Eon Matthews reflected on the morning's events, he thought that if his wife heard on the news that we had been hit, at least his family would be with her in Portsmouth since it was her birthday. In fact, she was alone, but when the ship returned she told Eon that *Glamorgan* was the only ship casualty that had been handled properly. She knew that all the next of kin of those killed and injured had been informed and since she had heard nothing she presumed that Eon was OK.

The news about our hit was received with considerable feeling in South Wales where the population had taken us to their hearts and where there was immense pride in 'their ship'. Sir Cennydd Traherne, the Lord Lieutenant for the Counties of Glamorgan, spoke for South Wales. He wrote: 'We are all very grieved to hear of the loss of life but relieved to know the ship is still operational. It has a very special place in the hearts of people here. The motto of the ship is *I fyny bo'r nod*. They aimed high ... very high indeed!'

Michael Barrow responded to those who sent messages of sympathy. His telegram to Mid Glamorgan County Council read:

Thank you for remembering us in our hour of need. Our sadness at the loss of friends is balanced by appreciation for the sterling efforts of all on board which prevented further casualties. The Welsh Guards, fighting so hard ashore with greater losses than us, are keeping the Welsh flag flying high.

Had it not been for the dedication, ship knowledge and selflessness of many of the crew, there is little doubt that the ship would have been sunk. After the war, the Royal Naval Damage Control School at *Phoenix* produced a poster entitled 'Damage Control - HMS *Glamorgan.*' The poster shows a photograph of the devastated hangar area captioned,

'Early morning in the South Atlantic at 0637 while on transit from coastal areas, an Exocet missile hit HMS *Glamorgan* and detonated in the vicinity of the hangar. A 5 foot x 10 foot hole was blasted in the hangar deck. The helicopter exploded and a major fire developed in the hangar. The galley was devastated, the Seaslug magazine started to flood and with half the ship's power lost the ship heeled progressively to 12 degrees with an increasing amount of water from firefighting and fractured high pressure salt water systems.

0652 – Boundary cooling achieved on all sides of the hangar.

0720 – Hangar fire contained. Free surface in crew's galley restricted by erection of dwarf bulkhead and removed by portable pumps.

0758 – Ship 12 degrees to port, ballast tanks flooded to improve stability.

0811 – Ship back to 4 degrees to port.

1054 – All fires out, flooding from fire fighting and fractured high pressure salt water systems pumped out.

THE PRINCIPAL LESSON - Not easy, but it can be done – Could your ship do it?'

Chapter 14

Recovery

Sunday, 13 June

Overnight the support team from *Stena Seaspread* came on board and completely cleared out the debris from the galley. That, more than anything else they did, gave John Holden the greatest lift. Standing outside the hangar that morning, looking at the devastation, John remembered an arm thrown around his shoulders and a broad West Country voice said, 'Alright John?' It was Pete 'Oggie' Waters whom he had last seen in 1971. Pete was one of *Stena Seaspread*'s, shipwrights. It was then that John cried.

I awoke at 0700 with a splitting headache, aching all over and short of breath due to the exertions and smoke inhalation of the previous day and then went to the bridge for the alongside with *Stena Seaspread*. *Stena* slid in sideways alongside us as we lay stopped. Once secured, we reverted to fifteen minutes notice. *Plymouth* was hove to 1,000 yards away, her repairs nearing completion.

I recorded: 'Familygrams have been sent but as yet nothing has appeared on the news; even from Argentine sources. The fact we did not stop may have fooled them but it was a clear night and everyone ashore must have seen the explosion as the missile hit and the hangar exploded.'

Stena Seaspread gave us a really excellent four-course lunch, especially when compared with the Leading Regulator's corned beef sandwiches. Chips, steak and peas with a choice of two types of gateaux and ice cream were on the menu. The Merchant Navy knew how to live well. We had not seen chips for weeks. Being in a war zone, our deep fat fryers had been emptied to reduce the risk of fire, enforcing healthy eating. Not only did *Stena*'s crew carry out effective material repairs, they conducted equally effective morale repairs to our crew for which we were, and remain, extremely grateful.

After lunch, *Plymouth* sailed to rejoin the battle group. She manned her ship's side to thank *Stena* as she went and signalled from the Bible, 'And your ancient ruins will be re-built. You shall raise up the foundations of many generations. You shall be called the repairer of the breach. The restorer of streets to dwell in.' The pastime of searching the Bible for suitable quotations remained alive and well, even in the South Atlantic.

We received messages of sympathy and support including one from Admiral Woodward who signalled, 'Whilst I am very grieved to note the casualty list, I am glad you are the first warship in the world to survive an Exocet hit.' Everyone was very kind and understanding. By mid afternoon the Argentinians were claiming to have hit, set on fire and sunk a frigate. By disappearing from view over the horizon, bearing in mind that no ship had ever survived an Exocet hit, it was not unreasonable for the Argentinians to believe that they had done so.

My splitting headache persisted all day and I felt exhausted. Although exhaustion was nothing new, I found it more difficult to deal with the mental anguish. I often found myself crying and tried to find a quiet corner so as not to be observed. Crying used to be viewed as a sign of weakness. I fought hard to bottle up my emotions, finding something taxing to distract my mind. I never saw Mike Barrow cry but knew how he must be feeling. I tried to follow his example.

On the night we were hit all the advance objectives were achieved, albeit with considerable loss of life. Mount Harriet was captured along with 200 POWs by 42 Commando. Seven were killed and thirteen wounded. We had been supporting 45 Commando, who had been late reaching the start line and experienced trouble in taking Two Sisters. They lost four and had ten wounded securing their position. The heavily defended Mount Longdon was captured by 3 Para who lost seventeen and had thirty-nine wounded. In the previous twenty-four hours we had suffered seventy-two casualties ashore. Forty-two targets had been engaged by 29 Commando Regiment, firing 2,807 rounds and they were now running short of ammunition.

Feedback on the naval bombardment confirmed it to have been very effective. The Royal Navy was also providing logistic support, equally important albeit less glamourous; *Sir Percivale*, for example, had completed offloading while *Sir Geraint* was due to offload at Teal Inlet the next day. The intentions ashore were to consolidate whilst

5 Infantry Brigade prepared for an assault upon Tumbledown and Mount William whilst 2 Para prepared for an assault upon Wireless Ridge. This was the second phase of the investment of Stanley. Preparations had also begun for Phase 3, the attack on Sapper Hill and Stanley itself.

At 1515 we slipped from *Stena Seaspread* for an airdrop ten miles to the west. We met up with *Andromeda* and the tug *Irishman* and waited for the RAF. Before our rendezvous, *Irishman* had been unaware of our misfortune but now, having seen what Exocet could do to a 6,000-ton ship, the Master asked what he should do if an Exocet came his way. 'Sink!' was our only suggestion. There were supposed to be two Hercules aircraft with twenty-eight members of the SAS and some stores but a defect forced one aircraft to turn back to Ascension. During the Hercules' first pass, the ten SAS parachuted into the sea; by the time they were to actually reach the shore, the war would be over.

After the SAS had been recovered, the Hercules proceeded to bomb us with cardboard boxes. When it went well, the parachute detached from the box as the latter hit the water but, of course, it did not always go well. Some parachutes detached as the boxes were pushed out of the back of the aircraft and others failed to detach on hitting the water. This caused difficulties for the recovery crews. Fortunately, that day the wind was light and the recovery was speedily concluded. We used our borrowed Wessex helicopter to lift the boxes out of the water once the boats' crews had cleared the parachutes. *Andromeda* embarked the SAS and stores for the battle group and headed back towards the action, leaving us to continue repairs with *Stena*. By the time we arrived the swell prevented *Stena* from coming alongside. We spent the night hove to a few cables away.

Monday, 14 June

Stena tried unsuccessfully to come alongside again at 0800. It was at about this time that some newspapers appeared in the ship. Amongst all the media speculation about the war, a poem written by a schoolgirl published in the *Portsmouth News* had the greatest effect on me. I never found out who 'M.R.' of Farlington was, but her words were nonetheless moving for that. They showed, vividly, the effect of war on families, including children.

A Little Girl's Prayer

The Navy has taken my Daddy away,
He's gone to the Falklands, so they say,
I don't think my Daddy wanted to fight,
But it sometimes takes courage to do what is right.

We went down to Portsmouth to wave him good-bye,
Some people cheered, but I saw my Mummy cry,
'God bless them all' said a man in the crowd,
I thought of my Dad and I felt very proud.

The house seems so quiet since Dad went away,
Mum listens for the news on the TV all day,
I hope he is safe and the seas aren't too rough,
I'm sure I'd be scared, but I know my Dad's tough.

In church and at school we all pray for peace,
And ask that the fighting may very soon cease,
I know when it does they'll send home my Dad,
So I try to keep smiling and not feel too sad.

The Navy has taken my Daddy away,
He's gone to the Falklands, so they say,
I don't think my Daddy wanted to fight,
I wish I could give him a cuddle tonight.

M.R.

On my way to the charthouse I read the latest intelligence signals which indicated that the Argentinians had suffered further heavy air losses, and we estimated they had now lost more than 25 per cent of their entire air force. The Harriers had strafed a fast patrol boat, causing it to beach and it was then re-attacked by *Penelope*'s Lynx, armed with Sea Skua. Despite the boat being close inshore, the missile hit and the vessel began to sink by the stern. On land, things were no better for the enemy. An action trial was carried out with a laser-guided bomb against a gun battery and the bomb landed right in the gun barrel – one cork the enemy would have trouble in removing. Back in Argentina, Galtieri had suffered a scathing interview by a female Italian reporter, who compared him to Mussolini. When asked if he had ever fought in a war, a real war, he had to admit that he had not.

As the morning progressed we received confirmation that the missile which had hit us had, indeed, been an Exocet. Some missile debris had been found in the gas turbine uptakes, possibly the safety arming mechanism and 'FRANCE' was inscribed on one piece; it was all the confirmation we needed.

Stena Seaspread tried again to come alongside, but conditions remained unsuitable, so maintainers were transported by boat, which hampered progress. Despite this, transformation of the damaged area was very swift. The Fleet Maintenance Unit embarked in *Stena* worked wonders and were masters at improvisation. They even 'stole' alloy/aluminium spoons from the wardroom for welding the hole in the deck, using steel plates 'stolen' from South Georgia and left behind by Davidoff's men. Around-the-clock repairs on the areas affected by action damage were progressing well. All damaged plating and cables had been cut away. The smaller, but still significant, shrapnel holes had been patched, while insignificant ones would be left with the ship for the rest of her days - the scars of battle. M2 breaker room was being dried out to allow some electrical repair work. Not much was left intact in there but work was needed to make damaged and burnt cables electrically safe. The engine on L1 diesel generator was now working though L2 diesel generator still needed spare parts and possibly a complete re-build.

Elsewhere in the Task Force, the frigate *Penelope* reported coming under attack from Super Etendards escorted by Mirage fighters but while missile launch was reported to have been seen, the missile missed. From where did this 'extra' missile come? Was it war nerves? Certainly there was an attack but it is doubtful it was Exocet.

During the afternoon I spoke to the Communications Officer about Radio Operator Roberts, whom I thought had done particularly well during the hangar fire. After drafting a formal letter in the hope of getting him official recognition, it was back to operational business and planning the next air drop. Bad weather was forecast, although when we detached from *Stena Seaspread* the wind was still light. Within one hour there was a full gale blowing and the seas were rapidly rising.

The first replenishment aircraft arrived at 1630 with eleven loads which took over two hours to recover; it was fortunate, therefore, that the second aircraft was cancelled. Using four Gemini dinghies belonging to ourselves and the tugs *Irishman* and *Typhoon*, plus the Wessex, we chased cardboard boxes all over the ocean. If the parachutes failed to disengage on hitting the water, they took the boxes downwind at about 30 knots until the parachutes eventually collapsed, sometimes miles down range. It seemed that the white parachutes were reliable, releasing as the load hit the water while the blue ones gave us problems, refusing to disengage. The high sea state made boatwork hazardous, and this was aggravated by poor visibility in passing blizzards. All the boxes, except those dropped without a parachute and which consequently sank, were successfully recovered, and this reflected the courage, stamina and skill of all involved in the operation which we were lucky to complete without any serious injuries or loss of life.

The recovery operation was perceived differently by Marine Phil Holding, the coxswain of a Gemini.

It was my job to keep the boat straight and keep an eye out for the cut away parachute so as not to get it wrapped around the propeller. 'George' was responsible for cutting away the parachute and hooking the load onto the helicopter winch. I remember it seemed that we were out there for an awfully long time and it was extremely cold. It was additionally somewhat worrying that *Glamorgan* seemed to be a long way away.

All did not go well. I do not know how he managed it, but 'George' succeeded in putting his knife through two of the inflatable sections in the Gemini. It was made of five sections and could stay afloat on two. However, it was getting dark, the seas were getting up rapidly and *Glamorgan* was nowhere in sight! We managed to put a clamp from the boat's bag across the split, holding it together and preventing it from getting any larger. With 'George' keeping warm by energetic use of the foot pump, we managed to limp back to *Glamorgan*.

In fact, *Glamorgan* sped to the Gemini to minimise the amount of limping which the latter had to do.

With the final load inboard and the helicopter secured, the recovery teams trooped below to get warm and dry. Awaiting them was some extremely good news. A white flag was flying over Stanley and negotiations were taking place. *Cardiff* had splashed a Mirage during the afternoon and I wondered if this would be the last air engagement of the war. In the previous forty-eight hours, the Argentinians had had over 400 troops captured during their retreat from the hills overlooking Stanley but the 'white flag' only applied to forces on East Falkland; no mention was made of West Falkland, the offshore islands or the mainland. Whilst the threat from East Falkland was gone, we were not immune from air attack from the mainland or airstrips such as Pebble Island.

Although there was a temporary truce, we could not afford to drop our guard. As if to reinforce the point, an electrical fire started outside M2 breaker room though it was quickly extinguished. Another problem was stability and being low on fuel, we had to ballast Number 3 fuel tank with seawater. After six hectic weeks, we had defeated the human enemy but not the South Atlantic weather. By 2230 the wind was up to storm force 10, gusting force 11 and the ship was groaning while water poured through the hole in the hangar deck. The storm blew all night and in the accompanying blizzards the ship suffered from icing. It was as bad as it could be but we survived the night.

Tuesday, 15 June

The wind moderated to a full gale but the barometer continued to fall throughout the forenoon, bottoming out at lunchtime before the wind increased again to a severe gale. The sea state was impressive. Our fuel was below 50 per cent and we hoped for some moderation in the weather; two more fuel tanks were ballasted to improve the ship's stability. Whilst Petty Officer Wiltshire was pumping water into the fuel tanks, Petty Officer Balston was pumping out rain and seawater which was cascading into the ship through damage holes.

Overnight, our borrowed Wessex became the last aircraft casualty of the war. With no hangar in which to shelter, it had been frequently 'goffered' on the exposed flight deck. By dawn, one of its rotors was clearly broken, the most obvious external evidence of damage, but the sea and salt water would also have caused less obvious damage. We thus lost our second helicopter. We were not overly concerned about this, however. At 0100, all Argentine land forces on the Falkland Islands surrendered. There were 11,000 in Stanley, 2,000 on West Falkland, 1,000 prisoners at San Carlos and another 800 prisoners at San Salvador. The number of Argentine dead was not known but we believed there had been about 18,000 Argentinians defending the Islands. The news of the surrender would be greeted with relief by the families but with immense sadness by those on both sides who had lost loved ones.

We were not surprised, either, to hear that the Argentinians in Stanley had no tents and had had to suffer blizzard conditions without proper shelter. We always felt the Argentinian co-ordinated logistic support was a weak area and we heard that they only had food left for another three days. It was easy to see why General Menendez saw his position as untenable but it was a far cry from the optimistic position he held six weeks before. Our job now was to see how quickly the prisoners could be repatriated; an extra 11,000 mouths to feed was a logistical nightmare. Later, we discovered that the Argentinians had considerable supplies of food on the islands. The immediate solution was for *Canberra* to take 5,000 prisoners to South America and return for a second trip, with *Norland* as back-up. Special category and senior officers were not being returned during this stage of repatriation. Another condition of surrender was that the Argentinians left all their impedimenta behind.

With prisoners being repatriated, there was a growing belief that the war was over; tension was ebbing and people had time for their thoughts. Some hated the enemy; but who was the enemy? Was it the dictatorship? Was it the Argentinian serviceman? For myself, I could not bring myself to hate the average Argentinian who had, on the whole, fought with courage. They had lost because we controlled the sea. To control the sea, you must control the air. On 1 May we took firm control of the sea surface, tightening our grip as each day passed. The Argentinians had had control of the air over the Islands while air control over the sea had been disputed. Slowly the air war swung in our favour and by the time of the landings we were disputing air superiority over the Islands. Enemy raids were, on the whole, severely mauled. The major lesson, learned yet again, was that it was not cost effective to fight aircraft with ships. With a proper fleet carrier at our disposal, how many ships might have been saved?

I thanked God that the war was possibly over. I was glad *Glamorgan* had stuck it out from start to finish and appreciated the team effort which had saved the ship. I felt that Mike Barrow had been a tower of strength and an inspiration throughout. The same applied to his wife. It took fortitude for the wives to keep the home front going. They would not get official recognition but we would never forget their support.

Many sympathetic signals continued to arrive. From *Brilliant*: 'All hands join me in saluting your great bravery in rising above such a horrendous attack. It is indeed good to see you again more or less in one piece.' However, the signal that we were all waiting for was the one that confirmed the surrender. It arrived on board at 0210.

In Port Stanley at 9 O'clock PM Falkland Islands time tonight 14 June 1982, Major General Menendez surrendered to me all the Argentine armed forces in East and West Falkland, together with their impedimenta. Arrangements are in hand to assemble the men for return to Argentina, to gather in their arms and equipment, and to mark and make safe their munitions. The Falkland Islands are once more under the Government desired by their inhabitants. God save the Queen. Signed J J Moore.

We fought the elements all day, steaming slowly into a head sea, but by dusk, the barometer was slowly rising and the wind slowly veering. I was contemplating turning down sea rather than steaming into it but the sea state was still too high to undertake the evolution with safety and Mike Barrow agreed we should keep our nose into the sea overnight.

* * *

A disaster brings out the best and worst in people. On the positive side, the Ship's Welfare Fund allocated £1,500 to the dependents of our dead while a collection on board generously raised a further £8,200. But no financial contribution could make up for the suffering of the bereaved; all we could hope to do was alleviate short-term financial suffering. Giving money was the easy task. Lieutenant Alan Watt, the Deputy Supply Officer, had the unpleasant but necessary task of sorting out the personal belongings of the dead and wounded which he nonetheless did in a thorough and sympathetic manner.

On the negative side, the tailor's shop had been looted after we had been hit and that left a very bad taste on board. The only redeeming factor was the return of the stolen gear after a pragmatic approach by the Master at Arms and then the incident was closed. The war saw some similar incidents amongst other units on both sides and perhaps the stress of war was the underlying cause.

Wednesday, 16 June

The gale moderated but the seas remained very high. We had *Atlantic Causeway* in company and she had a serviceable Wessex, though no aircrew, so we sent across the crew from our storm-damaged Wessex. It was an exciting boat ride for them, reminding them that, although they flew aircraft, they were still sailors. In off-duty moments, many of the ship's company surveyed the damage and the M2 breaker room in particular provided sobering moments of thought - the shrapnel had reached within 2in of the Seaslug magazine bulkhead.

At 1700 we started refuelling from *Tidepool* and it took more than six hours. Helicopter operations delayed the start by an hour. We tried the astern gunline method which was highly dangerous as both ships yawed about wildly on the downwind course. When we finally got close enough to pass the gunline, *Tidepool* then failed to pay out the hoseline which parted. Having sorted ourselves out we had a second go but *Tidepool* had further hoseline problems. We then tried reducing speed to 8 knots but the radio operator inside the bridge failed to inform the bridge wing, from where the ship was being conned, of the speed reduction and my first realisation of this was when we suddenly started to overrun the hose as the tanker's speed dropped. Revolutions were immediately reduced but as we dropped back the hoseline snagged and parted again.

We gave up the astern method as a bad job and asked *Tidepool* to prepare the alongside probe rig. We successfully settled into station but as *Tidepool* was passing the hose, rough seas led to the tanker getting a turn in her rig. More delay! Eventually the rig came across but this time the connection was defective and refused to mate. We broke away and asked *Tidepool* to prepare his quick release coupling rig on the other side. 'Third rig lucky!' This time we passed the rig without incident and embarked 450 tons of fuel. Shiphandling in these conditions was extremely difficult, and teamwork essential, but I actually found some sadistic pleasure in achieving our aim despite the unpleasantness and difficulty of our task. Even in the computer age, there are times where mariners have to rely upon brute strength and mental determination to overcome acute discomfort. It is easy to picture the glamorous side of a naval career but on this day I was frozen solid as were most of the upper deck crews. We trooped below to thaw out and were pleased to find mail dated 28 May waiting for us.

Logistics had been a nightmare in the appalling conditions but thanks to some excellent flying in darkness, despite atrocious weather, re-supply of rations to all units had been achieved. The arrival of support ships in Stanley harbour would markedly improve the logistic situation. Work had started on clearing the airport and the minefields but land mines would remain a problem for decades. It only takes seconds to lay mines from an aircraft but it takes years to clear them, and there is the ever-present risk that a few might remain to maim unfortunate innocents.

At last the weather moderated and normality returned to the TRALA, though we were now rapidly losing ships as they were deployed inshore.

Chapter 15

Clearing Up

Thursday, 17 June

Overnight *Glamorgan* groaned as she hogged and sagged in the heavy swell. We re-joined the carrier battle group and by dawn sea conditions were improving. I spent the morning plotting the mine positions and it was surprising to discover how few mines had actually been laid at sea; it was certainly out of all proportion to the impact which had been achieved. For the Argentinians, they had been a very successful sea denial weapon. Two minefields had been laid, both within the six-mile circle off Cape Pembroke. One field contained eight mines laid in two rows while the second field contained thirteen mines, also in two rows – just twenty-one mines in total. The mistake the Argentinians had made was in leaving us a mine-free area inshore of the field in which we could operate.

I also plotted the anchor berths issued by *Hermes* which was not simplified by some signalled anchorage positions amongst the hills around Stanley. Reciprocal bearings had been used, which called for a rude signal by light to *Hermes* but it drew no reply; I had struck a raw nerve.

For a change, the signal traffic made pleasant reading. The Chiefs of Staff signalled:

> At this historic moment, … send you … our warmest congratulations on the exemplary and brilliant way you have carried out all the tasks given to you by Her Majesty's Government against very considerable odds. We are enormously proud of the gallantry, stamina and professionalism shown … . Our thoughts at this time are also very much with the families of those who have lost their lives and those who have suffered wounds in the service of their country. We echo the admiration and gratitude of the nation when we say 'well done'.

The Argentine Junta called a meeting to discuss three options: to keep fighting, keep fighting whilst negotiating a peace, or sue for peace now. The majority favoured 'peace now'. At this stage we had not heard about the Junta's decision and the official ceasefire only extended fifty miles from the Falklands. Later in the day we were to hear that General Galtieri had resigned and that the news was received with cheers by the Argentinian prisoners in *Canberra*. Now that the fighting had ended my mind could not help but dwell on recent events, particularly the night we were hit. It had seemed surreal looking at the dead. When I had reached the hangar office door I had tried to move the casualty but bodies are surprisingly heavy and the task had been impossible with only one spare hand while the other held a fully charged hose. Inside the office, despite the fire, smoke had made it dark and the presence of bodies at the forward end of the office had not fully registered. The priority had been to get the hose through the shrapnel hole into the inferno in the adjacent compartment and subconsciously, I had dismissed a pile upon which I climbed, in the heat of the moment, as rags. What I had done was now coming home to roost and it resides to this day. Turning the ship had effectively sealed the fate of those men. Having been instrumental in their deaths, albeit in an attempt to save the ship, I had then climbed upon their bodies to fight the fire. How can one ever come to terms with that, even if it was for the common good?

Likewise, I thought about the wounded John Kelly. Could fire-fighting have waited a few minutes whilst I gave him first aid? As it was, I was high up when I poked the hose through the shrapnel hole, causing an eruption of smoke and steam, which drove me back coughing and spluttering once I had subdued the fire. It left me in no condition to assist John. All I could do was to call for first aid parties. Questions, questions, questions - if I had done this, if I had not done that, what would the outcome have been? Now that there was time to think everyone was soul searching; for many, this manifested itself as post-traumatic stress. We would be re-fighting this war for decades.

There was considerable understanding of what we had experienced and achieved, particularly by all those who had seen action. With pressure off the broadcast, there was space for supportive signals and, likewise, signal lanterns were kept busy. One example of an exchange by light was between *Invincible* and ourselves: 'Glad to see you still have your tails up!' and *Glamorgan* 'Tail's bent – head's OK!' Formal signals were distributed more widely and the MoD (Navy Department) signalled:

Now that the Falkland Islands are repossessed the Admiralty Board wishes to congratulate everyone in the Naval Service, whether uniformed, civilian or in the Merchant Marine, who have had a part to play in this brilliantly successful operation. Those who have seen action have shown qualities of skill, fortitude and bravery that have won the admiration of the whole nation. The hard work, dedicated professionalism and ingenuity of all those involved in support of the front line have also been superb. It has been a magnificent team effort. We all feel great sadness for the many who have been killed or injured. Their sacrifice has been for a good and just cause and our thoughts are with them and their families. We will remember them.

We were still unable to come alongside *Stena Seaspread* and the rumours were that we would be going into Berkeley Sound, and thence to San Carlos, to complete the welding jobs in calmer water. It would be a pleasant change to go inshore without 155mm howitzer shells landing around us. The seas moderated sufficiently to allow a crane transfer with *Stena Seaspread* to embark some more acetylene and the maintainers succeeded in restoring supplies to Seaslug while half of M2 breaker room was once again operational. Mike Barrow now believed we would stay for about ten days before being sent home and with these pleasant thoughts we detached with *Active* and *Stena Seaspread* for San Carlos.

Friday, 18 June
Admiral Woodward ordered us to 'get fixed and then go home'. Morale soared. There were to be two days of repairs, two days to 'back RAS', a day to collect mail and then, by 23 June, we would be heading for Ascension. By now we had improvised an emergency firing mode for the starboard Seacat and successfully test-fired it. Good progress was being made on Seaslug which we hoped would soon be operational.

At dawn, East Falkland was in sight and for the first time we could enjoy the view. Four hours later we led *Active* and *Stena Seaspread* into the crowded anchorage at San Carlos, anchoring next to *Blue Rover*. Helicopters were buzzing everywhere and *Stena Seaspread* came alongside without problem and repairs resumed apace. The gas turbines and L2 diesel were soon back on line and the Seaslug transmitting station was flashed up and proved, which was no mean feat of the maintainers. Work on the main galley was progressing well and it was soon back in use.

It was comforting to see Rapier batteries established on the surrounding hills and easy to picture the battles which had taken place a few days before. San Carlos was very beautiful though desolate, but desolation in this overcrowded world has a special beauty. However, with an 8,000-mile passage to plan, I could not spend long enjoying the scenery. I also had to prepare to anchor in Port William.

We could now use the upper deck though masking tape remained around the deadlights and we still had to carry our respirators, lifejackets and anti-flash gear. I contemplated eating the bar of chocolate and sharing the mints that I had secured inside my lifejacket as emergency rations but decided to keep them there just in case. Life on board and on the islands was slowly returning to normal. The Islanders were glad to see the Argentinians go, though island life would not be the same again with the inevitable enlarged garrison; but this was the price of freedom.

Saturday, 19 June

Overnight, we received a vertrep (vertical replenishment by helicopter) from *Fort Grange* which brought fresh provisions and urgent stores and allowed us to disembark unwanted stores. *Arrow* was returning home today, leaving us, the last of the Three Musketeers, on station. Commander-in-Chief, Fleet, signalled:

> As you prepare to sail for home you can be very proud of your performance and your most significant contribution to the success of Op Corporate. I was much saddened by your losses but pleased and relieved that you have overcome so much of the material damage. Your kind personal signal much appreciated. Would like my ceremonial lifebelt back sometime, that is if you did not ditch it going into battle! Well done and a quick passage.

Captain Barrow had previously offered congratulations on Admiral Fieldhouse's award of the GCB. The lifebelt had been embarked in Gibraltar, and never offloaded and was duly returned when *Glamorgan* reached Portsmouth and we certainly took the hint about a quick passage - economical steaming could be ignored.

A congratulatory signal was also received by the Task Force as a whole:

Personal from C-in-C. I have had the honour to receive the following message from Her Majesty the Queen and pass it to you all with great pleasure. 'I send my warmest congratulations to you and all under your command for the splendid way in which you have achieved the liberation of the Falkland Islands. Britain is very proud of the way you have served your country.' Signed Elizabeth R.

I thought of my Argentine counterparts and wondered what sort of reception they were experiencing. Some had fought with great courage and determination, but who, I wondered, would show them the gratitude they deserved for their selfless devotion to duty.

Stena Seaspread did us proud and it was our turn to thank her properly. The officers from *Stena* came into the wardroom for drinks and now the half pint of lager limit was history. The other messes similarly looked after their *Stena* counterparts. Two of our officers, Lieutenant Commander Paul Raine and Lieutenant Ray Harriss, had been lent to *Minerva* for fighter control duties. They missed our traumatic night on the gun-line but managed to return for the party with *Stena*.

We had further visitors in the afternoon. An Army Scout landed on board with the CO of the Welsh Guards and his RSM who had come to offer us their condolences and to say 'hello' and 'goodbye'. Condolences were also due to them for they had been hit much harder than ourselves, suffering forty-one killed. The RSM complimented *Glamorgan* on the accuracy of our bombardment on the night we were hit and told us that its effect on the Argentinians had been devastating, making the task of those ashore that much easier. He had seen us being hit and felt for us in our moment of trial. Before the CO and RSM left, their helicopter was loaded with a case of whisky and ten crates of beer, all it could take. It was a small gesture to the Welsh Guards with whom we had established a strong rapport and friendship.

That afternoon, *Broadsword* anchored in San Carlos. She too needed *Stena*'s assistance, having been damaged. We said our farewells to *Stena*, recording as she slipped, 'A great ship!' Those few words said it all and Mike Barrow sent a short signal by light, 'Thank you all for so much. Take a make and mend'. Their reply, 'Good bye, God speed. Thank you for the beer and personal message. Hope you have a good homecoming.' We manned the side and cheered ship for *Stena*.

After *Stena* sailed, the sole surviving Chinook helicopter arrived to remove the storm-damaged Wessex. It was lifted, rotorless, to San Carlos Settlement to await the arrival of *Atlantic Causeway*, for eventual return to Fleetlands. Shortly afterwards, as the sun set in the comparative still of the evening, I photographed San Carlos and Falkland Sound with the bridge wing Bren angled skywards in the foreground and the battered *Broadsword* in the middle distance. It summed up beautifully the uneasy peace that prevailed.

A photocopy of the Instrument of Surrender appeared on board, together with information about the opposition which told us that six more Exocet missiles had been found ashore. I acquired my own copy of the surrender document and particularly enjoyed one aspect of it. The Royal Navy had always joked about the Royal Marines being academically challenged and we could not help laughing when we saw Her 'Britanic' Majesty's Government.

The day at the anchorage gave some crew members the chance to fraternise with colleagues in the other services. Leading Seaman Dave Simpson managed to get across to *Sir Lancelot* to see his brother while one of our crew heard a rather unpleasant story recounted by a paratrooper. Allegedly, during one of the attacks, three paratroopers became temporarily isolated and were captured by the Argentinians and shot in the back of the neck. Shortly afterwards, the attacking paratroopers found their bodies and caught the patrol responsible. On being questioned, one Argentine soldier cracked and split on his three comrades and the paratroopers shot the entire patrol on the spot. Another story told of a downed helicopter pilot being bayonetted as he struggled ashore. This I did not believe but there was perhaps more truth in the report of other survivors in the water coming under fire. Was this the propaganda war still at work? My reflections were curtailed as special sea dutymen closed up in preparation for departure from San Carlos.

As we weighed anchor *Broadsword*'s aldis sprang into life: 'Have an enjoyable trip home in the sun and have a well earned leave.' Our reply, 'Very many thanks. We shall follow your fortunes with interest and feeling. See you soon.' Captain Bill Canning was an old friend of Mike Barrow and I remembered with fondness my time with Bill in *Cambrian* in the late 1960s.

At 2000 we sailed for Berkeley Sound with *Plymouth*, *Active*, *Elk*, *Baltic Ferry* and *Blue Rover* in company. Some of these ships accompanied us into Port William and others re-joined the carrier battle group. At last we were heading towards home.

Sunday, 20 June

We entered Berkeley Sound at 0900, conducting a boat transfer with *Dumbarton Castle* to collect *Plymouth*'s mail, before anchoring in the outer harbour at Port William. Once anchored, I calculated the distance to Portsmouth to be 6,774 miles. I then instructed the Yeoman to hoist the signal code for 'I am bound for GB' to make those remaining behind a little jealous.

Throughout the morning helicopters arrived with mail and stores but no spares for the 992. We then saw the Argentine hospital ship *Almirante Irizar* entering the bay causing us to lower our flag hoist. She passed close up our port side, cameras trained upon our battle scarred hangar. She had come to collect wounded prisoners and once gone, our signal was re-hoisted.

We eventually discovered where the 992 spares were supposed to be and *Fearless* did her best to hijack a helicopter to collect them for us by sunset. The Supply Officer, Commander Mike Croxford, and Chief Petty Officer Colin Phillips, went ashore to chase things up whilst we sat and watched the abundant marine life. That morning a large flock of rockhopper penguins had swum past the ship. There was nothing particularly remarkable in that; more remarkable was a crew member's claim to have seen three penguins flying up the port side the previous afternoon.

Mike Croxford and Colin Phillips eventually returned with two of the six required spares for the 992 but they were not pleased. Having re-captured the Islands, the RAF no longer needed to drop boxes of stores into the sea where some were lost and, instead, with a couple of islands the size of Wales, they dropped them in a minefield. All Mike could do was look at the boxes, shrouded in parachutes, and wonder which one contained our vital spares. Before returning to *Glamorgan*, Colin picked up a stone from the drive to the Governor's House. He pondered, 'Fourteen lives for a small piece of stone! Was it worth it? Yes.' In contrast, Petty Officer Wiltshire closed his diary with the words, 'Victory is ours, the Falklands are British, God Save the Queen, Rule Britannia.'

We weighed at 2300 to rejoin the carrier battle group and on the way heard that the Argentinians on South Thule had surrendered.

Monday, 21 June

At 0400, we closed *Tidespring* for another cold night replenishment and I realised that next time we replenished, it would be significantly warmer. However, for our last Falklands RAS, the weather was not too bad. In a way, I would miss the stormy replenishments and pitting my considerable professional skills against the elements. Having topped up, we took up our station and waited for *Plymouth* to collect her mail.

Hermes signalled overnight: 'We have been through a lot together and you have been through a lot more. BZ [well done] on an outstanding contribution. We shall miss you down here and look forward to seeing you on our return. Bon voyage.' The many inter-ship signals in the immediate aftermath clearly showed the deep feeling, togetherness and sense of teamwork which prevailed within the carrier battle group and it was this team spirit which had made the CVBG so effective.

Brilliant's Lynx delivered bags of outgoing mail and two passengers, Captain Andy Buchanan and Colonel Tom Seccombe. We also embarked Petty Officer Caterer Dunn who had an injured knee. He asked permission to bring some Argentinian wine on board, which he had 'liberated'! After this transfer, a steady stream of helicopters followed. My mind went back to early May when the homegoers were delivering essentials to us. Now we were northbound, offloading essentials to those who had to stay.

We remained in the northern part of our sector anticipating the order, 'go home!'. At 1330 we were released with *Plymouth* in com-pany. It would be rude to go without saying good-bye so we made a close pass, something in the order of 100ft, up *Hermes* starboard side at 24 knots. Our turret was trained 15 degrees to starboard and with permission to salute the flag, we used our gun, loaded with high explosive for the purpose. When abeam of *Hermes*, we woke them up with thirteen rounds. Numerous banners were displayed over our port superstructure such as, 'We came, we saw, we conquered!'. *Hermes* gave us a thoroughly rousing cheer. For them, this was their first opportunity to see at close hand the extent of our damage. *Plymouth* followed and was given a similar and well-deserved reception.

We put *Plymouth* on loose line abreast at 4,000yds to make stationkeeping a very relaxed affair. Within a couple of hours, the CVBG was lost on radar and we were no longer a member of the South Atlantic Battle Group.

Tuesday, 22 June
Overnight, we made better speed than anticipated. It was obvious that there was a spot of 'RA's revs', those few extra turns on the shafts,

over and above those ordered, so that the married men could get home early, but I turned a blind eye to the tachometers. In following the Great Circle route home, the seawater temperature had dropped markedly, leaving a chill on the upper deck and a real possibility of icebergs. The danger was from the bits that broke off icebergs, the bergy bits and growlers. The latter were about 10 to 15ft across, hard to see and virtually impossible to detect on radar, but a 15ft lump of ice could rip open our hull. The bridge and lookouts were briefed to be especially vigilant and a close watch was kept on the temperature as this would give clues as to the presence of ice.

News came in overnight that Princess Diana had given birth to a son and this, we hoped, would be followed by an invitation to 'Splice the Main Brace'. However, it was not the time to consume alcohol. We were still at defence watches and under possible threat from both the Argentinians and the ice. By 1100, the RA's revs were getting a bit out of hand. Since 0400 they had crept up an extra knot and a half so I had a word with the Chief of the Watch. Midday saw us relax to reduced defence watches and we began to feel out of the war if not out of the cold. The temperature dropped to 4°C and icebergs were reported further east. If we were to see any, it would be within twelve hours.

That afternoon Mike Barrow received information detailing the future of many of his officers. He was to leave the ship on 27 July and we would all be very sorry to see him go. The strain over the last couple of months had taken its toll and he seemed much older than on the way south, but I think we had all aged. A number of the younger members of the ship's company had been little more than boys but there were certainly no 'boys' heading north, only fully-grown men.

I was due to remain on board until Christmas, so I could look forward to a relatively relaxed time in the forthcoming months but I would be sad to see the break-up of such a good crew. The first newcomers were due to arrive in Ascension, including David Tinker's relief. A few of us quietly talked about that and wondered how it would feel to join a ship and take over the cabin of a colleague who had been killed; no hand-over, just the memory of a brave young man killed in his prime.

The sun set behind a grey sky as we left the chill of the South Atlantic.

Wednesday, 23 June

As the first glimmer of dawn broke we crossed 45 degrees south on what promised to be a calm and mild morning. It was so peaceful and such a change from the previous couple of months. The cold South Atlantic with its violence and war seemed a distant memory. For some, there was time to relax but not the Midshipmen who had their Boards to pass.

That afternoon, Colonel Tom Seccombe, the Chief of Staff to General Moore, and Captain Buchanan, one of the Staff Captains to Admiral Woodward, who were returning to the UK with us, gave us a briefing on the war as seen at high level and I made notes as they were talking.

The aim of the British Government was to re-establish British rule in the Falklands and its Dependencies. Early priorities were to re-take South Georgia, establish a MEZ (maritime exclusion zone) and then to maintain a TEZ (total exclusion zone). The next priority was to plan to land on the Falklands but this did not include their re-capture. CINCFLEET very early issued a directive not to plan for a political solution.

Planning factors taken into account were that the earliest possible landing was 14 May without *Intrepid* or 16 May with *Intrepid*. The latest possible date was 23 May. The limiting factor was the ability of the carriers to conduct four weeks of continuous flying. The actual date chosen for the landing was 16 May.

The Fleet Operations and Logistics Officer informed the staff that the Fleet had provisions, fuel and water until 27 July. It was only when *Canberra* reached Ascension that the decision was taken to send her into the AOA (amphibious operating area). This resulted in a massive cross decking operation.

There were only two options seriously considered, Port Salvador or San Carlos. As it turned out, San Carlos was the only place possible. The amphibious landing had to be carried out at night in sea conditions where *Canberra* and *Norland* could unload into LCUs via galley ports in the ships' sides.

The amphibious force was one hour late at 'H' hour. It was planned for 40 Commando to go in at 0630 with 2 Para at 0640. There was a forty-five minute delay due to difficulties in disembarking the heavily laden troops, each with 90lbs of kit, down the side of *Canberra* into the LCUs (landing craft utility). This resulted in 3 Para landing in daylight. The cardinal rule of having air superiority for a successful amphibious landing was broken. The landings were supported by NGS (naval gun support) against Fanning Head. Special Forces had been landed twenty-four hours previously to neutralise the Argentinians in the Fanning Head area and this was successfully achieved. The first wave of troops landed unopposed; complete surprise was achieved. Whilst 2 Para occupied Fanning Head, 40 Commando moved outwards to establish a beach-head perimeter and 42 Commando were then landed, after which the LCUs started to land stores and ammunition. *Elk* alone was carrying 2,000 tons of ammunition and had she exploded, she would have taken half the anchorage with her.

The first air attacks were mounted at 1030, by which time all the logistic ships were safely at anchor. The intensity of the air attacks led to 45 Commando, who were being kept in reserve, to be landed. This allowed *Canberra* to sail at dusk on the direct orders of Maggie Thatcher, removing a potentially prize target from the opposition. *Canberra* took with her plenty of valuable stores that had not been landed, but no one begrudged her departure. Fifteen volunteer female crew members were on board.

The air attacks carried on throughout the day virtually continuously. The LCUs and mexi-floats (mechanised pontoons) continued to ferry stores and ammunition ashore throughout, despite being strafed. The Sea Kings flew all the first afternoon, including right through air raids, landing Rapier missile systems and artillery field pieces, the two top priorities. In all probability we had been very lucky on that first day. Most of the warships had suffered varying degrees of damage. Had the Argentinians managed to launch just one more heavy attack, with fewer warships in a fit state to oppose them, they might have hit a rich target.

Once the initial landings had been successfully achieved, Brigade HQ was moved ashore and mounted in snow-cat vehicles. These tracked landrovers were initially designed for use in the Cold War in the snows of Norway. They coped with the Falkland Islands' terrain admirably.

The logistical build-up continued for the next five days. It was hampered by the loss of three heavy lift Chinook helicopters in *Atlantic Conveyor*. Only one Chinook remained. General Moore, the overall Commander, was coming south in *Queen Elizabeth II*.

The commander ashore had orders to stay put and consolidate until the arrival of 5 Brigade. However, he came under increasing pressure from the Royal Navy to break out to take pressure off the warships which were taking the brunt of enemy attacks in San Carlos. Of the enemy aircraft, those flown by Naval pilots were by far the best. They came in very low and pressed home their attacks with great tenacity and courage.

The Royal Navy took heavy losses and the only way to take the weight off the Navy was to set out for Stanley, recognised as the key to the islands. The dilemma was when to move. Too soon would have resulted in a battle lost. Goose Green was very nearly a battle lost thanks to the BBC who told the Argentinians the British were on their way there. This enabled them to re-inforce their troops. As a result there was a very close and bloody battle. The attack on Goose Green could not have been achieved without artillery support and the battery supporting 2 Para was itself one gun short, very nearly costing us the battle. It became clear the Argentinians would only give up after giving a very good account of themselves. From a psychological perspective, Darwin/Goose Green was a key battle. It was also crucial from a political point of view. From that moment on, there was never any chance of a political ceasefire dictating events.

After Goose Green, the next target, allocated to 45 Commando, was Douglas Settlement and Teal Inlet. For some reason, Teal Inlet was never subjected to air attack. Then, 42 Commando were air lifted to Mount Kent where they stayed for twelve days in very bad conditions. Much to 40 Commando's disgust, they were left to guard San Carlos until the arrival of 5 Brigade. Whilst these advances were going on Pucaras continued to harass the support helicopters with some success, shooting down three of them. The logistic lift was 500 rounds per gun and by the end of the battle, rounds remaining were down to single figures. The subsequent target was Mount Longdon where 3 Para finished their attack with a bayonet charge after hard and persistent resistance. On Two Sisters ridge, 45 Commando had a slightly easier time and 42 Commando surprised the enemy by going round and coming up from the rear, capturing 300 prisoners for the loss of just one Royal Marine.

The Scots Guards were then ordered to take Tumbledown, followed by 2 Para taking Sapper Hill. After that, it all folded. In the final attacks around Stanley the eighteen field pieces had been supplied with 600 to 700 rounds apiece. Negotiators had been in touch with General Menendez for a couple of days and he actually surrendered at 2200 and not at 2359.

'Flight Lieutenant Fray Bentos' who ejected above *Fearless* said the pilots had been specifically ordered to attack the warships. This helped explain why STUFT (merchant ships) had a charmed life.

The report on NGS stated it was devastating, causing a huge amount of damage to both material and the mind. It kept the Argentinians awake and got them up every night. They never knew where the naval artillery shells would land next. Likewise, they never knew whether or not they would receive a return visit on the same night, sapping their will to win. *Glamorgan* was very popular with the troops ashore. Our salvos always landed where and when they were wanted. British troops were quite happy to call down fire from *Glamorgan* a bare 150 yards away.

The briefing was most informative. I had a chance to talk to Tom Seccombe later that evening when I was invited with Gerry Hunt to have supper with Captain Barrow, Tom Seccombe and Captain Andy Buchanan. The dress was red sea rig (tropical shirt, Number 12 trousers and cummerbund). It made a very pleasant change from sweaty Number 8s in which I had been living for months.

Thursday, 24 June
The elements had declared only a temporary truce; by dawn, the wind and sea were up sufficiently to make us reduce speed to 16 knots and the barometer was falling sharply. The South Atlantic was having her final fling. We had a rendezvous with *Appleleaf* and I could only afford to reduce speed for a few hours but even at 16 knots *Glamorgan* was making heavy weather of it. As the gale and sea rose we were forced down to 10 knots and it was *Appleleaf* herself who announced a shift in rendezvous of nearly 200 miles. We compromised and suggested a revised rendezvous and then informed Ascension of our ETA.

As we were no longer in a war zone we had undarkened ship. We were now wearing normal sea rig, gratefully hanging up our life-jackets, respirators and once-only survival suits, and peacetime routines resumed with battles being fought in weekly planning meetings. Issue of Daily Orders and *Glamorgan* Temporary Memoranda began although for two months we had survived perfectly well without them. Peacetime comforts, such as curtains over the windows and scuttles, also returned. The ship's immediate future was being considered; our repairs, combined with a period of docking and maintenance, would see us through to the end of summer. Despite our mail diversion signal, seven bags of our mail were sitting in Port Stanley and they would now arrive in the UK after we had returned to Portsmouth.

Friday, 25 June

Well before dawn *Glamorgan*, *Plymouth*, *Appleleaf* and *Pearleaf* met in the wide expanses of the South Atlantic. The RAS was delayed by an engine defect in *Appleleaf* but we completed at 0930 and were followed by *Plymouth*, concurrently conducting vertreps until 1345. We then left *Pearleaf* and *Appleleaf* to complete their pumpover whilst we sped towards Ascension though the weather again forced us to temporarily reduce speed.

Saturday, 26 June

Overnight, the wind eased and *Plymouth* invited the wardroom across for lunch. I was greeted by Iain Henderson, *Plymouth*'s First Lieutenant, who had served with me in *Cambrian*. We were shown *Plymouth*'s damage which was worse than ours, the ship having been gutted by fire almost the full length of 2 deck. One bomb had gone through the funnel and a second had entered the dining hall area. The third bomb had hit the flight deck and had either exploded or had detonated a depth charge. The fourth bomb had passed through the mortar handling room. To survive one hit by a 1,000lb bomb is no mean achievement: to survive four hits was quite something. Despite all they had been through, they were in very good cheer.

We had painted the union flag on the bridge roof and on our return from lunch in *Plymouth* I decided to protect the flag from the ever increasing rays of the sun. Lying on a warm steel deck in pleasant conditions was bliss. After a couple of hours on the bridge roof, it was back to business as *Invincible* and *Andromeda* hove into sight. Captain Jeremy Black and a load of fresh bread from *Invincible*'s galley arrived by Sea King. The bread was particularly welcome since our own galley could only provide a limited service.

We received permission to conduct a steampast close up *Invincible*'s starboard side but *Andromeda* was to starboard of *Invincible* limiting our searoom and when we had effectively reached the point of no return a seaboat suddenly appeared from behind

Andromeda, nearly ruining the evolution. Both ships were stopped and, as they were drifting sideways at about 2 knots, the seaboat and the leeway were effectively slamming the door in our face. It required some very fine judgment to get through the gap, our stern passing within 50ft of *Invincible*'s bow.

Sunday, 27 June

We were greeted by a glorious sunrise and the sight of *British Tamar* ready to refuel *Plymouth* and ourselves. By 1030, both ships had replenished by the astern method and then we went alongside for a light line transfer to swap films and collect mail. This was the first occasion I had replenished from a civilian tanker and I was impressed by their cheerful efficiency. With the RAS completed we manned ship whilst *Plymouth*'s Wasp took photographs and then met the *Plymouth* team for return hospitality in *Glamorgan*.

Monday, 28 June

At 1130 we allowed *Plymouth* to detach ahead since she had a Sod's Opera planned for the evening, which required minimum wind speed over the deck during the performance. During the fighting I had not bothered to maintain any of the chart folios outside the war zone and hence there was a large backlog of corrections waiting in the charthouse. My Yeoman, Norman Richardson, had made a start and I gave him a hand. Throughout the ship it was an ideal opportunity to catch up on all those little jobs which had been left during the fighting. The routine work made a change, and a change was as good as a rest. The Midshipmen were even swotting.

Tuesday, 29 June

First light found *Plymouth* back in company and, as we headed north, the *Southampton* group were heading south, having just sailed from Ascension. *Southampton*'s Lynx closed to take a close look at *Plymouth* and ourselves, a pair of battered war veterans. *Leeds Castle* then came out of Ascension to escort us in, firing its water cannon and as the huge jet of water arced across the ocean, we flashed, 'We could have done with that fire hose a couple of weeks ago!'

Alvega, the resident tanker, was anchored in Clarence Bay and we banged alongside her port side in the heavy swell. Shortly after, *Plymouth* banged alongside her starboard side. The swell conditions could be described as 'cruelty to fenders!' However, they did their job. The advanced leave party was disembarked and mail received.

For the first time since we had headed south from Ascension we had an opportunity to exercise the divers. The first requirement was to inspect the hull, checking for action damage and the ravages of the South Atlantic. I was with the first team in the water and we started with the rudder and screws. The forward fairing plates on both shafts and the port rope guard assembly had been blown off by the bombs on 1 May and hull plating near the centreline had been 'dished'. In addition, there was a large dent in the port side hull plates just above the waterline which had been submerged at the time of attack. There were some small shrapnel holes in the starboard rudder and the surface of the starboard propeller was peeling in places. It was all too evident just how lucky we had been, coming within an inch of having our screws blown off.

Having checked on the damage I was able to enjoy the dive in perfect conditions. The sea temperature was around 80°F and the nominal visibility was 100ft plus though immediately around the hull, visibility was greatly reduced by the sheer mass of fish. On completion of our dive, the other team had their turn and then we secured the gear in preparation for sailing.

Replacements for some of our lost comrades had joined. We made the newcomers feel welcome and with the sun low in the west, we said farewell to Ascension and started the final leg of our journey home. *Plymouth* was to divert to Gibraltar to be kitted out before returning to Rosyth; many of her ship's company's uniforms had gone up in smoke in San Carlos.

Chapter 16

Final Leg

Wednesday, 30 June

We steamed steadily towards the equator. *Plymouth* was signalled to take station astern and we set about increasing the number of Line crossings experienced by the two crews. At 2006 we crossed the Line, making a figure of eight thereby crossing the Line a further four times. For good measure we did the same again. Everyone could now boast that they had crossed the Line at least ten times. It had been a perfect day with plenty of sunshine and Chris Gotto agreed to a 'make and mend' (an afternoon off), a rare event. I used the time to calculate how long we had been in the South Atlantic – 7,093,299 seconds. I left it to the ship's company to convert it back into weeks and days.

Having crossed the Line we officially moved from winter back into summer and as we had been working in GMT we now advanced clocks to British Summer Time.

Thursday, 1 July

After a quiet night we stopped temporarily for a boat transfer with *Plymouth* in ideal conditions. At 1500 we reduced speed for the official crossing the Line ceremony. We decided to hold the ceremony during daylight as we had crossed the Line in darkness and appropriate preparations were made to transform the flight deck from a mini airport into a royal palace. Everyone was guilty of disrespect since we had not paid our respects on the way south. Some came in for special treatment and I was ducked for grounding at Bandah Jissah. Seeing the activity, *Plymouth* enquired whether we knew where we were as the Line was now 200 miles to the south. We laid the blame for the navigational error on the Midshipmen.

We considered stopping for hands to bathe but a 15ft hammerhead shark and another large shark had recently been seen and so we prudently decided to defer our bathing until we were further north.

Friday, 2 July
We tested our anti-gas respirators and mine was rendered useless by my beard. With any gas threat, beards would have been shaved but Argentina posed no such threat so they had been retained. Those with beards now found their eyes and noses running and everyone's clothes reeked of CS gas but the test was a necessary evil.

The gunnery department calculated our total rounds fired in anger which amounted to 1,243 rounds of 4.5in, six Seaslug and one Seacat. As the sun set the ops room had to resume thinking operationally as we were the target for a surface action group exercise by the next south-going group and at 2200 we detected two sweeps of 993 radar. Under wartime conditions, we would have reacted.

Saturday, 3 July
The 'enemy' eventually found us at 0730 and one of their Wasp helicopters hovered overhead as the group closed. The Wasp would not have been hovering overhead had it been for real, however. The *Danae* group closed, a turn-over was completed, we wished them luck and headed homewards. We spent the next couple of hours conducting RAS approaches, giving young officers confidence in shiphandling. It was also an opportunity for Seaman and Engineering Officers to exchange duties. On completion, the Captain went below to conduct rounds. Peace had surely returned.

Sunday, 4 July
The weather deteriorated overnight and as we had a rendezvous to make, we increased speed to keep up. It was noticeably cooler now as we headed into the northeast trade winds.

Monday, 5 July
After breakfast we rendezvoused with *Plumleaf.* Whilst *Plymouth* fuelled, we conducted more practice approaches. *Plymouth*, on detaching for Gibraltar, made a close pass up our starboard side but we were ready for her. We 'tested' our saluting guns, trained hoses on her, fired verey lights, sounded sirens and gave her a thoroughly good cheer. In exchange we received cheers, vereys, hoots and Welsh music.

As *Plymouth* was not fitted with SATNAV, I had been passing twice-daily positions to her. Now that she would no longer receive them I gave her a few more directions, 'Past the Canaries, first turning on your right, then first left!' Having been stationkeeping with *Plymouth* for the last two weeks, Mike Barrow sent the final station-keeping signal, 'Take Waverley Station'. Her final destination was Rosyth.

We were down to 26 per cent fuel remaining and embarked over 500 tons, our largest amount in one go. In exchange, we gave *Plumleaf* 15 tons of water. A bottle of spirits was exchanged for a Chinese takeaway for the Captain. *Plumleaf* was an old friend and their Hong Kong Chinese crew were famed for their specialities. We also exchanged films. We broke away at 1230 and were alone once more. We stopped for hands to bathe, which proved very popular, prudently maintaining a shark watch. Before the war, I had ordered a new suit from Leung How Chiu, our Chinese tailor. It was now ready and fitted perfectly. Superficially, it had been a perfect day but I was reminded now of the passage of time and the passing of friends: and the dreadful memories of the war remained as vivid as ever.

Wednesday, 7 July
By 0800 we were west of Lisbon and further north than we had been when diverted south in April. The weather continued to be kind and so was the Commander who granted a second 'make and mend' which allowed volleyball to be played on the flight deck and hands to bathe.

Thursday, 8 July
Dawn saw *Glamorgan* 475 miles from Portsmouth. Overnight we had encountered fog and rain with lightning in an unusually calm Bay of Biscay. I discussed our arrival in Portsmouth with Mike Barrow and though we could arrive the following afternoon we agreed that Saturday morning would be better, allowing more families and friends to greet us.

Friday, 9 July
In the early hours, Cornwall was detected on radar and as we entered the Channel we were reminded of the South Atlantic with visibility down to just over a mile in good old 'West Country mist'. Despite the poor visibility, we hove to close to the Lizard to receive a vertrep which brought mail, strawberries and the vibration analysis team. We then sped eastwards to embark CINCFLEET off Portland Bill.

As we approached Portland, *Sirius* asked permission to make a close pass. She manned the side and gave us three rousing cheers and the gesture was much appreciated. The warmth of the cheers was very genuine compared to those put on for VIPs; to be cheered by your comrades was something special. For our part, we hung a large notice over the side indicating air raid warnings to the south.

We then tried to talk to Portland on VHF but the aerial had shrapnel damage and we resorted to a hand-held stornophone. Visibility was good and CINCFLEET's Lynx easily found us. Admiral Fieldhouse did not say much but what he did say was to the point. We had proved to the world that a dictator could not grab any country he felt like and our actions would have worldwide repercussions for years to come. He was delighted to be flying his flag in *Glamorgan* again but added that very soon he would leave because, 'tomorrow is your day!' He told us we were heroes and expressed deep sadness at our losses. After touring the ship, he was entertained to a strawberry tea on the flight deck attended by representatives of every mess on board. On completion, he went home for the first time since the crisis started. It was not only those in the front line who had been working extreme hours; fleet staff and others supporting us had also put in very long hours without a break.

With time in hand, I took the ship for a scenic cruise close inshore giving those on land an excellent view of a very rusty and battered warship and this seems to have prompted numerous telephone calls to the Coastguard and Naval Base. We then patrolled off the Needles overnight and spent some time assisting a dismasted Swiss yacht.

After supper, Commander Lyons (who had relieved Mike Croxford) gave a talk about the war as seen from the MoD. He passed on some generally unknown facts. Although the Americans were ostensibly neutral, behind the scenes they gave us all the material help requested. In addition to communications and intelligence, the most obvious items were Sidewinder and Shrike missiles. Sidewinders made a tremendous difference to the operational capability of the Harriers, while the Americans had their latest systems tested in wartime conditions. They also offered Harrier aircraft and an *Iwo Jima* LPH (amphibious assault carrier).

Commander Lyons explained that South American countries had been lukewarm in their support for Argentina, and that Chile had been distinctly frosty. The only help the Argentinians received was from Peru who gave a few Mirages. The French confirmed that the

Argentinians had only five Exocets and that they had increased an offer from £200,000 per missile to £1,000,000.

To silence the 'Wets' in her cabinet, Maggie Thatcher had witheld the news of the two Wessex losses in South Georgia until after the operation. The government was warned to expect 25 per cent losses but despite this, the loss of *Sheffield* had come as a major shock and only the Prime Minister's resolve had overcome the doubters.

The Naval Staff had met opposition from junior ministers when obtaining authority to bring ships out of reserve and even after five weeks into Corporate these difficulties were still being experienced. Mr Nott had eventually overruled his junior ministers, which must have been a very bitter political pill for him to swallow after the Defence White Paper on the number of ships required by the Royal Navy. The briefing was very enlightening and people drifted back to their cabins for a final night at sea. I returned to the bridge to check that all was well before setting my alarm for 0530.

Saturday, 10 July

As we passed the Fairway Buoy we attempted, unsuccessfully, to pass our position to Southampton Port Radio as required by the Solent traffic management. We called Solent Coastguard, explaining that our aerials were battle damaged and asked them to pass our intentions to Southampton. Radio Solent translated this into, 'Solent Coastguard are guiding the damaged *Glamorgan*, limping into the Solent!' We were anything but limping.

At 0800 we anchored at Spithead, the only ship of interest in the Solent that morning. Ferries diverted to make close passes, everyone waving and cheering. Yes, it was to be our day and our families' day. It was also going to be a very sad return as we remembered our lost comrades.

The press arrived in force at 0915. We wanted to be factual but we also had to consider security. Unsure of what we could or could not say, if there was any doubt we evaded the question. They concentrated on missile evasion but no one asked a single question about events after the missile hit, when there were plenty of stories of ingenuity and courage. They did not ask, so we did not volunteer information. We were the only ship to have ever survived a hit by an Exocet yet the press were oblivious as to how we had achieved this feat. They also seemed quite blind to our feelings. I left the press conference in tears, and went to my cabin to compose myself before returning to the bridge.

Once underway, we raced past Outer Spit Buoy at 15 knots. We were led in by *Adept*, water cannons going full blast. She also had her propulsion going full blast and as we rapidly closed her stern, she asked us to slow down; by escorting us in with his biggest tug, the Queen's Harbourmaster had unintentionally stopped us from speeding.

Thousands of people lined the harbour to welcome us. We made a ceremonial entry with our Welsh flag proudly flying from the mainmast and a button boy atop the 992 platform. We were surrounded by an armada of small boats, adding to the atmosphere, and the welcome came at us from all quarters by light, flag hoists, banners and posters. The entire foreshore and every vessel afloat was packed with people; even the Isle of White ferry *Brading* gave way to us. That made a change.

An American sailor in a destroyer, berthed close to the Semaphore Tower, asked what all the fuss was about. He was given a very succinct reply that summed up the entire affair, 'They won!'

As we rounded North Corner we could see and hear the band playing at our berth and behind them all the families were madly waving and cheering. This was the really meaningful welcome that we relished. Unfortunately, the families had to wait a little longer. We quickly came alongside but then spent five minutes adjusting position for the brow (gangplank). Despite doing everything to attract my attention, it took me fifteen minutes to spot Marianne and Katherine amongst the crowds. (My younger daughter Sarah, suffering from chicken pox, could not attend.) Eventually, the Deputy Captain of the Port was happy and the order was given to double up and secure. At 1115, Mike Barrow gave me approval to ring off. I passed 'Midships, Ring Off' on conning intercom, then passed to the machinery control room, 'Finished with main engines and steering, eight hours notice.'

Petty Officer Alan Carlisle was on the wheel. For him it was a day to remember although he could not see much whilst concentrating on his steering, but once the ship was secured, he was able to witness the extent of the joyous welcome. It was also at that moment that the full impact of losing shipmates struck home. I had sworn, come hell or high water, to see the ship back to Portsmouth and now that she was safely alongside I realised that the war was all over. I had given everything I had and the will to strive on was gone in an instant; my priority was to greet my family.

Chapter 17

Aftermath

Those who could go ashore quickly departed with their families. All over town, houses were bedecked with flags and it was easy to determine that they were the ones which accommodated members of the Task Force. My own family had put out the flags at home and made a welcome-home cake.

One of the many calls I received that weekend was from a London evening newspaper asking for a photoshoot with my family. I co-operated to minimise further intrusion and on completion, the reporter asked, 'Were you under threat of court martial when you were in action off the Falklands?' 'Yes,' I replied. The daily papers picked up on this and made the most of a story about sending people to war under court martial threat for striking an uncharted rock.

As the first ship back which had seen action from start to finish, we were the object of people's curiosity and interest. A day later, *Canberra* entered Southampton followed some time later by a very rusty *Hermes* which received a cheeky welcome from *Glamorgan*, 'Do not go too far up the harbour, there are scrap merchants there too!'

The first leave party returned at the end of July and were saddened to hear that Able Seaman McCann had died. With the majority of ships back, invitations flooded in. Some were genuine expressions of thanks and respect, others less so. A nightclub in Southsea invited Captains of Task Force ships as guests of honour to their 'Task Force Night' but they wisely ducked the invitation, sending a representative instead. It became distastefully clear that the presence of officers from the Task Force in uniform was purely to pull in more punters. In London, although Stringfellows entertained members of the Task Force with more sincerity, one of the invited 'pop stars' claimed that 'It was not as bad in the South Atlantic as the press made out' and the *Glamorgan* representative, with vivid memories of the recent horrors, was reduced to tears by this insensitive remark.

* * *

Fine men died in the ships that were hit. Others were scarred for life; some with physical scars, others with psychological scars. Many of *Glamorgan*'s crew were significantly affected by post traumatic stress but none attempted to receive financial gain for their suffering. After his horrific experiences, John Holden developed post traumatic stress and when serving in *Drake* he sought help. Unfortunately, the doctor who saw John was 'No help whatsoever', considering traumatic stress sufferers to be malingerers. Conversely, a few years later, I found the *Drake* Medical Officer most supportive. Another sufferer was Petty Officer Carlisle. He wrote in 2000,

> The thoughts and memories will always be with me ... . I have in the past found it very difficult to talk about what happened during 1982 ... In the ten years after the war my life was a mess. My whole character changed. I was sad, quiet, angry, moody. I drank too much, had nightmares and saw grotesque faces in the night. Strangely enough, it was the start of the Gulf War that was to be my salvation. It sparked off all the bad memories in my head. Every one of life's small problems seemed bigger and worse to me, and it was my wife Karen who suggested that I seek help. I honestly did not think I had a problem. My GP sent me to Haslar where I joined other veterans on a four-week Post Traumatic Stress ... course run by Commander O'Connell and his team.
>
> The course proved to be a lifeline for me and my family. It made me realise that I did have a problem and that talking about it was the only thing to do. Eighteen years on, and I finally feel I have come to terms with what happened ... Life goes on - but the faces of the dead never leave you.

Mrs McCallum was eight months pregnant when her husband Kelvin was killed. Her baby, Gemma Louise McCallum, was christened on board *Glamorgan* after the war. This required great courage and reflected the strength of feeling for *Glamorgan* amongst the crew and their families. It was this strong sense of unity that was instrumental in the establishment of the *Glamorgan* Falklands Association which is active today, providing friendship and support. The assistance of Alan Watt and others helped Mike Barrow get the Association started. Well attended re-unions are held every five years, providing an opportunity to support old friends. The Association also helps the next of kin of those who have died.

Petty Officer Dunn was drafted from *Glamorgan* to *Sultan* on our return and when the South Atlantic medals arrived, the Captain of *Sultan* held a parade and personally pinned on each man's medal. Others were disappointed to receive their medals through the post rather than at a formal ceremony though my 'medal ceremony' was even worse. Many had received their medals months previously. Then I heard a rumour that the medals for those serving in *Osprey* were in the Pay Office. There, I found a box full of them and so I extracted mine, without ceremony, and took it home to be mounted at my expense. Shortly afterwards, I was told my 'Mention in Dispatches' would be presented at the weekly staff meeting. And so it was. The Admiral read the citation and then flicked the 'Oak Leaf and Mention' across the table; the Staff meeting then continued.

Glamorgan came through Portland for work-up after a year of repairs. The day before the ship was due to fire her first Seaslug missile since the war, I was aboard and met Chan Lok Wing, the Number 1 Laundryman. We had a chat and as I turned to leave I said, 'No wandering about the launcher deck this time!' He reassured me in no uncertain terms that, unlike 1982, he would never again be on the launcher deck when the missiles were fired.

Sadly, *Glamorgan* did not remain in Royal Naval service for very long. She was sold to Chile as *Almirante Latorre*, where she featured on a Chilean postage stamp. She is not forgotten. On Pebble Island there is a cairn commemorating the raid, 'This cairn marks the site of the first landing of active British Forces in the liberation of the Falkland Islands on 13 May 1982. Units of the Second Special Air Squadron, flown by helicopters of 846 Naval Air Squadron and supported offshore by HMS *Glamorgan* succeeded in disabling 11 Pucara aircraft one of which is displayed in the Fleet Air Arm Museum, Yeovilton.' A memorial window in Portsmouth Cathedral, funded by the *Glamorgan* Association, was dedicated in 1998, and the name *Glamorgan* and those killed are recorded on memorials as far apart as St Paul's Cathedral in London and Port Stanley.

* * *

Some questioned whether the war was worthwhile. Weapons Electrical Mechanic Nigel Lowe returned to the Falklands in 1983 and after visiting some of the memorials, he walked up the main road and said, 'Good morning' to a passing couple but was totally ignored, the couple making it clear that servicemen were not welcome. Nigel was only eighteen when he saw his comrades buried; it was the first funeral he had ever attended and he felt badly let down and angry by these islanders for whom *Glamorgan* and her crew had given so much.

Conversely, I had a more positive experience in 1990, when I was offered lunch (mutton - what else!) by 'Biffo' during a duty visit to Saunders Island. During the war she had lived on Pebble Island. I apologised for any inconvenience caused by our bombardment and was horrified to learn that after the raid the islanders had been locked up, the Argentinians believing they had helped us. The islanders had been spectators, enjoying every minute, and Biffo considered it well worthwhile being locked up for a few weeks. Later, I visited Pebble Island, collecting some Juniper tree seeds which I successfully germinated. I gave one tree to Mike Barrow.

In March 2000 the Falkland Islands Memorial Chapel was formally opened as a focus for memorial at Pangbourne College by the Queen. Here servicemen, families, and future generations can reflect in tranquillity upon the events of 1982. In time, I hope there will be a memorial within the chapel to remember those servicemen and families on the Argentine side who also suffered. Responsibility for war lies at the feet of politicians. Servicemen do their duty and pay the price.

The Falklands Hymn

We entrust to the Lord our lost brothers.
They responded to duty's stern call,
And so far from their homes and their loved ones
Paid the price that is highest of all.
Flesh had failed them, but God was their saviour;
Bringing rescue from battle's alarms;
Beyond death he is always their refuge,
Underneath, everlasting, his arms.

We commend to the Lord those who mourn them,
Loving parents and children and wives,
From whose pride in their selfless commitment
Has been countered by grief for lost lives.
When so many returned, theirs was absent,
Leaving long years of anguish to face;
May the Lord heal the wounds of bereavement
With infinite power of his grace.

We commit to the Lord now our own lives,
And we vow in our turn to reply
To the call of the weak and the friendless,
Though the cost to ourselves may be high.
When the choosing is hard, may God grant us
The direction that strengthens and calms.
For we trust in the Lord as our refuge,
Underneath, everlasting, his arms.

Words by W H Moseley Esq.

☨ *We will remember them* ☨

POAEM(L) M.J. ADCOCK

Ck B. EASTON

AEM(M) M. HENDERSON

AEM(R) B.P. HINGE

LACAEMN D. LEE

AEA(M)2 K.I. McCALLUM

AB(R) D. McCANN

Ck B.J. MALCOLM

MEM(M)2 T.W. PERKINS

L/Ck M. SAMBLES

L/Ck A.E. SILLENCE

Std J.D. STROUD

Lt. D.H.R. TINKER

POACMN C.P. VICKERS

Glamorgan – Crew List

CPOCA B D ROBB
MEMN P A R SMITH
CWEMN J V SOWRAY
MEA R C SPOWART
WEA J F STEVENS
WEA P STUBBLES
WEMN R TARPEY
AEA(R) I L TATE
MEA(H) I R L THOMAS
WEMN G C WILLIAMS
CRS K WILLIAMS
CPOCK J S FROGGATT
CPOWTR S R HAMBLIN
CPOSTWD D HARRISON
MAA K J HOLT
CPOGI S A HORNE
CWEM(O) P D JAMES
CAEMN D LEE
CPO(EW) K C MARTIN
CPOCK D R MOORE
CMEM(M) R G PERRY
CWEA J L WETTON
CPO(SEA) D A WING
MEMN(M) K A GERRARD
MEMN(M) G MARTIN
MEMN(M) M A READ
MEMN(M) M A G SCOTT
WEMN R W TIPTON
POAEM(L) M J ADCOCK
PO(M) J ALLEN
POMEM(M) K S BALSTON
POSTWD B BENNETT
POSTWD P L BOWERS
PO(S) D P COWAN
POPT A CARLISLE
POMEM(M) D A NICHOLSON
   (On loan from *Fife*)
PO(R) M G FRYATT
RPO M J HAMMOND
POSA P HOPKINS
POCK J M PEARCE
POWEM(R) J A PORTER
POMEM(L) T S RALPH
WEA A B RAWCLIFFE
WEA R J SINCLAIR
PO(EW) J S UTLEY
POMA G WESTERMAN
POCK D J WILSON
POMEM(M) M R WILTSHIRE

POWEM(R) T P WOOD
POWEM(R) L A BERKS
WEA M S BLAND
RS D M BROWN
MEA(EL) S A BYGRAVE
MEMN(M) J CRANSTON
PO(S) D D CREESE
PO(S) A DOUGALL
POMEM(L) R DUNN
POCK P A EAGLE
POWEM(O) R J R GARDINER
POWEM(R) V J GRIMSHAW
PO(M) D HENDRY
POWEM(R) D J HORSLEY
POWEM(O) C M JAMES
WEA T P JAMES
WEA C A JAQUES
PO(R) T JONES
MEMN(M) P LAMB
SGT RM W H LECKY
WEA T M MEDCALF
AEA(M) K I McCALLUM
POMEM(M) D McLAUGHLAN
PO(R) T MICHAEL
POSA R W MORLEY
POMEM(M) P C MORE
POAEM(R) M R MORRIS
WEA M O'NEILL
POMEM(M) T J PETTERSON
WEA J B POLLARD
POMEM(M) T G K PRICE
POWEM(O) R D SMITH
POWEM(R) M H THORNE
WEA R J VERE
POACM C P VICKERS
PO(M) R F WETHERICK

*Junior Rates – Weapons Electrical
Branch*
WEM(R) I D FRANCIS (On loan
   from *Collingwood*)
LWEM(R) A BERRY
WEM(R) A J FORSYTH
LWEM(R) N C FRESHWATER
LWEM(R) S HEY
LWEM(R) R WALTERS
LWEM(O) G ALLEN
WEM(R) D L BIRT
WEA APP S A CONNOCHIE

LWEM(O) M S CROOK
WEM(O) W S CROSS
WEA APP S A CULPAN
LWEM(O) R DAVIES
WEM(R) P I DAVY
WEM(R) C ELLAM
WEM(R) P G FRENCH
WEA APP M P GABOUREL
WEA APP B D GREGORY
WEA APP J GRIFFITHS
LWEM(R) D J HAND
WEM(R) P HODGSON
LWEM(O) I HOWE
WEM(R) S HUGHES
WEM(R) J K IDE
WEA APP A ILEY
WEM(R) D W JAY
LWEM(O) P D JOHNS
WEM(O) R A JOHNSON
WEM(O) K JONES
WEM(R) R J KNOX
WEM(R) N R LEEMING
WEM(O) N C LOWE
WEM(O) C S MEADEN
WEM(R) S W MOXHAM
LWEM(O) I MUMBY
WEM(R) I D PARKES
WEM(R) W PARIS
WEM(O) G J PRAGNELL
WEM(R) A QUICK
WEA APP C D SHARP
WEM(R) T J SHEEHAN
WEM(O) K G SOWERBY
LWEM(R) J W SPENCE
WEM(R) D G WATTS
WEM(O) S J WHITTER
LWEM(O) J WILLIAMS
WEM(O) M WILLIAMS
WEM(O) A FEARNLEY (On loan
   from *Collingwood*)
WEM(R) D J PAYNE (On loan from
   Collingwood)
WEM(R) T W WHEADON (On loan
   from *Collingwood*)

Junior Rates – Supply Branch
LSTD R T C BENTLEY
STD R R BRITCH
STD P CARROLL

STD S P CARR
WTR C G DODDINGTON
LWTR M ENGLAND
LSTD N P FIELDING
STD A P GREENWOOD
LSTD M S JOHNSON
LSTD S R LAST
LCA J LAVENDER
STD A P MANUELL
STD M V MOUNTFORD
CA A M ORANGE
STD C PRESS
STD S P SMALL
LSTD ADR STILLWELL-COX
STD J D STROUD
WTR N D TAYLOR
STD R I TONKS
CA M T TURNER
STD C J WARD
LWTR W A WARD
CK K BELL
LCK G T BROWN
CK B R CROSSMAN
CK B EASTON
CK C J ELSON
CK K N FEARON
CK A C FLYNN
LSA P GARDINER
CK A K GRAY
J/A/SA D HODGES
CK N JENKINS
LCK A E KOGA
CK B G MALCOLM
CK T G McNALLY
CK M S McLATCHIE
SA D R PENNY
LCK T G RENDLE
LSA C SCOTT
LCK A E SILLENCE
CK K W SMITH
LCK M SAMBLES
LCK K R WEBBER
LCK G WINTERS
SA A J WILBRAHAM
LSA A J YORK

Junior Rates – Medical Branch
LMA(D) C HOLMES
MA D G WILLIAMS

Junior Ranks – Royal Marines
MNE D G CLAY
MNE P C DELL
MNE A K GREGORY
CPL J A G GREINER
MNE M HERRON
MNE P J HOLDING
MNE R J RANKIN
MNE A SUMMERS
MNE L M YELTMAN

Junior Rates – Ship's Flight
LA(MET) B CROSTON
AEM(M) M HENDERSON
AEM(R) B P B HINGE
AEM(M) I J MACLEOD
LAEM(M) P OKOPSKI
AEM(M) K RYLEY

Junior Rates – Communications Branch
LRO(G)T W ALLEN
RO(G) A BELFITT
LRO(G) T A BLOGG
LRO(T) P S BONAR
RO(G) C A BOYES
LRO(T) S A CAHILL
RO(G) M E C CHILDE-FREEMAN
RO(G)N P CLARKE
RO(G) G CLAYBOROUGH
LRO(T) C R CORBETT
LRO(T) B T GATELEY
RO(T) M E GENTRY
LRO(T) J GLAZEBROOK
RO(G) L M JACKSON
RO(G) P A JONES
LRO(G) K LANGSTAFF
RO(G) R M LA TOUCHE
RO(T) G J LOFTHOUSE
RO(T) K LOWE
RO(T) P R J LOWE
RO(G) G NGUYEN
RO(G) P M RAINE
RO(T) M ROBERTS
RO(G) R P STAFFORD
RO(G) R STEPHENSON
LRO(G) T P WILKINS
RO(G) R A WILKINSON
RO(T) I C WILLCOCK

RO(T) S P WRIGHT
RO(G) D V WORT (On loan from
    Mercury)

Junior Rates – Operations Branch
LREG K A CRUICKSHANK
AB(M) J A FRASER
AB(M) S A BELL
LS(M) D E BELLAMEY
SEA(M) M M BEST
LS(M) C S BLAKE
AB(M) C J BIRTWHISTLE
AB(M) S P BUTLER
AB(M) C CAVE
AB(M) J E DENHAM
AB(M) G D A FRY
LS(M) A J GILLARD
AB(M) I M GRAY
AB(M) P J HADDLETON
AB(M) J C HAINES
LS(M) C E P HARRIS
LS(M) S HARVEY
SEA(M) N J HILLMAN
AB(M) P HUTCHINSON
AB(M) S J JILLINGS
SEA(M) K LANDER
AB(M) T G LOCKETT
LS(M) A T MARTIN
SEA(M) C MEWSE
SEA(M) D R MOORE
AB(M) W J L MOORE
SEA(M) B C NIXON
AB(M) A RHODES
AB(M) G ROOT
SEA(M) M G SMITH
AB(M) W J TAYLOR
SEA(M) A R THOMPSON
AB(M) A J WELDON
AB(M) D W WOOD
AB(M) D L WOOD
LS(M) P J WRIGHT
AB(S) G S BANCROFT
SEA(R) J K F BANCROFT
LS(R) M D BARLOW
AB(S) S BOX
SEA(S) C BRUCE
AB(S) S BUTLER
AB(EW) S T CAMPBELL

AB(R) A G A CHRISTIE
LS(S) J W CLASPER
SEA(EW) R W CLAY
SEA(R) W G W COWAN
LS(R) P S DARE
AB(R) S M DOUGLAS
AB(R) A J FARTHING
AB(R) A G FLETCHER
AB(S) M E FORDHAM
AB(EW) A GILL
LS(EW) D G G HOGBEN
LS(EW) S HOGG
SEA(S) N D HUFFEE
AB(S) M D HUMPHREY
AB(R) S M C JACK
SEA(R) A C JONES
AB(EW) C M JONES
SEA(R) K R JONES
SEA(R) P B JONES
AB(R) G R KENT
LS(S) J LINTIN
SEA(EW) F I LONGMAN
LS(R) A J LUND
AB(R) S S MACMEIKAN
AB(R) G A MALLALIEU
LS(R) S A MELLOR
AB(R) A R MASSEY
LS(R) E C MATTHEWS
AB(R) D McCANN
LS(R) B G NEWELL
AB(R) P F O'NEILL
SEA(EW) P M O'NEILL
AB(R) A E PALMER
SEA(R) R L PATTINSON
SEA(R) C C POTTS
AB(S) T PRYOR
LS(R) W J READ
LS(R) C ROSS
AB(R) N H RICHARDSON
SEA(S) P SEFTON
AB(R) T S SIMMONS
LS(R) D B SIMPSON
AB(EW) S S TEAL
AB(S) M D TARINOR
AB(S) J L WALSH
LS(S) D M WHISKER
AB(R) A J WILLIAMSON
AB(S) B J WILSON

Junior Rates - Marine Engineering Branch
LMEM(L) D P CASE
MEM(L) F H CHILTON
LMEM(L) A B CONROY
MEM(L) R M COPE
MEM(L) S E EDWARDS
MEM(L) T A FRANCIS
LEMEM(L) J HALL
MEM(L) S E McCONNELL
MEM(L) G OKOPSKI
MEM(L) A J P STONE
MEM(L) J A WATSON
MEM(L) D J F WEIGHTMAN
MEM(M) M A CARTER
MEM(M) S AUDLEY
MEA3 D BRAITWAIT
MEM(M) G D BROOKING
LMEM(M) J E CALLAGHAN
MEM(M) S W FEENEY
MEM(M) R J BILLINGTON
LMEM(M) R J PEART
LMEM(M) R HILL
LMEM(M) F RYLE
LMEM(M) G STEWART
LMEM(M) R E WHALLEY
MEM(M) R J WILCOX
LMEM(M) G N MACDUFF
MEM(M) J M C BROWNE
MEM(M) K A BURTON
MEM(M) F J CAESAR
MEM(M) M R CAMPBELL
MEM(M) H G CARVER
MEM(M) M CAVANAGH
MEM(M) A J COLLINGE
LMEM(M) M COOKSON
MEM(M) A CROFT
MEM(M) P DADD
MEM(M) A M DAY
MEM(M) L J DICKSON
MEM(M) D J EDWARDS
MEM(M) P A EVERALL
MEM(M) M A FRANCE
MEM(M) A D GAFF
LMEM(M) M F GARNER
MEM(M) A GATHERER
MEM(M) G C GIBBS
MEM(M) M J GILBERT

MEM(M) D T GIRLING
MEM(M) R J T GRAHAM
MEM(M) D P HOARE
MEM(L) S J HOLDEN
MEM(M) I HOWELL
MEM(M) K A KINGSLEY
MEM(M) A P LAIDLAW
MEM(M) M J LAVERICK
MEM(L) A D MACEY
LMEM(M) J MACKELLAR
MEM(M) R O HURST
MEM(M) D A MARCUS
MEM(M) P S MCCARTHY
MEM(M) W T McDOWALL
MEM(M) B P McGLINCHEY
MEM(M) C MITCHELL
MEM(M) K M MULDOWNEY
MEM(M) N R PATTERSON
MEM(M) A J PEACOCK
MEM(M) T W PERKINS
MEM(M) R PETHERICK
MEM(M) D A PLUMMER
MEM(M) G W PULLEN
MEM(M) O QUINLAN
LMEM(M) P E ROBERTS
MEM(M) P S ROBERTS
MEM(M) J K SMART
MEM(M) M A STUBBS
MEM(M) P A WEBB
MEM(M) J A WHITTON
MEM(M) S A WILKIE
MEM(M) P J WILLIAMS
MEM(M) S A WILSON
MEM(M) A WOOD
LMEM(M) F J WORKMAN
MEM(M) M WOOLLARD
MEM(M) S WRIGHT
MEM(M) A G A YEOMANS

Army Spotting Teams
NGLO (Until 19 May)
LIEUTENANT COLONEL K H R
  EVE

WO2 MALCOME
LRO(G) L WILCOX

FO4 (Until 19 May)
CAPTAIN K D ARNOLD
BDR D J ABBOTT
LBDR R TURNER
GNR M BAYLISS
GNR M CLIFFORD

OF5 (To *Invincible* 5 May)
BDR R E OLIVER
LBDR N C FERGUSON
LBDR J P MUNCHER

OF2 (To *Arrow* 7 May)
BDR J R JACKSON
RO(G) B J HARDY
GNR S BARFOOT

NGLO (From *Arrow* 7 May)
CAPTAIN W McCRACKEN
CAPTAIN HARMS

Glamorgan Civilian Staff
MR R KITE - CANTEEN
  MANAGER
MR G E HUGHES - CANTEEN
  ASSISTANT
MR K L SAUL - CANTEEN
  ASSISTANT

Chinese Personnel
CHAN JOHNNY K P -
  CONTRACTOR ASSISTANT
LEUNG HOW CHIU - TAILOR
LIU TAK MING - SHOE MAKER
CHAN LOK WING - NUMBER
  ONE LAUNDRYMAN
SETO HO - LAUNDRYMAN
CHEUNG YU - LAUNDRYMAN
LAU TAT MING -
  LAUNDRYMAN

Glossary and List of Abbreviations

182	torpedo decoy noisemaker
184	medium range sonar
278	height finding radar
901	Seaslug guidance radar
909	Sea Dart guidance radar
992	E/F band target acquisition radar
993	target acquisition radar
966	long range air warning radar
1006	I band radar
AAA	anti–air artillery
AAW	anti–air warfare
AAWC	anti–air warfare co-ordinator
ADAWS	action data automated weapons system, i.e. the ship's computerised weapons system.
AOA	amphibious operating area
Area Maria	Argentine submarine patrol area north of Stanley
ASW	anti–submarine warfare
Avcat	aviation fuel
AWO	Advanced Warfare Officer
BA	breathing apparatus
BAS	British Antarctic Survey
Black Buck	RAF Vulcan bomber
blue-on-blue	engagement with own/friendly forces
bogey	unidentified airborne contact presumed to be hostile
box	surface gunnery fire control computer
Burglar	Argentinian surveillance Boeing 707
CAP	combat air patrol
chaff	radar reflective decoy material
chaff charlie	chaff delivered by a 4.5in shell for confusion
chaff delta	chaff delivered by 3in rocket for deception
chaff hotel	helicopter-launched chaff
Circle 5	circular station 5,000 yards from the guide
CINCFLEET	Commander-in-Chief, Fleet

CO	Commanding Officer
COL	Command Open Line – intercom linking Ops Room and outstations
Corporate	operation to re-take the Falkland Islands
CVBG	carrier battle group
DC	damage control
defence watches	two-watch system used in wartime at the second degree of readiness
Drumbeat	tracker surveillance aircraft radar
EW	electronic warfare
Exocet	MM38/40 versions: surface to surface missile. AM39 version: air to surface missile
folio	folder containing about 50 charts of a specific area
FPB	fast patrol boat
G6	main propulsion gas turbine
GDP	gun direction platform
goalkeeper	close-in escort for a high value unit
goffer	wave breaking over the ship
GOP	general operations plot
GPS	global (satellite) positioning system
guide	ship upon which a force takes station
gun-line	area of water used by warships to bombard
HAG	helicopter attack group
Handbrake	Super Etendard radar – associated with an imminent Exocet attack
HDS	helicopter delivery service
HE	high explosive
hostile	confirmed enemy aircraft
HP	high pressure
jackstay	high line between two ships for transferring personnel and stores
LCU	landing craft (utility)
link	action information data link
LSL	landing ship (logistic)
M2	subdivision location marking – port side of 'M' section
MAD	magnetic anomaly detector
Mark 46	air/surface launched active anti-submarine torpedo
MATCONOFF	Materials Control Officer

MCO	main communications office
MCR	machinery control room
MEXA	maritime exclusion area
MEZ	maritime exclusion zone
milestone	large wave which thuds against the hull and normally shipped green
MoD	Ministry of Defence
MV	muzzle velocity
NBCD	nuclear, biological and chemical defence - i.e. damage control
NGS	naval gunfire support
Northwood	Fleet Headquarters where Admiral Fieldhouse was located
nutty	chocolate
Oerlikon	20mm machine cannon
OOW	Officer of the Watch
Ops Room	operations room - war fighting nerve centre
pan	intermediate aircraft emergency
Paraquat	operation to re-take South Georgia
pop-up	sudden appearance/disappearance of an airborne radar contact
POW	prisoner of war
probe	type of fuel coupling
PWO	Principle Warfare Officer
RALONGS	Royal Artillery Officer (Naval Gunfire Support)
racket	electronic warfare intercept of radar transmissions
Rapier	radar controlled land based anti-aircraft missile
RAS	replenishment at sea
red-on-red	enemy engagement on their own forces
Rhondda Valley	2 Deck passageway
riser	sudden radar contact of short duration – normally associated with a periscope
ROE	rules of engagement
RPM	revolutions per minute
RSM	Regimental Sergeant Major
SAG	surface action group
SATNAV	satellite navigation system
SBS	Royal Marines Special Boat Squadron (Special Forces)

Seacat	short range surface-to-air guided missile
Sea Dart	semi-active homing long range surface-to-air missile
Sea Skua	helicopter launched air-to-surface guided missile
Seaslug	long range beam riding surface-to-air guided missile
Shrike	anti-radar missile
sitrep	situation report
'Sod's Opera'	a review put on by members of the ship's company, usually comprising a number of sketches and performances of dubious quality
SSN	nuclear powered hunter killer submarine
STUFT	ship taken up from trade
TARA	tug and repair area
TCM	torpedo countermeasures
TEZ	total exclusion zone
The Line	the Equator
Tornado	the amphibious landing deception operation
Tracker	Argentine maritime patrol aircraft
TRALA	tug repair and logistic area
TS	Transmitting Station
Type 21	*Amazon* class frigate
Type 42	*Sheffield* class destroyer
Unifoxer	noisemaker towed astern to decoy homing torpedoes
unknown	contact whose identity has yet to be ascertained
Vertrep	Vertical replenishment by helicopter
Warning red	attack imminent or in progress
Warning yellow	attack probable
Willie	*Glamorgan*'s anti-submarine Wessex helicopter
yellow high	intermediate threat alert state between yellow and red

Acknowledgments

This book could not have been written without the help of the Ship's Company of *Glamorgan* and their families. I am especially grateful to the following contributors: Keith Balston, Judy Barrow, Michael Barrow, Taff Callaghan, Alan Carlisle, R Dunn, Hugh Edleston, Paul Engeham, Nigel Fielding, Ian Forbes, John Gilbert, Chris Gotto, Elizabeth Gotto, John Holden, Phil Holding, Nigel Lowe, Geoff Martin, Eon Matthews, Barry Nixon, Michael Page, Colin Phillips, Francis Ryle, P Sefton, James W Spence, Roger Tipton, Mike Walton, Alan Watt, Michael Wiltshire, and other crew members of *Glamorgan* and their families whose experiences are recounted.

My appreciation also extends to the Ministry of Defence for permission to illustrate this book with official photographs.

I am particularly indebted to my wife Marianne, together with our daughters Katherine and Sarah for their encouragement, support and constructive suggestions. It was their willing acceptance of the impact of this task upon family life which made this book possible.

Bibliography

The following publications have been consulted:

OFFICIAL PUBLICATIONS:
The Falklands Campaign; The lessons, HMSO December 1982
The Management of Battle Stress, Defence Council Instruction 237/88

OTHER WORKS
David Brown, *The Royal Navy and the Falklands War*, Leo Cooper Limited, 1987
Mike Critchley, *Falklands Task Force portfolio*, Maritime Books, 1982
Adrian English, *Battle for the Falklands (2) Naval Forces*, Osprey Publishing Limited, 1982
Max Hastings and Simon Jenkins, *The Battle for the Falklands*, Michael Joseph Limited, 1983
Charles W Koburger, Jr., *Sea Power in the Falklands*, Praeger publishers, 1983
Martin Middlebrook, *Operation Corporate*, Viking, Penguin Books Limited, 1985
Martin Middlebrook, *The Fight for the 'Malvinas'*, Viking, Penguin Books Limited, 1989
Anthony Preston, *Sea Combat off the Falklands*, Willow Books, 1982
Nigel West, *The Secret War for the Falklands*, Little, Brown and Company 1997
Admiral Sir Sandy Woodward, *One Hundred Days*, Harper Collins Publishers 1992.
US Naval Institute *Proceedings*, March 1988
Peter Way (Editor), *The Falklands War*, Marshall Cavendish Limited, 1983

Index